THE
SILICON
JUNGLE

SHUMEET BALUJA

THE SILICON JUNGLE

A Novel of Deception, Power, and Internet Intrigue

PRINCETON UNIVERSITY PRESS   PRINCETON AND OXFORD

Published by Princeton University Press, 41 William Street,
Princeton, New Jersey 08540
In the United Kingdom: Princeton University Press, 6 Oxford Street,
Woodstock, Oxfordshire OX20 1TW

press.princeton.edu

Library of Congress Cataloging-in-Publication Data

Baluja, Shumeet, 1971–
The silicon jungle : a novel of deception, power, and internet intrigue /
Shumeet Baluja.
p. cm.
ISBN 978-0-691-14754-3 (acid-free paper)
I. Title. PS3602.A633S55 2011
813'.6—dc22
2010043865

British Library Cataloging-in-Publication Data is available
This book has been composed in Goudy
Printed on acid-free paper. ∞
Printed in the United States of America

1 3 5 7 9 10 8 6 4 2

The characters, companies,
and numbers are not real.
Don't worry.

In nature we never see anything isolated, but everything in connection with something else which is before it, beside it, under it and over it.

Johann Wolfgang von Goethe

Contents

Preface   xi

Endings   1
Anklets   3
Anthropologists in the Midst   10
Mollycoddle   13
Touchpoints   19
Checking In   26
Working 9 to 4   28
Predicting the Future and 38 Needles   33
Contact   39
Two Geeks in a Pod   47
An Understatement   53
Euphoria and Diet Pills   61
To Better Days   70
Marathon   75
The Life and Soul of an Intern   81
Candid Cameras   85
Episodes   89
Liberal Food and Even More Liberal Activism   92
Subjects   100
Newsworthy   105
Patience   110
Hypergrowth   113
Little Pink Houses   117
Truth, Lies, and Algorithms   122
Negotiations and Herding Cats   129
The JENNY Discovery   133
I Dream of JENNY   138
A Five-Step Program: Hallucinations and Archetypes   143
Over-Deliver   150

A Life Changed in Four Phone Calls   154

Giving Thanks   160

A Drive through the Country   166

Control   171

A Tale of Two Tenures   178

Prelude to Pie   183

The Yuri Effect   188

Apple Pie   195

Thoughts Like Butterflies   201

Core-Relations   207

Collide   212

Control, Revisited   220

Fables of the Deconstruction   223

Control, Foregone   232

Foundations   236

One Way   241

Sebastin's Friends   244

A *Tinker* by Any Other Name   251

When It Rains   262

I Am a Heartbeat   267

What I Did This Summer   273

A Permanent Position   280

For Adam   284

Faith   288

Counting by Two   291

Disconnect   298

Sahim   304

Epilogue: Beginnings   309

Acknowledgments   313

Know More   315

Privacy Policy of a Few Organizations   317

References   319

Preface

An interviewer once asked what the most interesting anecdotes and trends were that we'd uncovered with the data mining and user profiling system we had created. Fortunately, despite the meager amount of data we had at that time, there was still a tremendous amount of interesting material to draw upon. The discoveries about users and their online habits were always entertaining, sometimes awe-inspiring, and occasionally horrifying. Additionally, the process to uncover the findings was often illuminating in itself: equal parts technology, intuition, and black magic. There was certainly plenty of fodder for discussion. The interview, to this point, was going well.

The follow-up question by the same interviewer was what would happen if all of this information about our users was accidentally released and fell into the wrong hands? Silence. It was early in the Internet years, and everything was moving too fast—who had time to think about such things?

Almost a decade later, we find ourselves asking the same questions, still looking for answers. Now, companies routinely watch and record our actions—while in grocery stores, online, or in shopping malls with our families. We trust these companies because they provide safety and convenience, and to not trust them would require too much effort. But the seemingly inconsequential bits of information we so readily surrender every day can be meticulously pieced together into a rich mosaic that reveals more about our habits, goals, and secret desires than we would dare share with even our closest friends.

In a post-9/11 world, perhaps it is not surprising that we are willing to reconsider how much privacy we are willing to forgo. It is important to remind ourselves that the technology, policies, and sheer enormity of the amount of personal data amassed about all of us is new. It's breathtaking. It's unexpected. All of us, those who are being watched and those who are watching us, are, quite literally, in uncharted territory. To address this, some organizations have adopted or created policies that mandate how all of this new sensitive information should be handled and who should be granted access to the information. But few organizations regulate how and what information will be merged together, what disparate bits of our lives will be combined to reveal the ever-finer details of who we are. Such decisions are often left to young, inexperienced employees. In the end, our faith must reside in *each* of the individuals that comprise the companies we implicitly trust—we must believe they will have the wisdom and courage to make the right decisions about topics that did not exist just a few years ago.

The Silicon Jungle examines what happens when the brilliance, immaturity, and unbridled enthusiasm of an intern, Stephen, is mixed with unfettered access to people's most private thoughts and actions. Stephen's blind idealism and overwhelming desire to impress render him oblivious to the severe consequences of his actions and make him an easy mark for those willing to exploit his naiveté. The setting, a ubiquitous Internet company located in Silicon Valley, is chosen not only for the steady stream of innovative technology that consistently emanates from the area, but also for the prevalent maniacal pursuit of scientific immortality, "the next big thing," and, of course, unmatched material excesses.

A question that I am often asked is how much of this book is real. *This book is a work of fiction.* The events are fictional. The technology and science described are based in reality. The people are fictional. Their temptations are not. The justifications offered for the intrusions on people's privacy are fictional. The ability, brains, and computational power to do so are not. Importantly, as to whether the companies described are real and whether any single company holds enough data to do all that is described in this book, this I can answer definitively: The companies are not real. As far as I know, no single company holds all of the data described herein.

Like the meatpacking industry in Upton Sinclair's *The Jungle*, a new, rapidly burgeoning industry is laid open for your investigation. For anyone willing to peek behind the sleek streamlined services and offerings we take for granted on the Internet, a profound conflict will be uncovered between the intellect of the scientists and their latest inventions, and the very human limitations and frailties of the people who handle, consume, and trust the technology daily. I hope you will find the science and the possible discoveries truly exciting—the insights unearthed by large-scale data mining initiatives provide an understanding into individuals and groups of people that, prior to the last few years, was impossible. How this newfound ability is used is where trouble can begin.

Perhaps all of this leads us to a conclusion that we already intrinsically know: It's not technology or a newfound ability that should be labeled "good" or "bad," it's what we choose to do with that ability. Science and technology innovation will, and absolutely must, progress. It is up to the creators of new technologies to open our eyes to not only the mechanics of what can be done and how to do it, but also the limitations and dangers, as well as the beauty and excitement, of their creations.

I have encountered few places in the world that are using technology more effectively, directly, and for a more worthy cause than the *National Center for Missing and Exploited Children* (NCMEC). Their efforts to rescue children and stop the spread of violent and hateful images exploiting children are exemplary. I am humbled and amazed at the work they do. For this reason, I am proud to support NCMEC and other non-profit organizations that espouse the use of technology to explicitly make the world a better place.

Peace,
Shumeet Baluja, Ph.D.
P.S. A note to my former interns: No, this book is *not* about you.

THE
SILICON
JUNGLE

-ENDINGS-

"Is that your friend on TV, *baba?*"

He glanced up from the game they were playing to look at the news report flashing on the TV screen. He caught a glimpse of Sebastin's face before it disappeared. It never ceased to astound him that his son, Adam, only six years old, could play checkers so well while paying such close attention to all that was going on around him.

"How do you know about him, Adam?"

"I heard you talking to *ummi* yesterday," Adam replied with a mischievous grin. "You said you were going to see him."

"You're too clever, Adam. Yes, Sebastin was my very good friend. He answered our prayers."

"What did he do?"

"He found our lost brothers. He found 5,000 of our lost brothers," he responded. As he said the number aloud for the first time, he was overwhelmed again with his good fortune.

"Were they *really* lost?" Adam questioned with sincere concern.

He smiled as he reached over to Adam and pulled him into his arms. "Yes. They were *really* lost. They were so lost that they did not even know how lost they were. Can you imagine that?" With a flourish of his hand and a warm smile for his son, he said, "Now we can find them again."

But Adam still looked worried. At six, worry was not hard to see; the child's brow furrowed deeply and his face became unmistakably sad. "The TV says that he died today."

He looked proudly at his son. He was always listening, always absorbing.

Adam stared down at his hands in his lap, and picked at his fingernails, a habit since birth. "Are you sad, *baba?*"

"Why, Adam? Why would that make me sad? It is God's will. Why would I be sad that God has decided that it be so." It pained him a great deal to use the word "God" with his son; everyone in his family had questioned his decision. But he had made it, and so it stood. He, too, would have liked to call God by His proper name, but it would be easier for Adam to grow up in America this way.

"*Baba*, did he know he was going to die?"

Thinking back to less than twelve hours earlier, concentrating on the still vivid memories of the few minutes in which the inevitability of his actions must have been apparent to Sebastin as well, he replied, "I believe he did, Adam."

"I thought so."

It amazed him how his son could say such things. "Now, let's turn off the TV and finish playing," he said as he freed Adam from his arms. "You are growing older, Adam. You know so much. This time, take care. I may not let you win."

-ANKLETS-

January, 2009.

"Stephen, report to Allison's office immediately," the intercom blared. Stephen automatically walked past the all-natural sodas, recycled paper products, and the latest lawn and composting supplies toward the back of the store. GreeneSmart, Silicon Valley's humungous and freshly rebranded "Earth-aware, all green" answer to large retailers like Walmart and Target, was about to open its shopping doors for the day. When it did, for Stephen, it would be more of the same—rushing to respond to the countless calls for computer, e-mail, printer, network, fax, and telephone support from every corner of the building.

He instinctively made his way to the door marked "Employees Only." Crossing that threshold, the cold floors of the showroom were replaced with carpet that felt good under his feet. Hours of standing every day made him thankful for even the cheap stain-worn industrial carpet that had been laid years ago. He stopped at the open door to the inner HR office marked "Allison Glace" and walked in.

"Good morning, Mrs. Glace. What's going on?" He sounded like a child when he spoke, and he knew it. He'd been doing that ever since he left SteelXchanges.

"The usual. My keyboard isn't working again," Allison replied.

Stephen knew the problem before he began his investigation, and he strongly suspected she knew what the problem was, too. At least two or three times a month, Allison accidentally kicked the keyboard cable out from the back of the computer when she took off her shoes. The effect was that the computer stopped responding to any of her typing.

It was an easy enough fix, and he'd told Allison numerous times how to plug the cable back in, but here he was back in the office again.

He crawled under the oversized particle board desk that Allison had managed to obtain for herself (by saying HR must exude a good image if they were to make the best hires). He lay down on his back and scooted toward the rear of the desk. This wasn't even close to the work he was doing at SteelXchanges, but it wasn't nearly as bad as some calls he'd endured the past two and a half years.

> "We have to strike while the iron is hot!" Stephen's roommate, Arthur, implored. "This is a once in a lifetime opportunity. We do it now or someone else will," he continued urgently. "You're crazy," Stephen replied unconvincingly the first few times. But within three weeks, Stephen gave up completing his Ph.D. a year before he expected to finish. In exchange for a piece of paper that would proclaim him a doctor of computer science, he and Arthur founded their first company, Pittsburgh Steel Exchange. It was a company whose mission statement was primarily a number of in-vogue buzzwords strung together in a single wonderfully captivating sentence. It was 2004, the second coming of the dot-com craze was nothing less than a certainty. To not partake in the euphoria, especially after having cowardly shunned the first Internet boom in 1999, would have been regretted for eternity. Leaving the Ph.D. program was hard, but technically Stephen was still classified as ABD (All But Dissertation) at Carnegie Mellon University in Pittsburgh, Pennsylvania. Realistically, as far completing his Ph.D. was concerned, he might as well as have been classified as DOA.

Instead of just plugging the keyboard cable back in and being done with it, he lay there a few minutes, savoring the time he wasn't in GreeneSmart's loud showroom. By now, the doors would have opened, and the early shoppers would be swarming the store.

"Stephen, do you mind if I talk to you while you're down there fixing my computer again?" Allison asked in her motherly tone. It was a voice that could too easily comfort him to sleep if he wasn't careful. "I was thinking, while you're in here, we could talk about your career development. You know you were supposed to have your review meeting with your manager last month. Now he's gone on vacation and asked me to do it for him." Stephen had been avoiding the meeting as best he could; another review would mark another six months at GreeneSmart. He didn't want to think about so much time passing, but now he might be trapped. Perhaps she had planned it this way.

Arthur was standing on top of the mahogany conference table in front of the projection screen passionately urging, "You have to understand, we have an intimate knowledge of steel. We live in Pittsburgh. Steel runs in our veins." Stephen stood, too, though not on top of any tables, "Combine this with the world's best computer science talent at CMU, and it's going to be an unstoppable startup." The dog-and-pony show was airtight—the theatrics well rehearsed. This was their seventh meeting with top-tier venture capitalists, VCs, in Silicon Valley to fund their idea. Pittsburgh Steel Exchange proposed selling steel through an open auction, much like how eBay works today. And what had made all this possible? Simply, the Internet. It was declared brilliant, and they wound up with promises for more money than any graduate student knew what to do with.

Stephen plugged the cable back into the computer, no point in delaying the fix. He didn't bother to get up. If the career talk must happen, he would do his best to make sure he didn't participate more than he needed to.

"You're hired!" Stephen and Arthur had said thirty times in as many days. Flush with money, Pittsburgh Steel Exchange hired its core team without delay. "Thirty people? You've outgrown Pittsburgh," the VCs warned. "It's time to move to California. We're going to help you make it to the next level." The next level? That sounded promising. "And, what's with the name? We thought you guys knew the Internet," the VCs admonished. With thirty-two people in the company (all who eagerly relocated to the West Coast with their own visions of "the next level"), what had originally started as Pittsburgh Steel Exchange was reborn in Palo Alto, California, as SteelXchanges.com.

"Why are you here? Don't get me wrong; we all love having you here. But it's been more than two and a half years now. Isn't it time you found something better to do? If you don't mind me saying, Stephen, it's like you've given up, and that's ridiculous. Stop wasting your time here." Allison was the first HR person to be this honest.

2:10 a.m., nearby at the gas station food counter, while having coffee with a side of hotdogs that had been turning on the cooker long enough to be packaged as Slim-Jims: "This will be the last of our nightly food runs," Stephen began somberly once they were all seated. "I wanted you all to be the first to know. The rest of our promised funding is being withdrawn. We're closing down Steel-Xchanges in two weeks. I'm announcing it officially tomorrow." He noticed a few surprised expressions, but most had already suspected. Six months after they moved to California, the dot-com bubble burst, and the consequences to SteelXchanges.com were clear. "I'm going to help all of you find jobs. I promise. I'll make it right. It's not your fault, any of you. We did the best we could. I should have known better."

The brutality with which the funding was taken away even exceeded the excitement with which it had been given—the back-rooms, cigars, and dignified single malt scotches that were de rigueur for closing the deals where steel was bought, sold, and traded were working perfectly fine, thank you. And, despite the repeated and loud cries of "lack of efficiency" and "backwardness" and much worse name-calling from the technologists in California, the steel titans seemed little fazed, if they heard the cries at all.

Stephen turned his head, imperceptibly sighed, and waited. All he could see, from his vantage point under the large desk, was the bottom of Allison's grey skirt and her exposed calves as she rose from her chair to pace the office. He couldn't see her face, and she couldn't see his either. "There are so many companies around here that would hire you in a second. I think you could be part of something really big, who knows? I'm saying this to you as a friend, you know, and not as HR. As a manager, and as HR, of course I want you to stay here. But, come on Stephen, you and I both know you should be doing something else."

"What am I going to do now? I followed you and Arthur out here from Pittsburgh. I thought you guys were on to something. What happened?" a woman, mother of two and Pittsburgh Steel Exchange's fourth employee, asked. Stephen stammered out the now all too familiar consolatory words, "Give me your resume and I'll work with you on it until we find something for you. I'm sorry. I'm just really sorry for all of this. Go home and tell your family that it'll be okay. I'll find you something." Another heap of worries to add to his own. SteelXchanges.com had seventy employees when the news came of its closing.

He resumed his long list of calls to every VC and colleague he had met in the last six months. He began the conversations with "I need a personal favor," anything to help his team. They were, after all, his responsibility. It would have been nice if Arthur had made some of the phone calls, too. But Arthur had departed immediately, disassociating himself from the failure that was Steel Xchanges. No black marks on his resumé.

Allison continued on, but his attention was long gone. He was watching her legs as she paced around the room. She didn't have her shoes on, and he felt sorry she had to walk on such a dingy, disgusting, old carpet. He followed her legs as they moved back and forth across the office. Her voice was gentle. He wasn't sure what her words were, but he was positive he'd heard this conversation before. He knew it by heart.

He watched her. The anklets she was wearing on both legs—he'd never noticed them before. If she stopped speaking at just the right moment when her legs happened to touch, he could just barely make out the sounds of the anklets as they softly rubbed against each other. At every step, he held his breath for that extra little bit of silence, and listened for the quiet chimes again.

She spoke for a few more minutes; eventually it occurred to him that he'd been under the desk for too long. He clumsily maneuvered to sit up in his little space. Finally peering out of his makeshift cubby, he found Allison's face looking back from only a few inches away.

"Hey," she said in a surprised voice, "I thought that you had fallen asleep on me. Tell me you heard at least some of what I said."

"Yeah, I did. Thanks, Mrs. Glace," he replied quietly. "You're right. It's a lot to think about. You know that I really do enjoy it here, but I'll think about it. Promise I will."

Allison only half smiled back at him. He suspected she would do the same to her son. "Okay, but *really* think about it, Stephen. Life's too short, you know."

"Don't worry about me, Stephen. I've already found a job," said Ryan, one of Arthur's assistants and a friend to everyone in the company. "GreeneSmart was hiring, and I accepted a job there this morning. You should visit sometime. The café has better food than those gas stations you keep going to," he said, trying to cheer up Stephen.

Stephen did visit Ryan—two days after SteelXchanges closed permanently. Stephen ran into the head of tech-support at the store, a meeting he was sure Ryan had arranged. "So, you're Stephen? Ryan has told me so much about you; you're the tech whiz-kid. We could really use you—our PCs and fax machines are a mess. Think you can help us out?" The man was as welcoming as could be. It wasn't remotely similar to the type of work Stephen did, though he was certain Ryan had the best intentions. A lack of a backup plan, the need to get some rest from thinking about what he had done to twenty-one people, or simply the desire to be with a friend for a few weeks while he figured things out—whatever the reason, Stephen accepted a part-time job working directly for the head of tech support at GreeneSmart. Two and a half years later, Ryan had long since left and Arthur had returned to graduate school. Stephen was coasting, working full-time at GreeneSmart.

The conversation was at an end. Stephen sprang up, perhaps a bit too quickly since Allison had to hastily step out of his way. He thought about giving her a hug; it was good to know someone cared about him. He hoped he had been like this with his employees, too, but perhaps those were different times.

Seventy people had trusted him. For forty-nine of those seventy, he had found employment. But for the remaining twenty-one, the wreckage of the dot-coms around him was less forgiving—a fact Stephen could not forget. Weeks after SteelXchanges' closing, the calls started coming in: "Are you okay?" they all wondered. With tempers soothed, his former team remembered to inquire about how he had fared. Four weeks after the debacle, not a single person, not even those who had returned to Pittsburgh poorer and more in debt than they ever had been, blamed Stephen.

Instead of confiding any of this, or even just giving Allison the hug he had so wanted to, he awkwardly mumbled an excuse for his too-quick rise, and stumbled out the door.

-ANTHROPOLOGISTS
IN THE MIDST-

March, 2005.

Molly Byrne, age twenty-three, Cameroon, Africa. Seven months of applications and three months of training—yet, what the Peace Corps training had least prepared her for was simply feeling overwhelmingly isolated. Forty-two days into her assignment in Cameroon, and friends were still hard to find. The only person who treated her like anything but a novelty item was Sandrine, a beautiful fourteen-year-old girl with eyes that no National Geographic magazine cover could ever do justice. Sandrine had befriended her on her first day. Sandrine and her one-year-old son, Francis, were as close to friends as Molly had.

From Molly's Cameroon Diary:

> Day 42: Sandrine is now officially the only one who hasn't yet begged to see my cell phone or my stash of cigarette cartons that I keep for trading. Had I known, I would have brought plenty more—and Froot Loops, everybody loves Froot Loops here. I buy them at every chance. I try to teach Sandrine English, and she tries her hardest to keep me from embarrassing myself too much. fourteen years old, with a kid, and she's teaching me how to survive here . . . Life here is like living under a microscope. Everybody is watching me constantly. There is no break; I can't just go home to wind down. My host family is just as fascinated with me as I am with them. Everything I do is watched and reported on; the vil-

lage knows my every action and seemingly my every thought, too. I should probably be . . .

Molly had wanted to write more that morning, but when the stab-bing pain close to her shoulder was enough to make her cry out loud and writhe on the filthy floor in agony, she had needed to stop.

▼ ▼ ▼

"You are from America?" the doctor asked as he put his hands on her neck from behind, pressing his dark fingers deeply into her white skin. He already knew she was from America; everybody there knew she was.

"Yes," Molly replied. Say as little as possible. To talk more would only provide further interactions to misconstrue.

"Take off your shirt," the doctor said. "For your heart," he offered as an explanation. He took a step back and nodded approvingly as she pulled her shirt up. He looked disappointed when she didn't take it off completely.

The doctor was an old man with cold hands that trembled as he laid his stethoscope on her chest. He listened for a long minute, then moved in closer to her. She could feel his breath too close to her body. She stared at the bald spot on his head, hoping he would just once dare to look up at her face. He would understand what her expression was saying, that she knew what he was doing—and that she wasn't going to let it go any further. But he never looked up, he kept his gaze low.

She didn't need to be here, she thought to herself. The pain had subsided by the time she made it to the doctor's office. But Sandrine had insisted she should go inside to see the doctor anyway. He was a good man; he would know for sure if everything was okay, Sandrine promised.

His hand wandered lower. "Okay," Molly said loudly enough to dis-turb whatever fantasy was building in his head.

"Of course, of course. Everything is fine. Do not worry. Come back tomorrow, and I can check again. Maybe tomorrow, you bring a little gift?"

Molly pulled down her shirt quickly, self-conscious and furious at once—but saying nothing. She was fuming enough to know better than to speak. Blurting out anything now would only mean that the rest of the village would know about it long before she made it back home.

She opened the door out of the doctor's office without looking at him again. The room outside was overflowing with others waiting for his attention. Sandrine was, thankfully, standing by the door when she exited, ready to take her home.

"Sandrine, *comment ça va?*" the doctor called from inside his office as he spotted her through the open door. "You should come see me for a checkup," he suggested, nodding his head upward in a smile. Before Sandrine could reply, Molly took her by the elbow and pulled her quickly from his office.

"He's not a good doctor, Sandrine. Promise me you will find another," Molly whispered as they were leaving the waiting room. She was only 14. God knows what he would do to her.

"He is Francis's papa, Molly. He is a good man."

Enough. Molly left Francis and Sandrine standing at the entrance of the building. Before there was time to reconsider, she strode into the doctor's office, grabbed the first thing her hands could fit around, a half-filled heavy glass bottle, and swung it at the doctor. The woman on the examination table was yelling, the doctor's face was bleeding where two teeth had burst their way through the now dangling flesh of his cheek, and everyone in the waiting room was moving in for a closer look.

Seven months of applications, three months of training, and forty-two days in Cameroon. She was taken home before the week ended, having been deemed by the village, and the Peace Corps, to have "too intense a disposition to continue."

-MOLLYCODDLE-

February, 2009.

"Why do you need another computer again, Molly?" Trisha asked as she stepped into position behind the electronics center at Greene-Smart. "I've had mine for two years now, and it's doing fine. If you ask me, there are plenty of other things to spend money on."

"I know, I know. But it's for my research project. Anyway, just let me know later today if you find something back here that I can afford. I need to get one quickly." Molly scooted away to ensure she made it to her own station in the children's clothing department before her manager appeared. "I've got to run now. You know which department to find me in, okay? And don't forget, you promised to help me set it up when I get it." Molly gave an appreciative smile to Trisha before disappearing behind the shelves of DVDs.

"Whatever," Trisha muttered under her breath. In the three minutes before the store officially opened, Trisha checked their inventory, found a cheap computer for Molly, and had time to consider if she could convince Molly to spend her money more wisely. In the end, though, she decided it wasn't worth the effort, and resigned herself to finding a way out of setting up the computer for Molly.

Forty seconds remained before the front doors were officially unlocked; the intercom was fair game. "Stephen, report to electronics," Trisha's voice roared through GreeneSmart. For several months after Stephen first arrived, she had given him plenty of easy opportunities to ask her out. He was cute enough that she had even considered asking *him*. But she never did, and a good thing, too; he was far too quiet and shy.

Just like every other day, the first call came before the store opened. On the inside, Stephen thought, "What now?" On the outside, he happily declared, "Good morning, Trisha. What can I do for you?"

"Molly needs your help. She's setting up her new computer tonight, and she wanted me to ask if you had some time to help her?" He instantly agreed, as Trisha knew he would. What guy wouldn't gladly do anything for Molly? Long brown hair, smarter than anyone else she knew, intense, and intensely pretty. More than pretty when she actually tried, Trisha thought. Some people have all the . . . , Trisha started, but the rest of the thought was too obvious to go on.

Trisha hurriedly called Molly on her cell phone the moment Stephen left, "I can't make it tonight. But you know Stephen Thorpe? The tech-guy? He volunteered to help you with your computer." Before Molly could question her any further, Stephen anxiously showed up in the children's clothing section to make the plans in person.

▼ ▼ ▼

"All done!" Stephen happily exclaimed around 9:30 that evening. Molly's new computer was ready to go. "You just need to type your password right here, and you're all set." Stephen stepped out of the way to let her reach the keyboard.

So far, they hadn't spoken much. They had driven separately in their own cars to her apartment, and since then, he'd been busy with the new computer. Although they had talked a few times at the store, they were probably best described as acquaintances rather than friends.

Molly replied without moving, "Just use 'mollycoddle.' That'll be good enough. I always use that." Stephen's blank expression compelled her to spell it for him. "It means you're taking good care of me," she explained. Stephen finished typing it in, still a bit uncomfortable about Molly trusting him with her password.

"Thanks so much for setting this up for me. I'm sure it would have taken me days to figure it all out. I'm not really a tech person, as you've probably guessed by now." Molly sat down in front of the monitor to take the computer for a test drive.

"Oh, there's not much to it. It took so long just to get everything installed to protect it from viruses and all that good stuff. Just to make sure you're safe." The expression on Molly's face revealed nothing; it was impossible to tell whether she was interested, bored, or just being patient. He continued on, uncertainly, "It'll also keep your machine from being hacked into, and keep all your personal files and information private. Nobody should be able to break into it." Just stop talking, she doesn't care. Why am I saying this aloud? He was coming across like all the stereotypes he was trying his hardest to avoid.

But if she noticed his awkwardness, she was kind enough not to openly show it. "Thank you so much. I can't believe how nice you've been. Tell me why you're working at GreeneSmart if you can do all this so quickly? You should really be working somewhere else."

"Mmm-hmm. I've heard that before."

"You know, we *are* in the heart of Silicon Valley. Have you ever thought about working for a startup, or maybe working for Ubatoo? They're always hiring, and from what I hear, they treat their employees pretty well, too—better than GreeneSmart, I'd imagine."

"Thanks, but I don't think that's the right life for me. Setting up computers is one thing, but I think I'll need quite a bit more than that to get a job there."

"Don't they have a contest for finding summer interns coming up?"

He looked at her surprised. "How did you—"

"How did I know?" she interrupted. "You mean besides the billboard advertisements they have all over town? It's pretty hard to miss, even for an ass-backwards techno-phobe like me," she said jokingly. Then, she recited the all-too-familiar billboard to him verbatim, "Got what it takes? Prove it. InternSearch @ Ubatoo.com."

It was true. The quote was plastered all over Silicon Valley and heard on radio and TV constantly. She grabbed his hand and led him to the window. "Besides, I see their billboard every day—it's right there," she said, letting go of his hand far sooner than he would have liked. "Their offices are only a couple of blocks away. Besides, I'm sure you're just being modest; you'd get an offer no problem. All I'm going to say is that I think you should at least try it."

Before Stephen could argue about how different the required skills were between setting up her computer and what it would take to get into Ubatoo, Molly had changed topics. "How about some dinner? I owe you that much. I can order some amazingly good sandwiches. They're really much better than the hotdogs I see you stealing from Greene Smart's café."

Stephen was pretty certain Molly had reached her threshold for tech talk; he wasn't about to press his luck talking any more about viruses, her new computer, or Ubatoo. He did, however, readily agree to dinner.

▼ ▼ ▼

"Just make yourself at home," Molly said as she went to order the food. "I'll be right back."

Stephen stood uncomfortably next to the computer he had set up, not sure what to do next. All he knew for certain was that he wanted to literally move *away* from the computer. Of all the images he wanted to leave in Molly's mind, him next to a computer, having just talked about hackers and firewalls, was lowest on his list.

So what should he do now? Considering the favor he had just done, he assumed it would be okay to sit down and turn on the TV. On the other hand, given the amount of time they had known each other, it was probably best not to make himself too comfortable yet. He shook his head side to side, a little embarrassed, and frankly displeased with himself for thinking about this so much. He decided on a compromise. He would sit on the sofa, but not turn on the TV. *Dare I eat a peach, too?* he recalled, a line he had read years ago. Why all this thought? It had been a long time since he'd paid this much attention to his actions, and it was not at all obvious that any of his actions were ever worth so much thought.

Having made the monumental decision to sit, he absentmindedly looked around the cluttered coffee table, and piled together a few Xeroxed pages that were fluttering in the breeze from the open windows. Underneath the glass table top, five stacks of Xeroxed pages revealed themselves—each reaching up, at least a foot, from the floor to the table.

He couldn't help but be intrigued. Anything even remotely academic was a souvenir from a life he knew years ago as a graduate student. From the headers of the photocopied articles, he could see they were from publications such as *The Journal of Political Science*, *Urban Affairs Review*, *International Journal of Middle East Studies*, and *Politics and Religion*. His next thoughts came as a bit of a surprise to him: four years had passed since he had been a graduate student—and he missed it.

He remembered the pride and sense of accomplishment he had felt whenever an article he had written describing his latest research was accepted for publication into an academic journal. It was a testament to his discovery of something new, something that his peers, other scientists, found worthy of preserving and ensuring that future scientists had a chance to read about as well.

With these thoughts, though, also came the memories of what reality was for a graduate student. These fanciful ruminations were far from the day-to-day life of an academic. Reading volumes of academic papers and publishing regularly would simply be expected, not cherished. It would be little more than a concrete measure by which to confirm he wasn't simply wasting time.

Nonetheless, there remained a not-so-small twinge of jealousy in him as he surveyed the articles. With the same adoration that compelled some to covet and collect books, he looked at messy stacks of academic articles. Having them around was like having access to raw knowledge, waiting to be understood. Even if they were from fields outside his own line of study, it was reassuring that the world he had left behind still existed.

Dinner, and the hours of easy banter afterward, had been far more engaging than either could have anticipated. To start, Molly was a graduate student at Brown University in Anthropology and Political Science, doing part of her field work in Silicon Valley. How she wound up here he still didn't quite grasp, but there would be time for that later. That she was a graduate student immediately gave them a large set of shared experiences to draw from in their conversation. The fact they were both now at GreeneSmart provided even more fodder for the evening's exchanges. It wasn't until 5:30 in the morning that they decided to call it a night.

Thankfully, the night hadn't turned out anything like Stephen had imagined it might a few hours earlier. As he was leaving in the early morning, she implored him, even before it should have rationally had any impact on him, to at least sign up for the intern contest at Ubatoo. She was more certain than ever, she said, that he was underselling himself at GreeneSmart and he could be doing so much more.

But being an intern? Hadn't he just built up his own company, and managed a large team? he argued. No, she reminded him, what he had *just* done was waste two and a half years at GreeneSmart. His own company, she went on to state, was long gone. She certainly wasn't lacking in candor. In addition to the obvious realities she had pointed out, Molly also stated others he needed to hear. He had taken care of his employees better than anyone could have expected. He also needed to take care of himself.

However, in the six hours since Molly had first mentioned the Ubatoo prospect, the idea never left him, always rising up again in the few pauses between hours of conversations. Perhaps more pertinent was that, in the light of any budding new relationship, promises were all too easily made. Of course he had agreed to enter the contest; the only person who ever thought he might not was himself.

What Trisha could not have known just a few hours earlier, but would happily take credit for, was the instrumental role she had played in putting Stephen and Molly together, even if all she had really wanted was to avoid several hours of staring at a new computer in Molly's tiny apartment.

-TOUCHPOINTS-

September, 2002.

In 2002, Atiq Asad would have described himself as a modest man. He was rapidly approaching a tenured professorship in UC-Berkeley's Computer Science Department, his students were obtaining positions in the most highly regarded and prestigious academic institutions in the country, and his research in the emerging field of data mining was winning accolades and honors from his peers. There was good reason to be proud, though he would never talk about any of his accomplishments aloud for fear of being too boastful.

On average, Atiq received about one call per month from recruiters at startup companies in Silicon Valley that he had never heard of. To avoid common courtesy being mistaken as interest, he didn't normally bother responding in any way. But the latest company to contact him, *Ubatoo.com*, was not completely unfamiliar. When the recruiter called his cell phone for the third time, on a whim, he answered.

Within the first five minutes, he had already exhausted his patience, along with his usual cadre of excuses: "Really, I'm quite happy at Berkeley," or "I'm not in the market for a new career right now." It had been a mistake to answer the phone; the recruiter wasn't taking his not-so-subtle hints.

"Dr. Asad, just hear me out," the recruiter pleaded. "We've already assembled a stellar team of 40 people. We'd like you to come and create your own research group, as large or small as you like. I have to be honest with you, Dr. Asad—you have quite the reputation around here. At last count, five of our most senior scientists asked specifically that I recruit you. As far as they're concerned, you walk on water."

"Like I said, I'm flattered. But I'd like to meet those five delusional scientists sometime. Personally, I'd be leery of anyone with such a high opinion of me," Atiq replied, trying to cover his impatience.

"Dr. Asad, what are you looking for? Freedom to do your own research? Brilliant peers to work with? Is it money? Whatever it takes to get you here, I'll try my hardest to make it happen."

The words could be enticing if he let them linger. Focus. "In nine months, if all goes well, I'll be granted tenure at Berkeley. I can't give up on years of work when I'm so close. Thank you once again. I really must go now."

"I don't suppose telling you the salary we're offering could sway you? Or maybe telling you that the number of Ubatoo's stock options we're granting you is more than I've ever seen before? How about if we keep this offer open for you even after you get tenure? That will give you some time to think about it, too."

"Okay. Let's talk again in nine months, after the tenure decision is behind me," Atiq agreed. Finally, a polite end to the conversation. Besides, in nine months, these shimmery words would have already tempted the receptive ears of their next hiring targets.

The recruiter didn't call again.

The trouble for Atiq was that Ubatoo had insinuated itself in his life from every direction. Whether he used Ubatoo's search engine for finding academic papers, or whether he used it to buy Christmas gifts for his wife and kids, Ubatoo had become the single destination for finding all things on the Web. He was beginning to use their other services, too—e-mail and online credit cards, and occasionally their instant messaging service to chat with his son and daughter, both of whom insisted this was the only sure way for them to communicate. With each flash of the Ubatoo logo, it was difficult not to imagine what the recruiter might have offered had he not been so quick to close the conversation.

Ten months after the initial phone call, and a month after the long awaited tenure had been bestowed, the recruiter returned in person, with five friends. "Dr. Asad," the recruiter, and the only man wearing a tie, began, "As you requested many months ago, I'd like to introduce you to those five delusional scientists."

Atiq scanned their faces—faces he vaguely recognized from a few years ago, when he had taught them as graduate students. They looked like they had never left Berkeley's Soda Hall—worn-out jeans, faded t-shirts, scruffy faces, dirty hair, and the unmistakable aura of sleep deprivation. He reached out to warmly shake each of their hands and invited them into his office.

The small talk lasted only a moment before the recruiter steered the conversation back on track. "Have you given Ubatoo any more thought? Ubatoo has more than tripled in size since we last spoke, and we need you as part of our team more than ever. The offer is still open."

"Gentlemen, it's wonderful to see you all again. I can't possibly tell you how rewarding it is to have you all here like this, but I can't give all of this up." Atiq motioned toward the shelves of papers, books, and numerous framed award certificates haphazardly scattered amidst the mess. "I just received tenure. Let this old man enjoy it." He did feel old, very old, in the presence of the five sitting in front of him.

The recruiter spoke before any of the others had a chance. "Dr. Asad, we would never ask you to give up your position here. Just work with us for a while and see if it's a good fit. Keep your position as a Berkeley professor as long as you like. We're willing to share your time."

One of the five, the one in a crumpled old Berkeley t-shirt, stopped his furious typing on the laptop he never left home without and chimed in nervously, "Dr. Asad, listen. Don't you want to see how well your research works in the real world? We're facing all the same problems you studied and published about in dozens of your papers. This is what you've waited for; it's no longer just speculation and theory to ponder and write about. It's real. It's tangible. We live, breathe, and swim in the data every day. More data than you can imagine." He took a moment before continuing, his eyes wandering over the crowded shelves on all sides of the office.

As he started again, his gaze returned to resolutely focus on Atiq, "I know you use our search engine at least a dozen times each day and you use our e-mail constantly for sending personal messages. In fact, you checked it less than 45 minutes ago, just before you left your house to come here, right? I know you use our instant message service to talk to your kids, which I'm willing to bet was on their insistence. You probably talk to them more through instant messaging than you do in person considering the long hours you put in here. And last week, you used our credit card four times. This week, you've only used it once, yesterday . . . And that's just what I found from a few minutes of poking around our data while you were talking. Think about what you could do with this information on all our users."

The recruiter stepped a few feet forward and tentatively placed a thick sealed envelope on Atiq's desk, marked only with his name, the ubiquitous Ubatoo logo, and the words, "Welcome Aboard." The recruiter shifted his eyes from the envelope to Atiq, saying quietly, "I think we've probably said enough."

No one moved—all awaiting Atiq's response. He was subtly nodding his head up and down as he considered these five scientists, these kids, in front of him. He thought about the magnitude of what they had stumbled upon, wondered if they possibly understood what they possessed, or even knew what they should do with it, or *could* do with it. Then his eyes too wandered over the piles of books and dusty awards that engulfed him. "You seem to know me pretty well," he said as he reached one hand toward the envelope. "Tell me, have you figured out how to get all of your data to reveal what I am going to do now?" he asked with a smile, while deliberately smoothing a wrinkled corner of the waiting envelope.

The recruiter tried to step between Atiq and the scientists before any of them started talking again. But two of the five answered in perfect unison, as if this show had been perfectly choreographed just to deliver the final punch line: "Not yet. That's what we need *you* for."

▼ ▼ ▼

September, 2008.

Walking into the Ubatoo office building in Palo Alto, the heart of Silicon Valley, was just as overwhelming for Atiq back in 2002 as it is for those who visit Ubatoo today. Immediately he had felt the palpable energy in the offices, the vibrant animated discussions transpiring in front of whiteboards brimming with more equations and Greek symbols than words, and the furious clicking of keyboards punctuated only by rapid excited exchanges. But most of all, what he sensed—as clearly as if his eyes saw it—was the raw focused brainpower at work.

Six years later, Atiq was a vice president at Ubatoo, a company that had grown its ranks to 12,000 employees. Although he still held his Berkeley professorship, the vast majority of his waking hours, as well as a few of his sleeping ones, were spent on Ubatoo's sprawling grounds. Like Berkeley, there was no shortage of interesting and challenging problems to tackle. Unlike Berkeley, Ubatoo had the added thrill of allowing one's work to affect the lives of literally hundreds of millions of people within minutes of its completion. Change one thing on the web site and immediately a large portion of the world's population saw its effects.

Atiq's data mining division specialized in finding trends and patterns in massive repositories of raw data. All the data Ubatoo collected from every site on the Web, as well as each of the enormous number of interactions that any one of its users had with Ubatoo, were analyzed by some portion of the data mining group's computer programs. These programs ran all night and all day, every day, looking for patterns to better understand what the user was doing, what the user was trying to accomplish, and what Ubatoo could do to better serve the user's needs. And for his success, Atiq had been rewarded beyond his most spectacular dreams. His rewards ensured that his children would be able to support their children and maybe even their grandchildren without worry. The recruiter's exaggerations had proven true—the package, the people, and the work here were indeed extraordinary.

He thought about all of this today, in particular, since today was the day Xiao Ming, Ubatoo's CEO, would officially reveal Atiq's most ambitious initiative, *Touchpoints*, a project that had been over two years in the making. Atiq had waited patiently, and implored the rest of the Touchpoints team to be just as patient, until everything was completed before letting Xiao announce it to the rest of the company. Now, with the system's first round of tests completed, he was comfortable with the accolades he knew his team would surely receive. And though his intention was never to seek praise, it was impossible to deny his own tiny desire to have his work recognized by his peers at Ubatoo. It was because of these thoughts that he wondered if he could still accurately describe himself as a modest man.

▼ ▼ ▼

The auditorium where Ubatoo's "rally the troops" meeting was held was overflowing, standing room only. Xiao Ming had taken the stage fifteen minutes earlier and was reviewing the previous quarter's financial results and the latest technical milestones. The 1,000 employees who could fit in the auditorium were enjoying the elaborate aperitifs and hors d'oeuvres made by Ubatoo's master chefs in preparation for the event. The other 11,000 employees, scattered in buildings throughout the Palo Alto campus as well as offices in Tokyo, Beijing, Melbourne, London, Rio de Janeiro, Bangalore, and Moscow, watched Xiao's live video broadcast from the comfort of their desks—a small window on their monitors open to the video, and most likely a larger window still open to the project they were working on and were unwilling to interrupt.

Lynn Wiser, a recently appointed vice president at Ubatoo, who was easily recognizable by her disdain for business attire and penchant for loud colorful baseball caps, made her way to Atiq. "Atiq," she started. "Xiao's going to talk about your project today. I saw the slides before he went on."

Atiq couldn't help but feel excitement well up in his chest.

"I don't think Xiao is too happy," Lynn said worriedly.

Panic. "Why? What could he not be happy about? We've been working so hard. All the tests are working beautifully. What more could he want? What else could we possibly—"

"It's his usual rant, Atiq. He just wants more. He doesn't like that you kept the Touchpoints group so small. He's not satisfied with the job you're doing hiring, and thinks that's why the project isn't even further along."

He would have complained to Lynn, but what was the point? If Xiao was a reasonable man, Atiq could point out all the amazing things the Touchpoints team had done in just the last six months alone. But he knew Xiao would hear none of it.

"How bad is it going to be today?" Atiq asked reluctantly.

"Oh, it's the usual Xiao, damning us with faint praise. You know him—ever the diplomat. Sorry about this, Atiq. I know you were probably expecting more out of today, and God knows, you certainly deserve more."

The slide that Atiq had been waiting for, "Touchpoints: Understanding Our Users," appeared on the screen. Xiao spoke, "The Touchpoints project, led by Atiq Asad, typifies what makes Ubatoo truly incredible. The data mining group has been working for over two years in creating the infrastructure to, quite literally, harness the power of tens of thousands of machines to search for patterns—patterns in purchasing histories, in web searches, in e-mails, and in chat sessions. To date, in its pilot tests with some of our top advertisers, the revenue impact is estimated to be $65 million last quarter, and that's before it's even fully launched. Each one of you should find out more about Touchpoints; we're going to be integrating it inside all of our products. And to think, all of this was done with only eleven people in the Touchpoints group. We had hoped the group would be forty people by now; imagine how much more they could have accomplished. But let's keep our fingers crossed; hopefully we'll see that potential realized next quarter. Let's give Atiq and the Touchpoints group a hand for their incredible work—you're about to know more about our users than you ever have before."

The room reverberated with the boom of sudden applause. These weren't the half-hearted courteous claps of disinterested employees. Far from it. Engineering and scientific achievements were always well received, and when large monetary numbers were associated with them, they garnered even greater enthusiasm. Atiq suspected that the rest of the Touchpoints team would be delighted by the exuberant response—both from Xiao and the audience. Despite the accolades from employees as they left the auditorium, Lynn and the other VPs who were more versed in the nuances of the passive-aggressive Xiao-speak, were more consolatory in their praise, "You're doing great work. Don't worry about Xiao" they assured him. Truth be told, Atiq wasn't worried. This wasn't the first time his expectations had been too high—and there was a high probability, statistically speaking, that it wouldn't be the last.

-CHECKING IN-

March, 2009.

"Rajive here," the voice on the other end of the telephone line announced.

"It's Sebastin, from ACCL." The line went silent. "Hello, Rajive, you there? This is Sebastin Munthe from American Coalition of Civil Liberties, ACCL. Hello?"

Rajive finally spoke. "Yes, Sebastin. I know who you are. You're weeks late, again. I need you to be on time for this to work."

He was doing Rajive a favor, not the other way around. It was frustrating working with him, barely worth the meager amount they were paying. "Do you want the update or not?"

Silence again.

Sebastin continued, "I finally got a hold of Dr. Atiq Asad at Ubatoo. Unfortunately, I don't think that's going anywhere. Everything I tried led to a dead end. Either he wasn't getting any of my hints, or he wasn't willing to 'help.' I'm going to have to find someone . . ."

"Do you have a plan yet?"

"I'm getting to that, Rajive. Ubatoo's having some kind of intern contest this week. Atiq invited me to meet the interns at a party they're having afterwards. Hopefully one of the interns will work out for us."

"Names?" Rajive demanded curtly.

"I don't know. Like I said, they haven't even been hired yet."

"Will they have access to all the data you need?"

"I imagine they will. ACCL worked with a few Ubatoo interns last year. From what I recall, they were plenty resourceful. I can't imagine

it'll be any different this year. Besides, they will be part of Asad's group, so I'm betting they'll have access to everything. I'll know for sure once I actually talk to them."

"Any timelines yet?"

"Rajive, listen to me. I haven't even met them yet. What do you want me to tell you? I can't give you a firm timeline. I'll call them a few weeks after I initiate contact. If you want this to work, I can't scare them off. I'll give you more details the next time we talk."

"That'll put you almost a month behind schedule. Any good news to report?"

"No."

"Try harder with Atiq. He's likely still your best shot. Make inroads with the interns. And, Sebastin, make your next update on time."

"Always a pleasure, Rajive." Sebastin hung up, exasperated.

Rajive left the conversation pleased with himself. In person, he usually had to play the good cop, but on the phone, he could do whatever he wanted. It was definitely more fun being the hard-ass. Despite any indications he may have given Sebastin, everything was fine.

-WORKING 9 TO 4-

March, 2009.

Wednesday, 9:00 a.m. It was the sort of visit that one actually brought cameras to and literally wrote home about. Few visitors were allowed in through the guarded gates without an explicit invitation. But, today, over 600 potential interns were being herded around the "grounds," as Ubatoo's campus was called, and taken on guided tours through all the usual tourist stops created for just this sort of thing. At every stop, whether in front of one of the five-star cafeterias, or in front of signs with names designed specifically with tour groups in mind ("World Operations Monitoring," "Cyber Crime," "Web Memory," "Advanced Research Group"), flashes of cameras were steadily seen.

Of perennial interest to tour groups was the stop in front of two very large bulletproof windows. Here, onlookers were given the opportunity to see what most people not on the tour would find unconditionally dull. In the room beyond the glass were racks of several hundred computers. In there, the tour guide explained, 70 percent of Ubatoo's public e-mail flowed through these computers. If you had ever used Uba-Mail, your message had flown through here before finding its way to its recipient. Despite the "No Photographs" signs, it was too hard for many tour members to resist, some hurriedly trying to snap pictures through the glass. Many had used Uba-Mail since it was first launched, and this was just one of the many things they wanted to memorialize with a photograph.

The more technically savvy members of the tour were less impressed, as it seemed highly unlikely that any machines "on the grounds" would hold such sensitive data as e-mail. It was much more likely that the data was spread to undisclosed datacenters, warehouse-like complexes with thousands or tens of thousands of computers, in remote locations around the world. And, of course, they were right. The computers behind the glass had been in the process of being decommissioned when one of the junior members of Ubatoo's public policy team suggested this exhibit to impress a tour group of first graders—or so the legend goes.

Eventually, the tour guides deposited their charges in Ubatoo's largest auditorium—a large room that the CEO, Xiao Ming, had personally taken an interest in creating. Like all the excesses of Ubatoo, this room, its cost, its designer, and its construction, took on a life of its own in the local newspapers of Silicon Valley—a geek's episode of *MTV Cribs*. The peculiarity of the ornately decorated room, which gave the overwhelming impression of solid gold, was made complete with chandeliers, oversized drapes, and enormous oil paintings on three of the four walls of the Ten Tigers of Canton—a group of ten top martial arts masters in Southern China. The fourth wall consisted solely of a giant white projection screen, in front of which the speaker stood and any presentations took place. The room's existence was, in every way, an ode to Xiao.

In time, Xiao's excesses were forgiven, and the room became "Xiao's Ballroom." Xiao's only comment on the room was to say that he wanted a place to entertain in style when actors came to share their worldly insights, charities stopped by to raise money among Ubatoo's employees, or when, more importantly, the media was invited for a product launch.

As Stephen entered this room, he faced rows of cafeteria-type plain white tables set up with LCD monitors, keyboards, and computers. The tour guide instructed them to find a seat at any empty computer and get started filling out the forms displayed on the screen.

"A bit of advice. Get comfortable with your surroundings," the tour guide said. "You'll be in here for a while." With that, she left Stephen and the rest of the group standing in the entrance way. The room was strangely quiet given the number of people in it. A few times the staccato of a quick laugh broke through above the din, but these were few and far between. The members of Stephen's tour group, who had been so closely huddled when the tour guide departed, soon dispersed in every direction.

Ubatoo was infamous for its intern selection process. Anybody could apply, whether a student, an experienced professional, or something in between. Based on resumés and entry questions, the initial screening was conducted. Those who passed were invited to participate in today's event. Here, the remaining candidates were put into a single room and given a series of questions to answer. Sometimes the questions were programs that had to be written or sometimes they were riddles that required finding the one spark of insight that would unravel the entire puzzle. The answer was entered on the computer, and the cycle continued, for hours on end. The top scoring competitors were offered internships, and the others were sent home. Although nobody as yet knew how many people would be selected, it was a foregone conclusion that the competition would be difficult. No matter who you were, most likely you wouldn't be coming back.

Stephen knew he should be worried about his chances, but he wasn't. He hadn't traveled more than a few miles, knew he was good at what he did, and was comfortable with the fact that he wouldn't make it through. Moreover, he still wasn't convinced that transitioning from running a company to being an intern wasn't foolish. But Molly would be happy that he tried, and so would he.

Each computer screen offered a few multiple choice questions used to determine which department at Ubatoo was the best fit for the candidate—Ubatoo's equivalent of Harry Potter's Sorting Hat. After answering those, there was little to do but anxiously wait. The person seated in front of him was animatedly expounding to his neighbor about how the questions asked on the screen had a deeper meaning and that Ubatoo was probably already psychographically profiling the contestants. The ongoing conversation to his right, although not quite as overtly paranoid as the one in front, had its own set of quirks. Someone was describing why he was expecting questions on aerial image processing, and talking about satellites and Ubatoo's ability to use the imagery to create detailed models of people's houses. "It's truly wonderful," he continued in a thick accent, "I worked on this for my Ph.D., but I never thought anyone would actually be using any of it." The person he was talking to was plainly waiting to tell his own tale, but by this time Stephen had stopped listening. The conversations weren't helping his nerves.

On the far wall, on the stage in front of a large white screen, a man approached the microphone set up in the middle of the stage. "Good morning, everyone," he started. "My name is Atiq Asad. It's my pleasure to welcome you to our 5th Annual Internship Competition."

The room didn't just quiet down, it fell silent instantaneously. Atiq continued, "You all should be proud of making it this far. From the more than 3,700 applicants we received this year, based on your resumés and the sample work you sent us, we've invited 619 to take part in today's competition. It's truly an illustrious crowd; you have an amazing set of peers sitting with you. The brain power in this room is the stuff that Ubatoo was built on. It's what keeps us always inventing, always creating, and always being the most innovative company in the world. Over 60 percent of the people invited have completed, or will complete, their Ph.D. this year. But don't think that a Ph.D. is a requirement for success. Last year, one of our hires had not yet graduated high school. This year, we have two high school students competing. Next year, who knows, maybe elementary school. It's truly an eclectic, brilliant crowd. Welcome to each and every one of you. Now, I'll hand it over to Lynn Wiser, co-organizer of today's event, to fill you in on how you will proceed. Again, good luck. I look forward to working with you."

As Atiq left the stage, a brown-haired woman in torn jeans and a yellow baseball cap replaced him. "Welcome, everyone. Let's get right down to business, shall we?" Her words began before she even reached the microphone. "By now, I hope all of you have finished answering the questionnaire on your screen. We used this to help determine which group you would be appropriate for. This year, based on your preferences and our needs, we'll give you a set of tasks to accomplish. You figure out how to solve the task, design and write the program, gather the results, and submit them—as fast as you can. At 4:00 a.m., your results will be automatically analyzed and the scores tallied. The tasks chosen are as close to real world as possible. They're the type of problems our groups are actually working on and solving today. You can use any tool you have to answer the questions. I don't care if you phone a friend, use a lifeline, talk to the person next to you, or search the Internet. Do whatever you want; your answer is all that matters. Let me join Atiq in wishing you good luck."

"By the way, the fridges in the hallway are stocked with all the caffeinated drinks, juices, waters you could possibly want. Coffee, tea, whatever—it's all out there. You know the drill. Lunch and dinner will be served in the hall, starting in a few hours. The bio-break rooms, umm, excuse me, restrooms, are down the hall. Enjoy this, people; this is supposed to be fun."

-PREDICTING THE FUTURE
AND 38 NEEDLES-

March, 2009.

The computer screen had come to life. Stephen could no longer hear Lynn or anyone else talking. Having been assigned to the data mining group, he now stared at the screen intently, puzzling over the first task:

Data Mining Task 1: Predict the Future

At Ubatoo, we strive to know our users better than anyone else. Last year, we launched a series of cell phones with the ability to browse the Internet on-the-go. To help our users, we would like to predict what they are going to search for *before* they type it. How good are you at predicting the future? Design and code a system that predicts what a user is likely to search for next.

You have access to a month's worth of logs: all the search queries that 50,000 of our users typed into their cell phones. With each query, you are also given the geographical location of where the user was at the time the query was made, the time the user made the query, and the query itself.

Your TASK: Through the analysis of the logs provided, as well as any other information you can find, you must predict what the next ten queries typed into their cell phones will be for all 50,000 users. Points will be awarded for the number of matches between your prediction and their actual queries. We suggest spending no more than four hours on this problem.

This may have seemed more solvable when he was in his graduate student mode, but plugging in keyboard cables and fixing fax machines for the last two and a half years had done nothing to prepare him for this assignment. The only consolation he had was that he knew the task was do-able, or they wouldn't be asking him to do it—hopefully. It wasn't the number, 50,000, that was troubling. If he could accurately predict the search queries a single user would type, he could accurately predict them for 50,000. The problem was in developing the algorithm to make that first, correct, prediction. All the answers were in the logs kept of everyone's searches. It was just a matter of figuring out how to extract the right set of information from the data—in under four hours.

Let's start with the basics. Going back to his courses in grad school, *Artificial Intelligence 101*: To predict what a subject will do next, find other subjects like him, and see what they did in similar situations. He just had to match each of the 50,000 users with others who had also typed in a few of the same queries. By looking at similar users, he could find similar interests and other queries they might type. Once he had the idea, writing the program was easy; he was done before an hour passed. As he examined a few of the predictions, some seemed possible, but most seemed poor. For a moment, panic set in; he thought about trying to fix them manually. After fixing fewer than ten of them, he verified what he had known all along. There was a reason they had asked for predictions for 50,000 people—to ensure that any manual approach would simply be a disaster.

Stephen rose to get a drink, and glanced around the room for the first time. It was a scene he hadn't been a part of in years, people working frantically, absolutely oblivious to their surroundings, and all of them here because they wanted to be, not because they had to be. He looked for telltale signs of stress—anyone with their head in their hands, or leaning back in their chairs—but noticed none of this. Maybe it was just too early in the day—though he had hoped to see some cracks in the competition.

He looked back down to his screen, already filled with horribly written computer code from the last hour's work. It was ugly, it barely made sense, and it certainly was nothing to be proud of. He knew his college professors would probably take back his degree if they could see the mess of code and logic he was stumbling through right now. He also knew it was pretty unlikely that his undergrad professors would have made it into Ubatoo. Need to stop getting distracted with these thoughts, he cautioned himself. He sat back down without getting the drink. He put his hands on the keyboard, fidgeted with keys, and started thinking in earnest about what to do next.

When the epiphany did come, it was, as it always seems to be in retrospect, obvious. The fact that the users were on cell phones meant their location was probably an important clue. People searched on topics that were relevant to them, and if they were using a cell phone, they were traveling, and if they were traveling, then their location was probably important to them. If you were in California, you were more likely, based on empirical data, to search for sushi than if you were in Nebraska. Now the task became easier since the location of every user was recorded. When he searched for people who were similar to another, he added location to the profile he had built of the users (*i.e.*, the only way Jane would be considered similar to John is if Jane was in a similar place, geographically speaking, to John).

Two coffee breaks and a snack run later, he felt that what he had done was enough to improve his answers substantially. He was already running 45 minutes late. It was now 2:45 p.m. He tried the new modifications on a few of the 50,000 users. The results looked better than before. He let the program generate the answers for all of the users, and avoided looking at the answers it returned. If he had looked, he wasn't sure he would be able to resist tweaking his program further to squeeze out more improvements, all while the clock was ticking away. The moment the answers were produced, he submitted them and held his breath. By the time he leaned back in his chair, a message had appeared.

Congratulations, Task 1 sufficiently completed.
Press any key for Task 2.

Stephen surprised himself with how happy he was. Compared to the work he had done when he led his own company, the magnitude of the task just completed was miniscule. But, still, the thought of working at Ubatoo with access to all that Ubatoo had to offer (not that he was quite sure what all of it was, but he knew it was a lot), he couldn't help but feel excited, almost giddy. But there would be time enough for all that later. Task 2 was waiting on his screen.

Data Mining Task 2: Needles & Haystacks

Out of the 100,000 users who were pre-screened to fit the profile we were looking for, 78 of them bought a car that cost over $161,000. We're going to tell you who 40 of them are. Your job is to find the other 38.

You will have access to the emails they sent through Uba-Mail over the last year, their purchasing history when they used any of our credit cards, and the Zip code of their home address. Access to all of the searches they performed in the last year is provided.

The suggested time to work on this problem is twelve hours; we strongly suggest using outside information sources to help with this task. Whatever you find is fair game.

Twelve hours—it would be past 3:00 a.m. then. This task was big; not only because of the time allowed, but because of the data he was permitted to see: e-mails, Zip codes of home addresses, and credit cards. This was how Ubatoo made money, understanding their users, and knowing how and what to sell to them. Despite providing the tremendous number of services Ubatoo offered, it was, at its core, an advertising business, a relentless and unflinchingly efficient advertising machine.

Looking around, Stephen found half the seats empty. Maybe everyone was taking a break. He went to find food, but didn't hear the expected sounds of all those who should have been there. "Where is everyone?" he asked the first person he encountered at the food buffet. The guy was stuck at the entrees, trying to make a decision between the salmon and the buffalo fillets.

"I don't know," he replied, "I think most of the others didn't do well. I guess they weren't given the next round of questions."

"Oh," Stephen replied. He wasn't in a frame of mind to think of anything cleverer to say.

"In my group, cryptography, I heard a rumor that more than half of us were already given the boot." Finally, he decided not to decide and heaped a serving of both salmon and buffalo on his plate. "What group are you in?"

"Data mining. Just started the second question."

"Hope you make it. I've gotta run. Plenty more work to do," the indecisive eater said as he hurried back to his seat, inhaling his meal on the way.

Stephen sat at an empty table, trying to eat slowly, trying to convince himself that fifteen minutes of rest was imperative and would surely serve him well. But to no avail. Stephen wolfed his food down in under three minutes, burned his lips and tongue inhaling a scalding hot coffee, and almost ran back to his computer.

Once again seated in front of his computer, he felt foolish for having run. The problem was still as unsolvable as before. Talk about finding a needle in a haystack: He had to find 38 people from a set of 100,000. He just stared at the screen, which still impassively displayed the second task.

Stephen shoved his keyboard back and rested his elbows on the table with his head in his hands. He didn't bother opening his eyes. Start with what you know. Okay, first and foremost, what he knew for sure was that it was solvable. The information was accessible, and it was right there at his fingertips. Zip codes, e-mails, spending habits. What does a Zip code reveal? It could reveal a lot: how wealthy a person is, what type of house they owned. All of that information was publically available on the Web—the Census Bureau collected that much and more. He also knew he could eliminate almost anyone who shopped at GreeneSmart too often, come to think of it. He hadn't seen a $161,000 dollar car in the parking lot in quite a while. But what other patterns were there? He could eliminate anyone who regularly did their own errands or shopped at the dollar store. Okay, this was all available from their credit card usage information, to which he had access.

What else is an indication that someone will buy an expensive car? Their jobs? Maybe. That correlates well with Zip code, too. What else? What would convince *him* to buy a car that expensive, he wondered. Nothing, really. But his friends might try to convince him. Which friends? Those friends who had purchased some crazy car themselves? Yes. If he was the type of person who bought a car for $161,000, he might try to convince his friends to buy one, too. At the very least he'd tell his friends about it. Some of that must be in e-mail trails. What about pictures of the car? That would probably help, too. And if you were about to be convinced to buy a car, wouldn't you search the Web and research it? He certainly would.

So, let's start the groundwork. Find out which cars cost over $161,000. We know forty people who bought them. Who were their friends? Read their e-mails. See who they told about it. Which ones of them also searched for these expensive cars? We have the names of the cars, and now we have the potential set of friends who bought them. We know where they lived and approximately how much their houses were worth, too—just by looking at the Census Bureau's stats and a few real estate web sites. Could it be so easy to put this together?

Thinking this through, Stephen was as still as humanly possible, except for the small rapid eye motions beneath his closed lids. The lack of apparent motion concealed the swarm of activity in his mind. His thoughts scurried in a dizzying game of tag, charging through the minefield of false leads and the countless pieces of data requiring analysis to expose the missing thirty-eight people. Eleven hours remained.

-CONTACT-

March, 2009.

Half of Stephen's shift had already ended by the time he woke up at 1 in the afternoon. Thirty minutes later, he was in the children's department at GreeneSmart, on his way to find Molly. She was the only person he wanted to see.

"Well?" Molly asked anxiously, as she peered from behind a clothing rack. "How was—"

"It was incredible. I haven't had to think that hard in years. The people there were so smart . . . 600 of us were there . . . just working, hacking away on these ridiculously difficult problems. It was unbelievable. We were working until 4:00 this morning."

Even Stephen was taken aback by how fast and excitedly he was talking now, and he wasn't sure how to stop. ". . . and the data they had, well you understand how hard it is to get data, and they had it all laid out for us, and they just let us play with it, dissect it, and . . ."

By this time, Molly had taken his arm and guided him to a slightly less crowded aisle, where fewer people were watching them. Then, she finally inserted her fourth word into the conversation, "Well?"

Stephen stopped in mid-sentence, "Oh, I made it. They made four offers for my group this year, and I got one of them."

Molly was already giving him an enormous hug. "Congratulations! I knew it. Let's go out to celebrate. It's on me." She gave him another hug. "But you might want to change first—you're a mess," Molly said, happily. She grabbed Stephen's hand and started walking back toward the exit doors as if encouraging him to go home and change that instant.

"Sorry, I didn't have time to get ready. I just wanted to come and tell you about it."

"I'm really glad you did. That's all I've been thinking about. When did you finally get back to your apartment?" she asked as they were walking.

"Around 6 this morning, but we were at Ubatoo until almost 5. It was a complete disaster . . . baseball with Coke cans in the hallways, others running around the desks playing laser tag, being totally obnoxious. Then, the PlayStations and Xboxes came out. They projected them on this giant four-story screen in the room we were in. Okay, that was actually kind of cool."

"Sounds great." Sarcasm. Eye roll. "Out of control, sugar-high kids. Delightful, Stephen."

By this time, she had successfully led him to the front doors. "Well, you made it. That's huge. Tell me more about it tonight, okay? What time do you want to go out to celebrate?"

"I think I'm going to have to take a rain check," Stephen hesitatingly replied. "They're having a party tonight for the new data-mining interns. I think I'm expected to be there."

A look of disappointment crossed Molly's face for an instant, but just as quickly disappeared. "Well, the offer stands whenever you want," she said as she gave him a quick kiss and started walking away. "By the way, congratulations again," she called back to him.

"Hey, Molly!" he yelled out, loud enough to startle the kids and moms walking by. She stopped and waited. "You were right! Thanks!" With that she disappeared behind an aisle full of office supplies.

▼ ▼ ▼

That night, the four data-mining interns, distantly familiar from the previous night, were looking at each other uncomfortably across a formally set, candle-lit table to which they had been directed. Although they had no notion of what to expect, it certainly hadn't been this.

"Anybody know what this place is?" asked Stephen, the first to speak. His voice was barely audible over the noise of all the other party-goers, some Ubatoo employees, others from Ubatoo's large advertising clients. Stephen pointed to the two frescoed palatial domes in the four-story ceiling above him and shrugged. The surroundings married the imposing architecture of a gothic church with the gaudiness of newly minted millions.

The only woman in the group of four, Aarti, answered, "This is Xiao's house." She spoke with the speed and deliberateness of a southern drawl, yet with the unexpected sophistication of a British accent.

All eyes were upon Aarti and the oddity who happened to be sitting to her left, Kohan. It was a peculiar sight, seeing the two side by side. Both were Indian, but that was where any similarities ended. Kohan was a short rotund man with a prominent thick black moustache that he was constantly pressing and smoothing down with his fingers. If his hand wasn't at his mustache, he was typing something furiously into his BlackBerry, which he had already done numerous times since they sat down. His plaid shirt with cowboy-styled piping over both pockets, complete with bolo tie, oversized belt buckle, and brown leather riding boots, provided a perplexing thought experiment as to what calamity could have possibly produced this modern Indian Cowboy.

Then there was Aarti. She could best be described as Audrey Hepburn with a tan. Everything about her, from her tiny body to the way she was dressed (with her fitted pencil skirt and demure dove grey sweater set) to her hair, set in a neat twist at the nape of her neck, put her in a class different—above—everybody else at the table.

"Xiao had to buy and tear down six houses to build this place. This—this is what Ubatoo is all about," Kohan replied reverentially. They looked around at the marble expanses, the several stories high glass walls, and the paintings that they now suspected were originals. "The question I have is: Why are *we* here?" asked Kohan. "Maybe we're the entertainment," he said again, answering his own question with a smile.

William, so far silent, took his turn in adding to the conversation, "Our being here is likely an ill-conceived scheme some marketing person came up with at the last minute to show how big the data-mining team is. I wouldn't let it go to your head. I can't imagine they really care if we're here or not."

"You've become more of a curmudgeon than I remember," Aarti declared, a healthy dose of disdain in her voice.

"No more so than usual," William replied irritably.

"Don't mind him," Aarti explained to the others. "I've known William for years. His humor is on the dry side."

"Champagne?" A voice called out to them. A man dressed in a uniform of red and gold with a giant peacock feather looming high above an exaggerated turban on his head was holding a tray out to them with crystal flutes filled with champagne. Stephen grabbed one immediately, as did everyone else in turn, except Kohan, who didn't hesitate in grabbing two.

"Gentlemen, and gentlewoman, of course, I propose a toast," Kohan said. "To arriving, and arriving in style."

Taking Kohan's lead, Stephen tried to change topics. "That was tough last night. I'd heard the entrance bar was high, but that was beyond anything I imagined. I struggled for an hour before I had an insight into the car buying problem."

"Last year, when I was an intern, we did that kind of work all the time. This one was almost a textbook case," Kohan replied. Then he quickly added, "But if you hadn't done this before, I can imagine it being pretty tough, especially in a time crunch."

"The first question was trivial, if you ask me," William said. "I finished that in half an hour. The second one, I wound up finding the group of thirty-eight in two different ways just to double-check my answers. No issues here."

Stephen thought that possibly "curmudgeon" wasn't an appropriate description for William—the little runt of a man. Not to stereotype, but it was hard not to picture William as the maladjusted, snippy, peevish, repulsive part of every stereotypical computer scientist. Maybe "jackass" was a more fitting description.

"Everybody having a good time, I hope?" a voice called to them. Before anyone felt compelled to try a third attempt at conversation, Atiq had thankfully found them. He was dressed sharply in a black tuxedo with black tie. "I'm glad to see you all could make it." He looked around the table happily. "I wanted to tell you what's in store for the four of you tonight. Xiao is going to introduce you as Ubatoo's next generation of knights in shining armor. He'll probably tell everyone that, during your internships, you'll work with them to help them learn

more about their customers. It's all part of the 'Touchpoints' program—
our data-mining initiative you'll be working on."

Atiq spied worried expressions on at least three of the four faces—
excepting William, who was confident he would do a good job.

Atiq continued, "Don't worry about it. Normally, we have a team
who does the business side of things. Sometimes, though, it's good
for the advertisers to talk directly to the eggheads in the operation. It
makes them feel good. All you have to do is be enthusiastic; they know
you haven't even started yet. I'm sure you'll dazzle them. Trust me, it
will go well." He looked around for a moment and smiled at Kohan,
"By the way, nice shirt, cowboy."

Stephen couldn't recall a single employee he'd ever hired at Steel-
Xchanges who he'd let within ten feet of a customer without extensive
training. Maybe this was another indication of the type of talent Ubatoo
managed to attract. Or, maybe, interns could do very little that would
actually hurt an enormous company like Ubatoo. The latter thought
comforted him a great deal.

Atiq reached into his pockets and pulled out four decks of business
cards, one for each of them with their names proudly displayed next to
the official Ubatoo logo, and a title of "Software Intern—Touchpoints
Team." E-mail addresses and phone numbers were already assigned and
waiting for them to start.

"By the way, why are all of you sitting by yourselves? Meet some
people. They're quite friendly, I promise." Atiq turned around and motioned for someone to join them. "I'd like to introduce you to Miss
Erion," he said. "It's thanks to her company, Aston Martin, that we had
the second question in the internship contest. We worked on that very
problem for Miss Erion last fall." Introductions being made, Atiq hastily departed to find the next set of people to meet and greet—another
table of helpless guests needed to be rescued.

▼ ▼ ▼

"What were you doing before Ubatoo?" the man asked Stephen.
The man, who had introduced himself and his company a few minutes
earlier, was still completely anonymous to Stephen. He was the fourth
to talk to Stephen since dessert had ended less than thirty minutes ago,

and nobody's name had stuck. Stephen replied mechanically about his startup, SteelXchanges. Although he had muddled through the answer the first time he was asked the question that night, he knew better than to talk about GreeneSmart again. It had led to numerous increasingly derogatory questions that he didn't care to face a second time.

"You mind if I have someone from my team call you sometime? I keep hearing about the great returns you guys get for all the other advertisers." The man spoke with a slur, the sour telltale hints of too much alcohol invading the air between them with his every breath.

"Of course," Stephen replied. "Here's my card. I'll do whatever I can."

"Listen," the man continued in a more hushed voice, putting his hand clumsily on Stephen's shoulder, "when your internship is done, we could always use smart entrepreneurs on my team."

Stephen had heard that job offers came easily for anyone associated with Ubatoo, especially for interns. Still, getting offers before your first day of work was a bit unexpected. If the grapevine was accurate, the most coveted offer, the one from Ubatoo that would make an intern a full-time member of the team, was rare.

"Why don't we let him start working for us before you steal him away?" a voice said from over the man's shoulder. As the man stepped aside, they both saw Atiq smiling back at them.

"Ah, Atiq. Good to see you. But it'd be only fair if he came with us. Ubatoo has managed to take two of my best. You've got them sequestered far away somewhere in your organization," the man replied as he shook Atiq's hand. Bitterness, despite the toothy smile.

"I warned both of them they were leaving the best boss they could hope for," Atiq replied graciously. Just how many of the same conversations had he already had that night?

"Of course, Atiq, I'm sure you did."

"I'm afraid I must steal Stephen for a few moments," Atiq said.

The man took the hint, shaking Stephen's hand a final time. But the anger in his face, which he did little to hide, hadn't diminished.

"Stephen, I want to introduce you to a dear friend of ours, Sebastin Munthe." Atiq motioned to someone who, as if on cue, stepped forward with his hand extended.

As Stephen and Sebastin shook hands, Atiq continued, "Mr. Munthe, besides being a successful serial entrepreneur, serves a much higher function now, as Silicon Valley's moral conscience. He's the head of the ACCL—the American Coalition for Civil Liberties. A non-profit that I believe was started right here in Silicon Valley several years ago. This man single-handedly protects our civil rights that Washington, DC seems to take great pleasure in whittling away. I've offered to create any position he would like in order to work with us at Ubatoo, but he keeps telling me he has more important things to do," Atiq said with an easy laugh. "I'm sure you'll be hearing from him when you start here. Be sure to give him whatever he needs."

Stephen's confusion as to what to say at this point must have been apparent. Although unmistakably Stephen's turn to talk, he was naturally uncomfortable meeting new people, and the fact that Atiq was standing there, watching, wasn't helping. Thankfully, Mr. Munthe volunteered a few words before the awkwardness reached the point of no return.

"First, Atiq, as I mentioned earlier, please do call me Sebastin. That mister stuff is a bit too stuffy for a party. And, second, Stephen, let me assure you that Atiq is being far too generous with his kind words," Sebastin said in a thick, dignified, perhaps German, accent. "I hope that I will not take too much of your group's time. My colleagues who worked with your group last year offered nothing but the most outstanding praises for your team." Then he lowered his voice. "I firmly believe it was because of the work we did together last year that we were able to protect several dozen innocent people from God knows what forms of harassment and privacy invasion from certain parties in DC. Our entire team, and of course the people you helped, owe Ubatoo an immense amount of gratitude."

Some conversations you can nod along with, hoping that the tiny bits you understand will be enough if you are called on to contribute. This conversation, though, was not one of them. Stephen wasn't sure how his group could have possibly helped Sebastin, "Silicon Valley's moral conscience." Atiq was still watching him, and the fact that Atiq hadn't yet left to find another guest to talk with made it abundantly obvious that Atiq highly valued Sebastin.

"I'm certainly glad we could help," Stephen replied awkwardly, choosing his words too cautiously. "I hope I can be as helpful as my colleagues were last year. It would be great to do some good for the world together." He wasn't quite sure if it was appropriate to stop yet, so like he was too prone to do in such situations, he continued talking. "You'll have to tell me more about how we actually helped you preserve people's rights, though. That's a use for our data that I hadn't foreseen, I have to admit. Anything I can do to help further your work would be an incredible way to spend the summer." Sebastin seemed quite enthusiastic about the response. Atiq left—his work was done.

Besides a few minutes of vehement agreement about the evils of privacy invasion by governments around the world, and the witty, acerbic comparisons to the previous administration in the U.S., it was difficult to embark on a new topic. Sebastin kept returning to this one. It would have been beneficial to have been more prepped for the night, Stephen thought. They could have dived straight into the technical details of the projects, a conversation that Stephen would have been much more comfortable having.

Nevertheless, listening to Sebastin fervently speak about all that ACCL did and all the further good they could do with Ubatoo's help was the first conversation that excited Stephen. He was sold on the importance of Sebastin's work, especially when compared to finding thirty-eight more buyers for luxury sports cars.

As for Sebastin, as far as he was concerned, seeds were planted, doors were opened, lights were turned on . . . Whatever the appropriate analogy, the night went exactly as planned, and his plan was set in motion.

-TWO GEEKS IN A POD-

April, 2009.

"So what do you think of my new thesis title?" Molly asked as she crawled into bed next to him. It took Stephen a few minutes to wake from his sleep enough to focus on the piece of paper dangling a few inches from his face. "It's my eighth tweak this morning," she added, seeing his eyes open.

Dirty Laundry:
Quantifying the Transformational
Effects of the Internet on the Perceptions
of the United States among the
People of the Middle East

by
Molly Byrne

A Dissertation Submitted in Partial Fulfillment
of the Requirements for the Dual-Title Degree of
Doctor of Philosophy in the Department of
Political Science and the Department of
Anthropology at Brown University

Providence, Rhode Island

"It looks impressive," he said, squinting at the title. He had promised yesterday that he would be a sounding board for her latest thesis plans, though he hadn't expected it to be before he got out of bed. He read the page again. "I could never have come up with anything like this. I'd be embarrassed to tell you what I was working on for my thesis years ago."

"I didn't come up with the topic by myself. If I had, you can bet it would have had something to do with migration and Cameroon. But that's how my advisor and I *compromised*," she said with a roll of her eyes.

She climbed on top of the covers and stood up, straddling his chest. Stephen waited without saying a word. "You ready to hear my thesis pitch?" she asked. She was still wearing the tiny baby blue shorts and tight tank top she had worn to bed last night.

He sunk down further into the bed, continually looking up at her. He held on to her long smooth bare legs as she started immediately gesturing with her hands. "Before the Internet, there was no way for us to record what effect something had on a closed culture, or a town that we weren't allowed to enter. Imagine us throwing a bunch of books at some school in some village and the villagers actually taking the time to read them. We wouldn't know whether they appreciated them at all until we could study their changed behavior, and who knows how long that would take. Maybe years." She glanced down to make sure he was still paying attention. "But think about it. If the Internet really has an effect, people will write back and create their own web sites and blogs, post messages, or at the very least just search for more information. Its use alone will tell us the effect that it's having. Best of all, it's a closed system that we can monitor, track, and quantify. This is the first time in history we could ever do this and get immediate results and not wait for years like researchers had to before."

She finally took a breath. "I want to be the one who does it first. Come on, you've got to think that's pretty cool."

Just a few weeks ago, when they first met, he would have shied away from asking any questions or challenging her. Not anymore. If there was one thing graduate students were taught from their first day, it was to be critical of anything they heard, especially when it didn't come out of their own mouths. "It seems like the effect is kind of . . . ," he paused a second, knowing the reaction he was about to incite, ". . . obvious. I'm not sure your findings are going to be that interesting."

Molly's expression became stern as she wrested her legs free of his grasp and jumped onto the floor to look him in the eyes. "No, Stephen, that's not true at all. How can you say that? We don't know how things are going to turn out. You're thinking of what you see around you in Silicon Valley. Here, people are already skeptical of anything they read on the Internet; they know what to believe and what not to believe. Try to think about other countries just getting access to the Internet. It's not the same as here. Let me think how I can phrase it in terms *you* can understand."

She was pacing around the bed. "Imagine, Stephen, you live in a world without access to many books or to more than a single TV station. Now, all of a sudden, you get an Internet connection, maybe even for just a few hours a week. But, for those few hours, you get to see what's out there. You see new ideas, religions, politics, places that you never have before. All of a sudden, you're connected. How can you ever go back? Think about how incredibly transformed people will be when they learn about this other world out there. Sounds good, right? Now, instead, imagine that all you saw were hate messages on some discussion forum, or all you saw was even worse—just unabashed, un-forgiving calls to violence or God knows what other extremist views."

She stopped to scan Stephen's face for any reaction before continu-ing, "We really need to understand how people are influenced by this type of propaganda on the Net. It's easy to see the need for understand-ing it in some terrorist-laden remote village, or some extremist camp far away where we can't see it, right? But think about it here, in the U.S. When someone uses the Internet, what would happen if all they encountered day in and day out were hate messages and hate discussion groups? There are plenty of them out there. What do you think they would believe?"

Stephen ignored the question; he was fairly certain it was rhetori-cal. "I know. I got it. You're going to measure the influence of Internet propaganda in countries just getting Internet access. And that's impor-tant because—"

Before he could finish, Molly had taken over. The next few hours were filled with politics, religion, technology, and back again. Molly had clearly been looking for a sparring partner, and Stephen was happy to oblige—one of the many relaxing Sunday morning coffees in bed with his half-naked girlfriend that he could look forward to.

▼ ▼ ▼

Because of the myriad PBS and National Geographic documentaries (particularly those on the Maasai tribe in Kenya) that her parents had substituted for shows like *Three's Company* and *The Facts of Life*, her mind had been set on doing something good for the world for as long as she could remember. Hence, the Peace Corps.

When that came to an all-too-quick end, she didn't abandon her resolve to make the world better, even though she accepted that she might have to take a more circuitous route. Still, she wasn't about to find some vague justification of how some "normal" job did the world good. No, to make up for not being in the villages herself, she felt that her impact needed to be just as long-lasting and much bigger. From this, rose Molly's ambitions to help people like Sandrine escape the villages that offered them no opportunities and to give them hope of finding those opportunities elsewhere. She would study, from an anthropological and political science perspective, the migration from, and within, Africa.

In her department at Brown, this was considered a radical departure from the norm. It was a far more pragmatic topic than what her contemporaries in the Department of Anthropology chose to study—the cultural mores and social constructs of a long-past tribe or civilization, and the inevitable conclusions about how that particular tribe was uniquely relevant to the development of modern culture as we know it.

Molly and her advisor, Gale Mitchell, didn't see eye to eye on just how pragmatic, pragmatic should be. This starry-eyed idealism about changing the world was all well and good. She was absolutely free to select any topic she desired, but if she wanted funding from the department to continue her studies, it would have to be much closer to a topic that Gale actually cared about. And what Gale cared about was whatever she could obtain funding for, which didn't include "making the world a better place."

And so the thesis topic, the title of which Molly had just revised for the eighth time, was cemented. Molly would study the way the Internet changed how people felt about the U.S. Gale was happy. And Gale's funding, through whichever defense agency was currently backing research on the Middle East and the Internet, two of the trendiest topics in her field, was secured.

The topic was a far cry from migration in Africa. But Molly felt that though she may have compromised on the topic, she had not compromised on the magnitude of the positive effect her work would have. If she had her way, the effects of her research would do more long-term good for the world than she could have done with her old research ideas, and far more than she could have done in the Peace Corps by herself. It was an ideal compromise, one in which both parties felt like they wound up getting the upper hand.

▼ ▼ ▼

From the outset, Stephen had numerous reasons to be drawn to Molly. She was smart, passionate, attractive, and had a quality he never thought he would attribute to anyone in real life: She was inspiring. He admired what she had done in Cameroon—from the fact it was the Peace Corps to the reason she was kicked out. Like most people, he wouldn't have ventured to Africa by himself and he wouldn't have gone back into the room with the doctor, but he deeply admired people who possessed the courage to do so.

Since the first days of their relationship, there had been a small inkling of her feelings, too. In his own way, Stephen had cared about the people he felt responsible for at SteelXchanges. He didn't abandon them as would have been so easy, as even his co-founder, Arthur, had. That, she understood whole-heartedly at a personal level. She hadn't found that quality in many; her colleagues in graduate school were far too jaded and sarcastic, too removed to care, and her acquaintances in California were far too hurried and self-absorbed.

The intensity with which Molly lived her life was exactly what Stephen needed to remind himself of what his life had been like before

GreeneSmart. For Molly, the intensity she reignited in Stephen only served to increase her own, a renewed reminder of the responsibilities she had felt with Sandrine. It was like why so many doctors married each other—a shared base of fervency and experiences that didn't need explaining and didn't need repeated justification. It was simply their reality that others on the outside needn't understand.

On top of all that, there was the fact that neither of them had been in a relationship for over a year. That, coupled with their intensity, gave them enough passion in the less-than-cerebral pursuits of each other's bodies to keep them lavishly distracted in the precious little time they had together.

-AN UNDERSTATEMENT-

June 1, 2009. Start of Intern Season.

Stephen didn't mind the extra few minutes in the car. Today was the first official day of his internship. He knew enough about himself to recognize that once he started at Ubatoo, he would not be able to avoid, even if he wanted to, the irresistible ease of falling back into his old habits: no sleep, too much caffeine, and a complete lack, and even disdain, of "balance." He would happily neglect everything else in his life for his work. He had done it before in college, in grad school, in his old company, and now he would unquestionably do it again.

Since Ubatoo's party, Molly and Stephen had managed to spend at least several hours together every day. They could often be found sitting next to each other on a small sofa in GreeneSmart's employee lounge, anxiously talking about one or the other's "other job"—how Molly's research was going or how excited Stephen was about his internship. It wasn't long before their co-workers just gave the couple their space; neither had many close friends at GreeneSmart anyway.

Hopefully, the time lost not seeing Molly at work would be made up for by the fact that they would be moving in together this week. Though the decision had been made quickly, only three months after meeting each other, it came naturally, and neither of them had needed to think twice. They decided to move into Molly's apartment since it was within walking distance of Ubatoo. Like the rest of their very deliberate lives, it was well reasoned—there was no point in waiting to do something they would ultimately do anyway.

▼ ▼ ▼

Upon entering Ubatoo, Stephen was escorted to a large cafeteria where more than a dozen other interns were quietly waiting to be greeted by their sponsors. He joined the other data-mining interns, Aarti, William, and Kohan, who were already sitting together.

Beyond the standard beginning-of-job litany of forms, a nine-page document describing Ubatoo's code of ethics required his signature. Like everyone else, Stephen signed it without reading. Then, like with all tech companies, there were the non-disclosure and non-compete forms. These forms ensured that any thought from this day forward, valuable or otherwise, Ubatoo owned. No problems there either, Stephen thought.

By far, the strangest form was the one marked "Rules and Conditions for Data Access." In no uncertain terms, it clearly specified Ubatoo's immediate right to terminate employment, without recourse, if there was any unauthorized use of Ubatoo's data that it collected on its users. The data included, but was not limited to:

e-mail
e-mail response times
deleted e-mails
e-mail attachments
contact information
contact usage statistics
home address
work address
addresses explicitly provided
addresses automatically extracted from correspondences
age inferred
age explicitly given
birthday
maiden name
nickname
viewing history – videos watched
viewing history – online TV watched
length of online activity

time between online activity
location history given
phone number
location history inferred
calendar entries
online activity timings
personal photos
faces recognized in photos
objects recognized in photos
travel destinations recognized in photos
clothing recognized in photos
search terms entered
ads clicked
ads shown but not clicked
web sites visited
web sites receiving a click
images viewed
images clicked
image magnification
image linger time
sexual orientation inferred
sexual orientation explicitly given
mobile phone call logs
purchase transaction records
billing records
bill payment dates
profile updates
profile update frequency
personal documents
stock portfolios
credit checks
credit card numbers
credit card purchases
credit card spending trends inferred
credit card balances
travel information given

travel information inferred
personal files uploaded
spreadsheets uploaded
music preferences given
music preferences inferred
medical records
medical conditions inferred
preferences implied
preferences stated
Social Security numbers
instant messages
instant message statistics
searches on maps
searches on mobile phones
typing speed
hours spent online
sms messages sent
sms messages received
friends and contacts stated
friends and contacts inferred
social network stated
social network inferred

The list went on for six pages and had 220 items in it. The document ended with the statement that it was also reason for termination if, for non-company business, any individual's information was identified, unencrypted, un-anonymized, or even examined for personal use, monetary or otherwise.

The strongly worded document was intended to instill respect for the privacy of all of Ubatoo's users. But, at least for the four sitting at the table, it would have been difficult to construct a better combination of words to get them more titillated than ever before.

"Six full pages!" Kohan exclaimed. "I bet there's more data at Ubatoo than has ever been collected by any company. Probably more information on people is on their, I mean our, servers than has ever been collected in all of recorded history."

No one said anything. "Judging from the lack of arguments, I think we all agree. That's a first for us," Aarti said, smiling.

The first thing Stephen wanted to do, the minute he had access, was to find out what they knew about *him*. Though he did wonder if that was within the legal bounds of the documents he just signed. He didn't think it was, and he was right.

▼ ▼ ▼

Each time someone used Ubatoo's services for sending an e-mail or typing an instant message, a copy was stored in their massive databases. Every search ever conducted, whether at midnight in the privacy of your home or during business hours for your company, was the same for Ubatoo; each was logged and queued for analysis. Update your profile for your friends to see, and instantaneously seven copies of your page were updated across all of Ubatoo's servers, no matter where they were located in the world. All the presentations and the files you stored with Ubatoo for safekeeping and for sharing with colleagues, mothers' groups, and company boards were redundantly backed up in Ubatoo's "cloud"—vast farms of servers located in dozens of sites on six of the seven continents. The exact locations of these farms were known only to a few people within Ubatoo.

Where were all the places that your file was located? Nobody knew; only a sophisticated set of algorithms determined where the content was stored and where it was backed up. The algorithms automatically adapted to usage patterns, volume of inflows, and size of requests, just to determine where best to store your book report, your MP3 files, your stock portfolio, your e-mails, and your electronic greeting cards. The benefit to you was that even if all of Europe suddenly was hit by a me-teor, you would still have multiple copies of your e-mails and pictures of your vacation ready for perusal without interruption.

And when these servers weren't busy writing and storing your data, what did they do? Each set of servers crunched the data they had amassed, twenty-four hours a day, seven days a week, 365 days a year. No break required. Click something on Ubatoo's site, find a search result you wanted to read more about, an image you thought looked good? Immediately those clicks triggered dozens of machines to spring into action, ensuring those clicks were logged and saved for analysis. Even more immediate action was taken when someone used an Ubatoo phone or Ubatoo's virtual or plastic credit cards. These were high-value pieces of information that revealed much more personal and interesting insights about you, and so were queued to be processed immediately.

What the interns suspected was accurate: Each piece of this massive information repository amounted to more information about an individual than had ever been collected before, in all of recorded history, integrated through time. Although Ubatoo may not know the color of your eyes (unless you decided to upload a picture of yourself to their photo sharing services), enough data existed on their servers to tell a detailed story of you, down to the most minute details of your life. Everything was there, from your buying habits, to the e-mails you sent that you wouldn't want your boss to know about, to the pictures you searched for behind the privacy of closed doors. And why was this information collected? The simple answer was so Ubatoo could show you a better advertisement.

Create a profile of every user and utilize those profiles to personalize the temptations they see—flash an ad before their eyes for something Ubatoo knew they would crave before they did. Everything Ubatoo did, and every service it provided, seemingly for free, actually came at a miniscule price: your time, your attention, and hopefully, your click. An advertisement was shown to you. If you clicked the ad, the advertiser paid Ubatoo. Though almost nobody clicked regularly, almost everyone clicked sometimes. In the end, it was a simple numbers game. Make services that people used so they kept coming back, and each time they did, show an ad. Eventually, something would be enticing enough to make you click.

Adamantly against clicking? Not going to be swayed? That's okay, too. The profile built on you helped to understand others. Plenty of people like you existed, people who searched on the same things, who spent the same amount of money per week, and maybe even who lived in a house close to yours, and these people were more amenable to advertisements. So use the services all you want, your data was as good as your neighbors, and both sets of data were equally welcome.

The extremely grounded and ruthlessly capitalistic mission of better advertising was well understood among everyone who worked at Ubatoo. It stood in stark contrast to the idealistic and infamously liberal demographic of the "talent" employed there. This did not go unnoticed by management. For most of the workers at Ubatoo, the mechanisms behind Ubatoo's capital successes were placed in the same category as knowing that the sun rose in the morning: It mattered—they wouldn't know what to do without it—but it wasn't something that needed attention. For the technologist who worked on the "front-lines," there was the everyday battle of keeping the almost 3,650,000 servers located around the world up and running. For the hundreds of engineers working on their e-mail service, little was on their minds except meeting the growing requirements of a user base that was expected to triple in size by the end of the year. For the several thousand Ph.D.s working to make Internet searches more efficient, the thought of money and advertising never crossed their minds; the rapid growth of the Internet and all the information being produced was enough to keep their intellect entirely occupied.

For almost everyone at Ubatoo, the pace was so frantic that the only way to keep up was to keep their heads down. Immerse yourself in whatever project you were working on; everything else was taken care of for you. The only people who worried about finances were the "money people," who were intentionally housed in a building on Ubatoo's grounds separate from the scientists and engineers. The influence of the money people on the technologists was small; they were never allowed to make decisions regarding products or the activities of the technology talent. Instead, the sole job of a tiny number of selected individuals was to bridge the gap between the technologists and the money people. These selected individuals had two offices, one with the technologists and one on the other side of campus with the money minders. These individuals shielded both sides of the company from each other.

It was because of this carefully constructed shield that the four data-mining interns could remain blissfully enamored of the company despite, or in their case, because of, the papers that they had just signed. The thought of using all this data for producing money wasn't a connection they had made. What they knew, instead, was that they were about to be offered the keys to a kingdom of pure raw information. Few people, outside of Atiq's group, ever considered the number of actions, thoughts, and desires of users stored in Ubatoo's cloud, waiting to be mined.

And absolutely nobody, other than Atiq, ever grasped the enormity of what it meant to have profiled almost every user on the Internet. Almost everyone who had touched a computer had used at least one of Ubatoo's services at some point, whether it was through one of their partners or through Ubatoo directly. For each user, a profile had been constructed, waiting to be filled in with countless tiny bits from their lives, significant or otherwise, be it done over an hour or a year. All that the interns knew so far was based on the document they signed, which meant all they really knew for sure was that there was a lot of data. They would soon realize the magnitude of such an egregious understatement.

-EUPHORIA AND DIET PILLS-

June 1, 2009.

Two-wheeled razor scooter, flames painted on the handles, driven by an unidentified emaciated Indian guy with really big hair—heading straight for the table. He stopped inches from Kohan's boots and smiled as he looked over the cowboy. Without dismounting the scooter, he said, "I'm Jaan Ramamurthi—your sponsor. Follow me."

If there was such a thing as "royalty" in the data-mining community, Jaan Ramamurthi certainly qualified for that distinction. Although there may be fewer people in the world who recognized Jaan compared to the other more widely known royals found in castles and the tabloids, the respect his name evoked at this table certainly rivaled the respect any royal hoped to receive. Of the four, only Kohan knew what he looked like. He had watched Jaan accept the prestigious Breakthrough Award at the invitation-only banquet held in his honor at the *Pattern Recognition and Machine Intelligence Conference* last summer.

As they left the building and tried to keep up with Jaan and his scooter, they were surrounded by idyllic greenery, the obligatory gently gurgling fountains, and pristine building façades. All of this was in stark contrast to the scene that soon emerged. The stern concrete buildings to which they were headed were a drab mix of dark tinted brown glass and the just-slightly-less-brown concrete. From the outside, the buildings were as functional and austere as could be designed. Every hundred feet or so, a sign was posted next to the walkway: "This area is for employees only. Absolutely no guests permitted."

Jaan finally dismounted his scooter outside Building 11, in the mini parking spaces especially designated for scooters. A little receptionist, barely visible behind a high brightly colored desk, pressed a button, and a large door behind her left shoulder silently opened. "Good morning, Jaan," she called out loudly, the first sound they heard other than Kohan's boots on the shiny concrete floors. Jaan passed her with barely a glance, and a quiet mumbled thanks. The four followed close behind.

The labyrinth of corridors they had expected to find was instead a large open room with a mix of brightly colored low cubicles in the center, and small glass offices around the outer perimeter. Not only did it allow one to see from one end of the enormous room to the other, but it also allowed natural light to be seen from everywhere. A soft constant humming permeated the room—the sound of hundreds of computers running, waiting for something to do.

The offices were nothing special to look at, but they did house some of the more senior people at Ubatoo or those who had earned their place by performing a superhuman engineering feat or product release. Each office held two or more whiteboards filled with countless arrows and boxes and barely legible formulas, all liberally sprinkled with giant "DO NOT ERASE—¡No Borres!" magnets.

Building 11 was the home of the research group. The nameplates identifying the occupants of the offices were the latest source of wonder for the interns. The nameplates, subtly lit with solar-powered LEDs, held the names of the professors who wrote the textbooks they had used in graduate school, the lecturers from whom they had taken their courses, and the numerous classmates and school alumni who they had heard about or had vaguely known. They had all managed to find their way to Ubatoo. No other institution, in academics or in industry, had been able to amass such a stellar cast of computer scientists in its halls.

Most of the scientists were amicably chatting away or staring out their windows with glazed expressions. If work was in progress, it certainly wasn't apparent to the casual observer. Like any research lab, innovation happened in fits and starts. Long periods of frenzied work and creativity were followed by stretches of thought and play.

When Jaan stopped suddenly, the four interns who had been walking single file behind him, as if taking a cue from any Saturday morning cartoon, abruptly crashed into each other in their attempt not to run into Jaan. Jaan did his best to ignore them, and instead pointed to a group of about seventy desks in the middle of the room.

"Find good spots to sit in. Most of the desks will be taken by day's end. Interns from the other groups will also be sitting here. As for computers, I'm sure someone from IT will be around later to help you get set up. You don't have to worry about any of that—let someone else handle it," Jaan directed.

Jaan gave them a few moments to look around and scope out potential spots before continuing. "Normally, the first set of intern orientation meetings would take place at 11 o'clock. I'd like you to skip those. Instead, let's have our first meeting." He waited to see if anyone objected, but no one said a word.

"So, how about taking thirty minutes to drop off your stuff and find your way around? The snack rooms are back towards the lobby, as are the all-important coffee baristas. When you're done with that, meet me in the *Huckleberry Finn* conference room at 10:30. See you in a few minutes." Jaan then left them, and walked about a dozen feet to his own office.

Without knowing what else to do, the four found seats close to each other and near Jaan's office. Next, once the four confirmed what they had heard was true—all the perks and food and drinks on the grounds were free—the first and only stop during their thirty minutes was the closest coffee bar they could find. With double cappuccinos and extra-large gourmet coffees in hand, along with an enormous number of cookies, biscotti, and candy in their pockets, the four interns made their way at 10:25 to the Huckleberry Finn conference room. All the conference rooms were named after famous figures in children's literature.

Jaan was already seated and waiting. "Excellent. Good to see you found the conference room." They unloaded their pockets onto the table. "Glad to see you've already begun looting the place. It wouldn't be intern season if you hadn't."

"Let's get down to business, shall we? Atiq is in a bit of hot water for only hiring four of you for the Touchpoints project, so he's asked me to step in for a few weeks while he goes on a recruiting tour again. I'm going to make sure you get up to speed quickly. The best way to do this,

I imagine, is just to let you jump in and do something constructive." No comments arose, so he continued.

"I was thinking I'd just give you the project I'm working on. It's a marketing study, and not quite as sexy as selling sports cars like you did last time. I need you to find buyers for diet pills. Why, you may ask, do we care about diet pills? Well, it turns out . . ."

Diet pills. The long anticipation Stephen had felt in coming to Ubatoo was culminating on his first day with selling diet pills. It was, without overstating the obvious, an utter letdown. This is not the way he had anticipated spending his summer. He vaguely heard Jaan go on, rather unconvincingly, about the market capitalization of diet pill manufacturers, how much they spent on Ubatoo's sites per minute, the importance of this market, and so on.

Jaan finished his discourse with a question to all of them. "Now, it's your turn to talk. How would you start finding the best buyers for diet pills?"

Stephen tentatively raised his hand to offer a suggestion, but William started spewing half-baked thoughts without a moment's hesitation. "I think we can easily tackle this using the formulation in the paper by Redmon and Soffti that was presented at this year's *Knowledge Discovery and Data Mining* conference," he said with authority. "They showed the effectiveness—"

Jaan didn't let William finish his sentence. "You're talking about the paper in which they analyzed the buying habits of several hundred of their students over a period of two weeks, right?"

"Exactly. That's the one," William exclaimed, delighted at having his suggestion at Ubatoo recognized by Jaan.

"I see. Well, that's *exactly* the wrong way to go," Jaan replied harshly. "This isn't an academic exercise where we analyze a few people and come up with some ridiculous . . . ," he cut himself off midsentence, remembering that the four in front of him hadn't been here long enough for him to speak freely. "Look, this is your first day here, so you might as well learn this quickly. First, none of you have ever worked with the amount of data we have here, so whatever you think you know, you don't. Second, you don't need all those complex models and algorithms you studied in school. With enough data, try something simple first—it usually works just fine. We have so much information on so many people, rather than worrying about coming up with an esoteric complex approach, what you really need to concentrate on is how to put all of our tiny bits of information together in a way that makes sense. Third, the reason we hired all of you isn't because of what you've studied or what papers you've read. It's because we hope you know how to *think*. That means you know how to tackle new problems—and for you, these are all new problems. Without getting too Zen, let the data reveal its own secrets; just apply a little gentle coaxing. That's all you need." Jaan's voice softened. "Oh, and Stephen, you can put your hand down. There's no need to raise your hand in here."

William, immediately defensive, started again, "Okay, I got it. Let's start with people's buying records. Hey, Jaan, do we have access to them? We could always cross-reference that by scanning their e-mails to see if they talk about diets. Jaan, if it's possible, I'd like access to their e-mail as well. There's also the possibility of—"

Jaan cut him off again. "If we have the records, you have access to them. This is an important project, so if you can find a way to use the data, don't ask me about it—just use it. But, before we do anything, I'd like you to formulate a plan. Brainstorm something coherent; don't run willy-nilly through our data. There's too much. It'll waste your time and get you nowhere."

"How long do we have for this project?" Stephen asked.

"Well, I promised to launch experiments by tonight, but I think we can push that back a day."

Stephen and the other interns were dumbfounded. "Even if we do come up with a plan, there's no way we can search all of your logs and all of your users so quickly," Stephen worried aloud.

"Relax," Jaan replied, "you don't need to look at all of it. We're just doing this study for U.S.-based users. Start with the 200 million in the U.S. Some of the prebuilt user profiles we have will help you."

"200 million? By tomorrow night?" Stephen asked incredulously.

Jaan's seriousness faded, he smiled an enormous grin and stood up to address his charges. He'd been anxiously awaiting the right time to bring this up. "I give you all of India," he said in a tone that could have been mocking or sincere. No one could tell.

He continued, eyes wide, looking more than a tad possessed. "We have 139,000 machines in our India datacenter set up to handle the high volume of traffic we have in the middle of the day there. Fortunately, by the time you're ready to crunch data, it will likely be nighttime in India, so our traffic to the datacenter will have dropped dramatically. We'll easily be able to reroute all of India to other datacenters in Asia and Europe. You'll have all the machines completely at your disposal. Do with them what you will. The data is prepped and ready to go. See, all you have to do is ask, and we shall provide."

Diet pills or not, the enormity of the problem was enthralling. They were about to tap into Ubatoo's massive computer cloud, and use all those machines, sitting idly in India, as a single colossal computer, sifting through user profiles and all the other evidence that had been gathered on virtually every user in the U.S. It would have literally taken months anywhere else to do what this massive computation machine would complete in under a minute. This was a statistic that each of them figured out before Jaan's smile had time to fade.

▼ ▼ ▼

Jaan had a vested interest in ensuring that the interns did well. He was the brains behind the technology powering the Touchpoints project. He had designed how the data was stored, how it could be accessed rapidly, and how the trillions of little pieces of information Ubatoo collected were ready when needed. The interns were a good test case. If novice users could utilize the system effectively, it would go a long way to proving how well he had designed Touchpoints.

The brainstorming session progressed as Jaan had hoped. Like everyone Ubatoo hired, when working, the reason why the interns were selected was clear. They were good—excellent, in fact—at what they did. Schemes of how to best incorporate the pieces of information Ubatoo gathered were created, torn down, and rebuilt, all progressing to the solution they were seeking. Whether analyzing people's e-mails, chat transcripts, web sites visited, search terms used, or recent purchases, everything was fair game. Each one of these pieces of information—information "signals"—yielded small but vital clues about how likely a person was to buy diet pills. Find the people who matched these signals, and show them the right advertisements—do that and their ability to resist will disappear as fast as, well, chocolate cake at a Weight Watchers meeting. It was as simple as that.

It didn't take long for the subject matter, diet pills, to become just another abstraction, another signal to predict. The fact that more computer power than most countries have would be used to efficiently find consumers in the U.S. who were susceptible to the next diet pill fad was just something that would soon be, if it was not already, taken for granted.

With the pieces of the puzzle falling into place, the hours slipped away quickly. It wasn't until almost 3:30 that Jaan spoke of something other than the task at hand, "You all must be quite hungry. I entirely forgot to feed you." Nobody immediately volunteered to own up to the fact that they were famished (or point out they weren't babies/pets/plants). Nevertheless, it was clear from their willingness to look away from their computer screens that they were ready to eat. "I'll get us something. Why don't you head over to the patio? I'll meet you there."

They made their way through the vast maze of unoccupied cubicles—empty because the other interns were still at the orientation class that they too would have attended had they been assigned to any other sponsor. The bright sunlight, which burst on them as they exited, burned their eyes instantaneously. Four new interns, lost, temporarily blinded, stumbling into each other, with tears streaming down their cheeks—it was quite a sight to behold.

"I figured I had to make up for forgetting about you earlier," Jaan said when he met them a few minutes later. "So we shall have a feast! I told the chefs that we're working on a crucial project for Atiq. That was all it took."

Conversation about data and the task was shelved as Jaan told them what he had ordered (all done through an e-mail with the subject "Food-Needed ASAP" sent to food-help@ubatoo.com). Soon, they were rewarded with the arrival of three catering carts, holding enough food for at least ten people. The appetizers were excellent, but the entrees, seared scallops and filet mignon for the carnivores, and a Japanese tofu dish for the vegetarians, served by waiters dressed in clean white uniforms, exceeded even the already high expectations set by the first course. Despite the quality of the food, that deserved to be savored, the meal started winding down only ten minutes after it started.

"I don't suppose you have people's medical records online do you?" Kohan asked, returning to the task at hand. He had said it half jokingly, but still, they were all curious how far Ubatoo had ventured into that territory.

"No, unfortunately not yet," Jaan said with real regret, silently considering the possibilities. "When we do, though, it'll make this project a lot easier. We'd have you targeted from birth." He stood up abruptly, "Ready to go back to work? Let's get some drinks—we'll hit a coffee bar on the way back."

With caffeinated beverages of choice—two cappuccinos, one latte, and two extra-caffeinated waters—in hand, everyone was soon back at their desks, furiously working on the latest variation they had conceived on their walk back from lunch.

▼ ▼ ▼

Think, Type, Caffeine. Think, Type, Caffeine. One a.m. came quickly. Most of the denizens in the surrounding offices had long ago called it quits for the night. When Jaan announced that the four should probably think about going home, all of them were genuinely taken aback that he would suggest stopping so early.

"You think we've done enough?" Aarti asked.

"So far, so good. I think we've come a long way since the beginning of the day. We'll deploy the results you found in the morning, when we can use the servers in India to crunch the data. Within a day we'll see if we've convinced America to buy more diet pills. We'll know for sure by tomorrow night."

Without looking away from his computer, William asked, "Can you give me thirty more minutes, Jaan? I've been working for the last couple of hours on squeezing more information from all the overweight support groups. There are so many . . ."

"You want us to stay, too? I can stay or come back later if you need me?" Aarti offered.

"No, you guys go ahead. I just need thirty minutes. Is that ok, Jaan?"

"No problem," Jaan replied. "It's early. I'll be here for hours. Let's plan on meeting at 11 o'clock tomorrow morning."

With that, the three took their leave. More excited than tired, it had been a good, actually awesome, first day.

-TO BETTER DAYS-

May, 2006.

They had rented out the entire restaurant, *Il Fornaio*, in Palo Alto, and everything was on the house. There would be no talk of money tonight, unless it was at least a million or more. It had been almost eight years in the making and this very restaurant was where it had begun. This was the location of the final meeting the four of them had held—where these four friends cemented their business plan and fortified their resolve to quit their regular jobs and take a chance with founding a new company. It all took place in the same booth in which the champagne fountain was flowing tonight.

It was almost 11:30, and Sebastin sat by himself at the bar near the front of the restaurant. The boisterous crowd of over 180 employees and guests were outside on the back terrace, laughing, talking, making deals, and making connections. Likely, the seeds of the next company were already being planted out there. Another eight years, and this whole scene would be repeated, but Sebastin wouldn't be there then.

Mark had come to find him. "We did it, Sebastin. This is what we've been waiting for." Mark, along with Elizabeth, Nate, and Sebastin had been the founders of iJenix.com—as of this morning, with papers freshly inked, an officially wholly owned subsidiary of the Mahabishi Keiretsu.

Sebastin raised his glass. "Cheers," he said, and took another sip, his third drink in the last forty-five minutes.

"Come on Sebastin, cheer up," Mark said. "This is our night. To-morrow, when you wake up, you'll have nowhere to be, and you'll take your place as one of those who made it in Silicon Valley. It'll hit you tomorrow how lucky you are."

Sebastin raised his glass again and thrust it against Mark's, spilling most of both drinks. "I'll drink to that."

"Lighten up, Sebastin," Mark said with a grin as he nonchalantly wiped the mix of drinks from his shirt. "Good things are on their way. In a few months, when we're all refreshed and bored to tears from not doing anything, we're going to open up our first new office for our next gig. What's the latest name you came up with, again?"

Sebastin tried to manage a smile as he repeated the name, "Ameri-can Coalition for Civil Liberties."

"Right, right. What a wonderfully serious name. ACCL—it just screams official and powerful . . . and *good*. And we'll head it together, and lead it to great things—bettering the world, and all that." Mark was flying high tonight. "We've dreamed about doing this. We knew that after iJenix sold and we'd each made our first million, we'd do something good together. Come on, Sebastin, cheer up—we're actually going to do it finally—things are coming together."

"For you," Sebastin muttered under his breath.

"No," Mark replied firmly, his smile still intact. "They're coming together for both of us. We're going to do ACCL together, just like we did here."

"Just like here?" Sebastin was trying to hold it together, but that was too much. "Is that a joke? We weren't in it together here, Mark. You took care of yourself pretty damn well. Took care of Elizabeth and Nate. But, me, no. Me, nothing doing."

"Sebastin, we're not going through this again," Mark said quietly, any trace of a smile finally extinguished. "Not again. We've been through this—yesterday, the day before, and the day before that. I did what I could for all of us. You know that."

Sebastin toasted his own reflection in the mirror behind the bar. "I know." A minute adjustment of his eyes, and he could see Mark watching his reflection, too. "I know that in a few months from now, when we start a do-good non-profit, *then* we're going to share every-thing equally." He wasn't speaking as loudly anymore, but the bitter-ness didn't dissipate. "What about right now, Mark? What about the last eight years?"

"You're drunk, Sebastin. Maybe you should just call it a night."

"We were in this together, remember?" Sebastin was furious. "We're back in this same restaurant. Remember, Mark? This is where *I* invited the four of us to meet to hash out our plans. Or have you forgotten?"

"I haven't forgotten."

"You could have done something more for me."

"Sebastin, you know I tried. You know that all the Mahabishi guys wanted to fire you. They didn't trust you or want to deal with you again. You nearly single-handedly torpedoed the entire deal. You were way too aggressive—way, way out of line. They called your bluff, and we almost all paid the price for it."

"I did it for us—we could have gotten more."

"You shouldn't have, and you didn't need to. Nobody asked you to start making up stories, making up sales numbers. What were you thinking? You didn't talk to us about it—you just did it on your own. You got greedy. We were in the home stretch, and you had to start opening your mouth, coming up with anything to milk them for more money. You were out of control."

"I told you, it was for us."

"And I told you, you shouldn't have," Mark said resolutely, though he couldn't look at Sebastin as he said it. "Look, you and I—we've got to get past this. We both did okay in the end. The rest of the team came together, saved the deal, saved your ass, and it's behind us now. It's done."

Sebastin finished off the remaining drops of his drink without look-ing outside the bottom of the small crystal glass. "Tell me again, Mark, how is it that you wind up with more than $17 million out of this deal, and I have only two? How is that, Mark?"

Mark was gritting his teeth, his breath was shallow and his mouth barely opened when he spoke. "Maybe we should just forget about working together after tonight, Sebastin. You've got to figure out if you can get past this. You need to figure out what matters to you."

"Oh, screw you, Mark," Sebastin said as he reeled off his stool.

Mark grabbed Sebastin's arm before he could walk away. He wouldn't let him ruin this night completely. "Where you going?"

Sebastin waved his empty glass inches from Mark's face. "Empty. Or should I 'just get past it,' and 'figure out what matters to me,' too?"

"Damn it, Sebastin. Sit down. Stay here." Mark ordered as he grabbed the glass. "Don't talk to anyone until I get back."

Eight years. Two million dollars. This is what he had been working for? Two million? That's not what a startup is about. Nobody moves to Silicon Valley for two million. Where are the private jets and the islands he was supposed to buy? What a waste of time. Was he really going to work with these three again? A bullet in the eye sounded better.

Another drink was placed before him, along with a glass of water, which he immediately cast aside. He lifted the fresh drink to his mouth and turned fully to face Mark. "To better days," he said. A pleasant numbing burn warmed his throat.

"What are you going to do with all your money?" Sebastin asked.

No response. Mark looked away from Sebastin, back toward the party. The music was pouring in from the terrace, flowing across the terra-cotta tile and filling every silent moment with irrelevant noise.

"You could have done better for me, Mark. You know it. You made sure Nate and Elizabeth got their share. You could have done more for me," Sebastin said distantly.

"Sebastin, you're walking away with two million dollars. Two. Why don't you take some time off, I mean really off, and get away? You've got nothing else to do. You owe it to yourself to get away for a while."

Sebastin didn't reply.

"I've got to get back to the party, and you should go home—now," Mark directed.

Sebastin clumsily slid off his stool and stumbled to the front door, only a few feet away.

"Call me, Sebastin, whenever you're ready to work together again. We'll take care of each other on this one, okay? For what it's worth, again I'm sorry I couldn't have done even more for all three of you. Especially you, Sebastin. We've been friends for a long time. Don't let this last month mess up what we've been waiting for. We've worked too long to piss it all away. Let's go do something good for the world. Let's start ACCL and get out of this miserable rat race. We've been in it too long. It's driving us crazy. What do you think, buddy?"

"Asshole," he muttered. He wasn't sure Mark heard him or not. He hoped he did, *buddy*.

Sebastin stepped outside into the orange glow of the streetlamps and the flow of the college kids and night traffic. He sipped the drink he had managed to stay levelheaded enough to take with him, and started walking toward home. Two million—that's not what he'd signed on for. Maybe it really was time to do something else. He knew he'd call Mark in a few months, and it infuriated him. But Mark was right—ACCL changed the game; it didn't have to be the same rat race anymore. ACCL was about doing something good, not just about making money. That had to be better than this. Even so, doing ACCL in the Valley, with all the publicity it would garner and the personal cachet it would bring, there would inevitably be money, too. There had to be. Downing the rest of the drink, he sucked the ice clean and let the glass shatter on the pavement. Seven miles to home. He'd see how far he could go it alone; he had nothing better to do.

-MARATHON-

"Good God, Stephen. That sounds horrible," Molly said.

Stephen had stopped by GreeneSmart to see her on his way into work. He realized only after he'd begun telling her about his first day that everyone might not see it in the same light he did. "No, no. It wasn't horrible, it was amazing. I can't believe how much we did in one day."

"You're worse than I am. I've lost you to Ubatoo, haven't I? We're never going to see each other, are we?" Molly said, enjoying her dramatic words and exaggerated swoons.

"We'll see each other all the time. We're moving in together on Sunday. I know you haven't forgotten that!" Stephen replied happily.

She stopped laughing too quickly.

She took his hand in hers timidly. "No, I haven't forgotten." She lowered her gaze so that she wasn't looking at him anymore. "But I think we need to talk about Sunday."

This was coming out of the blue.

"I've been thinking," she started. "I've been thinking about this a lot."

He held on to her hand tighter. She squeezed back, but not for long enough.

"I don't know about Sunday," she said. "I don't know if that's a good idea . . . I don't know . . ."

Stephen reached for her other hand, too. But she wouldn't let him hold it. She pulled it back gently, but resolutely. They were facing each other, he looking at her, and she looking at the floor. He hadn't expected this. He should have known something would happen. Too much was going right. Whenever things started going well, something always happened to bring it to an end.

"I mean, I think—" Only silence.

Go on. Say it. Get it over with. "What's wrong?" he said, finally unable to wait any longer. His voice cracked, letting on more than he wanted.

She just stood there, looking at the floor. "I think . . . I think Saturday would be better?" she said without a hint of smile.

Stephen stopped. With her face lowered, her eyes looked up at him through a veil of messy hair, waiting for a reaction. He let out a loud groan while she broke out giggling.

"That was completely uncalled for, you know," Stephen said, as the weight of what could have been lifted. The conversation flowed easily from that point. Though, after finding out that everything really was okay—better than okay—Stephen's mind didn't take even a full minute to turn back to Ubatoo.

▼ ▼ ▼

A normally shy and exceptionally mousy woman in her self-reported late thirties, Mary listened for a few moments with the devilish satisfaction that only comes from hearing something she wasn't meant to hear. The conversation coming from one aisle over from where she was standing—it sounded like this girl was breaking up with her boyfriend. He probably deserved it, she thought, satisfied with the parts she heard.

Mary was working her way back and forth through the store to kill a few minutes before she had to run her next errand. She'd been careful to avoid all those aisles holding the colorful snacks to which she was so readily drawn. No candy aisles; no aisles with the yummy fruit drinks. She would not put herself in a place of such temptation. Just stay away. She walked to the books instead and picked up the first diet book she saw with a glitzy cover, vowing to read it the moment she got home.

Her problem wasn't severe. A few pounds to lose. Maybe a few more than a few, but still not severe. Any number of excuses rationalized her current weight, and they all applied equally well: no time to find something healthy; portions are too big everywhere; there's no time to cook; money is tight and it's too much stress; it's what happens when one gets older; no time to exercise; and so on. But Mary wanted to change; the mirror wasn't as friendly as it once had been.

Now that she was home, how to start? She had a book. But that was a lot to read and she wasn't nearly as motivated to read it at home as she had been in the store. Besides, from looking over the back cover, it looked like a lot of steps to follow. Surely someone had found an easier way? What's the latest in dieting breakthroughs? she asked herself. She walked to the computer in the family room, and searched on the Internet. "Diets," "successful diets," "latest diets"—all these search queries led her to more information than she knew what to do with. But she was diligent in her pursuit; she needed to lose that weight.

Mary scanned through the list of web sites returned looking for nuggets of truth among all the claims. She knew better than to trust all of them; some were probably just lies. She clicked a few links, believing the promises they flashed, but they didn't go anywhere she needed to be. After all, she wasn't looking to lose *that* much weight. The people on those sites had *real* problems. Not her.

Maybe she should just start with something easier, maybe just a beginner weight loss program. She searched again using "weight loss programs," and voilà, numerous suggestions. But which one was right for her? There were so many to choose from.

Another search: "Weight loss program reviews." There she found what she was looking for—in-depth reviews of the programs, along with links encouraging her to join support groups associated with those programs. Maybe there she would find people with the same set of problems. She joined. Finally! People she could relate to. All of them were more than willing to respond to personal questions so they too could share their stories and be helpful. She wrote to one of them, a man who lived, coincidentally, in Los Angeles, a place she had always wanted to visit. He seemed particularly trustworthy. It was a short e-mail, little more than "how do I get started" and "congratulations, you're an inspiration to me."

She signed up for the diet plan the man swore by, even used an online calendar to schedule what she should be eating every day and when to eat it. The man strongly suggested finding a doctor, too, a nutrition specialist, to make sure this diet was appropriate for her. Good advice, she thought. Good man. She searched again for "nutrition specialist, doctor." The first link returned was a doctor in her area; she wouldn't even have to drive that far. She scheduled an appointment with him as soon as she could and set a reminder on her calendar to make sure she didn't forget. She was ready. Let it begin.

▼   ▼   ▼

Despite trying his hardest to stay away from work until at least 10:30, by 10:15 Stephen found himself back in Building 11. The intern pit was crowded. More than three quarters of the desks were occupied. The interns from outside the data-mining group were staring rather absent-mindedly at their screens or talking in hushed voices with each other. They had nothing to do yet except wait for their next orientation class.

The four data-mining interns, though, were in an entirely different state of mind. They were eagerly looking over the work they had done last night. It was only 10:30 when Jaan walked by. Since all four were present, the meeting started early, and he called them all back into another conference room, *Despereaux*. Both Aarti and William, who sat next to each other, were acting as giddy as school girls sharing hushed secrets about boys. Aarti looked tired, but William looked like crap. He had coffee stains on his shirt with matching drips on his pants, his eyes were bloodshot, and his hair was an assortment of greasy clumps that he had obviously been pulling at for hours. Worse, he smelled as bad as he looked.

"So, want to tell everybody what happened last night?" Jaan said from the head of the table. "Or should I?"

William quickly spoke up. "Aarti and I spent the night here with Jaan. I think we came up with something pretty awesome. It's not just about their social groups like we had been thinking all along. It's about what they do when they're *not* online."

Aarti stepped in. "The people who are the most desperate for help with their weight problems are going to be the ones we want. They're the ones who buy the diet pills we're trying to sell, right? We need to find the desperate ones, not just the talkers in the social groups. There might be a correlation, of course, but we can do better. We only had to look at their—"

William took over again. "—at their calendars. If you make an appointment with a doctor to do something about your problem, wouldn't that mean you're probably going to do anything that might help, like buying the latest pills?"

"How did you find what's on their calendar?" Stephen asked.

Aarti answered Stephen directly. "Ubatoo launched an online calendar almost a year ago, Stephen. Don't you use it?"

Stephen grimaced. He didn't use it, or for that matter, even know about it.

"How did you know that the appointment was for a weight problem, or even for a doctor?" Kohan asked.

"Not an issue," said William. "For every appointment on every calendar for the past year, we just checked if it had the term 'doctor' or the letters 'D' and 'R' in it. Then we just looked up that doctor's name, and found whether there was a match geographically close to the user. We searched for the doctor's name on Ubatoo, like everyone else does, to find out what type of doctor he was. See? Easy." He was beaming, having impressed himself. Then he added for flavor, "This is all predicated on the fact that nobody, fat people especially, wants to travel far to see a doctor if they don't have to."

"Charming, William," Stephen almost said aloud.

William was still speaking, "Overall, though, I think the lesson learned is that the calendar is definitely a pretty strong clue, especially when you know where someone lives."

"The calendar was what I came up with," Aarti said, "but as you're about to say next, Stephen—" With that, Stephen perked up. He really wasn't about to say anything. "—the set of people who actually use our calendar is pretty small compared to all the people Ubatoo has profiles on, right?" Aarti stopped, but just long enough to catch her breath. "This is when William's social group profiling from last night actually became useful. For the people who had appointments with weight loss doctors, we examined who they talked to most often on the phone, or who they sent e-mails to most often, and which self-help groups they joined. If their friends also had appointments with doctors, they were probably both feeding each other's desperation. Come to think of it, just imagine all those people we found who had two or three friends who had appointments with weight loss doctors. Those could be prime targets for—"

"It'll work fine just the way it is," William interrupted impatiently. He was annoyed that Aarti was speaking so much and even going off on a tangent they hadn't yet explored. "Okay, okay," Jaan broke in. He could see the deer-in-the-headlights look Stephen and Kohan shared. "This is fantastic. First things first, we'll let India finish applying your findings to each and every one of our users. I'm sure we'll unearth some excellent targets with your approach. Later today, we'll start our first live trials. If everything still looks good, I'll pull some strings and see if we can't bypass the rest of testing—meaning, we could have a full-scale deployment running by tomorrow."

Jaan continued, "But guys, remember, this is a marathon, not a sprint. These are some early interesting results. You tried something new and innovative, and it looks like it'll pay off. If we can get a win this quickly, that's great, but we have plenty more difficult problems to tackle. This is only your second day. So, good job." After a small pause, he concluded with, "To all of you." With that, Jaan opened the door, and they filed out.

As they reached their desks, Jaan called out for Aarti and William to join him. As the three were walking away, he could be heard saying something about "face time" and "sharing their findings with Atiq." Becky, Atiq's administrative assistant, who had been sitting at her desk waiting for Aarti and William to catch up to Jaan, led them into Atiq's empty office. There, a video-conference with Atiq, who was waiting to hear the good news, was ready.

It was the second day at Ubatoo, and already Stephen had lost any vestige of his former position as the leader of his own company. At that moment, he became just one of the struggling interns hired for the summer. Marathon or not, everyone was sprinting.

-THE LIFE AND SOUL OF
AN INTERN-

June 5, 2009.

Two thick envelopes rapidly found their way through the miles of inter-office mail stations onto the desks of Aarti and William. The envelopes proudly displayed the Ubatoo logo and the words "Welcome Aboard," for anybody and everybody to see. Aarti and William were offered full-time jobs the day after their diet pill breakthrough was officially deemed a success. Advertisements for "miracle pills," "diet of the year," and "no exercise needed, burns the fat for you" were reaching the most susceptible demographic faster than ever, and the meticulously targeted audience was vigorously buying everything they were selling with renewed hope. The advertisers were ecstatic.

Before they had unpacked their belongings in the "intern pit," Aarti and William found themselves seated in their own offices close to Jaan. Whether their good fortune was a reflection of their impressive work or the desperate need for Atiq to hire wasn't clear. But one fact remained—in the first week, they had received what the other interns would struggle to obtain throughout the rest of the summer.

▼ ▼ ▼

June 22, 2009.

Walking through the doors into Building 11, it was impossible for Stephen not to instinctively peer into the offices he passed, hoping that one of the occupants would be serendipitously looking up at just the right moment and would engage him in conversation about their latest project or even inquire about his. But that didn't happen. If Aarti needed something, she found Stephen herself, Jaan's only communication was through e-mail, and William—well, he was better left alone in his office anyway.

Despite the lack of communication with those three, Stephen had little to complain about. In exchange for every last bit of his ability to think, Stephen's waking hours were taken care of entirely. A typical day's schedule deviated little from the previous day or the next day, and consisted of the following:

8:00–8:30 a.m.	Wake up.
8:30–8:45	Walk to Ubatoo.
8:45–9:15	Get omelet, cappuccino, or fresh smoothie on way to desk.
9:15–11:45	Work.
11:45–12:00 p.m.	Gather group of other interns for lunch, and debate about the best café to try.

12:00–1:15	Lunch
	    Get sushi at least two times per week.
	    Get lobster if featured.
	    Get veal if it's on the menu.

1:15–1:30	Walk to a far cappuccino stand to get a bit of exercise.
1:30–2:00	E-mail/chat with other interns about work.
2:00–3:00	Meet with data-mining team to get updates.
3:00–5:30	Work.
5:30–6:45	Dinner (Any café other than where lunch was eaten).
6:45–8:30	Goof off.
8:30–12:00 a.m.	Work.
12:00–1:00	Walk outside with Kohan and any interns who want to join.
1:00–2:15	Late night snack and coffee at desk while working.
2:15–2:30	Walk home.
2:30–3:15	Hang out with Molly.
3:15–8:00	Sleep.

Between meetings and dedicated work time, more than eleven hours a day were spent working. It wasn't that Ubatoo demanded this schedule; distractions, if desired, were ample. A few weeks into the internship, the annual intern versus scientist baseball outing was held on a perfectly manicured field on the grounds. When Kohan and Aarti left to join the others, Stephen promised to catch up later. He knew he wouldn't, though. The similarity between these events and a senior citizen three-day all-inclusive cruise with perky, vacant, over-zealous "fun-directors" relentlessly reminding everyone how best to have fun was inescapable. He had just spent the last two and a half years in a too comfortable, too easy job—he had no need to relax now.

One notably absent entry in the schedule was Jaan. He rarely spoke to the interns after the first week. Jaan's e-mails, which he sent every few days, were terse: the name, contact information, and relevant background about the latest advertising client who needed help. Stephen's job was to determine how to improve the client's advertisement campaigns—just like Aarti and William had done in their first days. If not diet pills, it was gym equipment, lawyers, videogames, movies, banks, airline tickets, candy, and the list went on and on. Whatever it was, it was advertised on Ubatoo.

The moment a new advertising client learned that their assigned contact, Stephen, was "just an intern," they rattled off a litany of projects for Stephen to complete immediately. But the five minutes of thought that some mid-level manager had given to his marketing campaign the day after his boss had yelled at him for being sloppy, simply couldn't compare to the concentration that Stephen put into his work, into finding what information the raw data held and how to best coax it free. None of the clients had played with the raw data from their company's competitors. Most hadn't even bothered to play with their own. Before the first conversations were through, nobody remembered that they were talking with "just an intern." Many were just silently thankful that Stephen wasn't vying for their own job.

The little discoveries and breakthroughs Stephen made for the advertisers were appreciated—and expected for all of the interns hired. This work was too easy. But boredom was never a concern. Stephen spent hours beyond what was expected, even for an Ubatoo intern, learning how to leverage Ubatoo's vast infrastructure and harness all the computation power available. He was also one of the few interns beginning to recognize what was possible with all the data Ubatoo had amassed. Nobody limited what Stephen did; the data, resources, and knowledge were ready for the taking by anyone who bothered to reach for them.

Ubatoo's cocoon—this was why it was created. He knew it. Ubatoo knew it. However anyone wanted to spend their time—working, playing, learning, eating, relaxing—it could all be done without leaving the sanctuary of Ubatoo's grounds. From the moment of waking to the moment before sleep, his thoughts stayed at work. If not yet his soul, at least his mind and wearied body belonged to Ubatoo. The ivory tower of research in academia was never as completely pristine as the world he was in.

As for the little part of his life that occurred almost four blocks from Ubatoo's grounds, he and Molly had moved in together, as planned. It worked out without any of the hitches everyone had warned him about. Though his schedule would have destroyed most relationships, with Molly being just as enraptured with her own work it made their absences all the less pronounced. In their times together, they rarely talked about work. They were both too far in the trenches and minutiae of their own research to bring the other one up to speed; it would require too much effort. Besides, the relationship was still new, and there were plenty of other, more typical, ways of spending the forty-five minutes they had together before they fell asleep.

-CANDID CAMERAS-

July 7, 2009.

Pink. It was rare to see anyone who works at Ubatoo blush. Topics usually didn't veer that way. But there Yuri was, turning shades of pink to match the color in question, a noticeable variation from his usually stark white complexion. His to-the-point words and lack of any intonation didn't confess his emotions, though his face certainly did. Yuri succinctly replied, "Pink. That's people searching for porn."

▼ ▼ ▼

Though Yuri frequently accompanied Stephen and Kohan on their nightly walks around Ubatoo's grounds, the attempts to coax him into joining the conversation weren't met with success. Yuri Wegovich remained exceedingly quiet and his characteristic vacant expression rarely left his face. It was only when, on one of these walks, Yuri sprinted a mile to return to his cubicle's whiteboard to hurriedly jot down a thought that had apparently been percolating in his mind, that Stephen questioned his initial explanation of Yuri's perennial vacant expression—perhaps it wasn't simply an indication of an empty head, but rather the unconcerned obliviousness of deep thought.

Five weeks into the internship, on a nightly walk, Yuri, in his thick Polish accent and peculiarly formal English, spoke of his own accord. "When we have completed this walk, I would very much like a moment with you both."

Stephen and Kohan immediately stopped walking and turned to face Yuri. Yuri stood silently, inexpressively observing the two concerned faces fixed on him. A few uneasy moments and several self-conscious blinks later, Yuri volunteered, "After listening on many walks about what you two do, I wanted to try it also. I would like to have a few minutes of your time and show you what I have created, if that is okay."

"We knew we'd convert you, hanging out with us for so long. It was all just sinking in, wasn't it? Forget all that computer vision stuff, or whatever it is your group does, Yuri. It's all about the data," Kohan said.

Whether it was the thick accent, the pause between words, or simply his distraction with Kohan's all-denim outfit of the day, Yuri's response sounded impatient. "Yes, yes. Just look at my demo, and you let me know what you think. Okay?"

The novelty of Yuri contributing to the conversation outweighed Stephen's need to stick to his normal schedule, so he didn't give in to the strong pull of his midnight snack and coffee ritual. Instead, he walked with them to Yuri's desk.

Yuri grabbed a remote control, and immediately four enormous LCDs around the room blinked to life as the recognizable outline of California came into view on the map displayed. He clicked his mouse a few times as he zoomed in tighter and tighter until the neighborhood surrounding Ubatoo's grounds was prominently visible. Then, each house, one by one, blinked and then glowed red, blue, or green or some other hue, until the whole screen was awash in myriad colors. "The red houses mean someone in that house is currently using our search engine. The house is blue if they are chatting or e-mailing; the really dark blue means they've been chatting for hours; purple if they are looking at our photo site; and green if they have just bought something using one of our credit cards. Black just means we have no data on that house, but there aren't too many of those."

They were silent for a few seconds as Yuri virtually steered the camera through the streets of one neighborhood and into the next—all the houses emanating a bright glow, disclosing, across the four LCD screens, whatever activity the inhabitants were doing in their homes. Yuri stopped at a randomly chosen two-level house, glowing red, and clicked it. In a moment, a bubble surfaced above it, displaying all the searches and images the user in that house was looking at, only a few milliseconds after the user saw it himself. He moved his mouse over other houses and clicked, until he had repeated the motion a dozen times. All of the houses had bubbles above them, showing the activities in progress.

Stephen was the first one to speak. "You're going to make some product marketing person ecstatic, Yuri. This is really beautifully done. Some of the houses are pink, by the way. What are they looking at?"

It was then that the blushing started. Yuri didn't want to respond, but Kohan and Stephen were waiting for an answer, watching him squirm uneasily. Then came Yuri's embarrassed explanation for pink: "Pink is for Porn." Stephen glanced at Kohan, hoping somehow he would convey the message not to poke too much fun at Yuri for monitoring this, as Kohan would inevitably want to do. Whether Kohan picked up the hint or decided it for himself was uncertain, but thankfully Kohan let it go. "I get all the data-mining stuff, Yuri. We do that everywhere on everything. But how in the world did you get such detailed, high-resolution images of the houses? I've never seen that before," Kohan said.

Stephen replied instead since Yuri was still taken aback by the pink conversation. "It's all available on the Web, Kohan. There's a small company that provides them for anyone to use how they want. Just do any search. You'll find them." Kohan just shrugged his shoulders.

Yuri had regained some of his composure. They were now talking about his area of expertise, and though he would never bring up his own work, he welcomed this opportunity to talk about it. "Actually, Stephen, we don't want to rely on anyone else's images for too much longer. I do not know if you are aware, but we are building our own neighborhood scanning vans with many high-resolution cameras to have this data all to ourselves. We have only a few right now that are driving through California taking pictures, but we'll have more soon. That's my project this summer, integrating all the images we're collecting from the vans ourselves with the images we're getting from satellites."

"What have these two done to a nice boy like you, Yuri?" an unexpected voice called out behind them. They turned to find Aarti standing and watching the monitors with the same fascination they had.

"These two look harmless, Yuri, but be careful. Don't let them corrupt you, okay?" she said smiling. If Yuri had blushed a bit earlier, he was beet red and sweating now.

Aarti walked closer to the LCDs. "All that's pink is porn," Aarti said to herself, or maybe it was a question. She was watching the bubbles above the now pink houses reveal image after image of explicit sexual acts of every sordid kind. "Amazing, isn't it, Stephen?" she started as Stephen walked up to her. "For everything else we do, this is what people decide to look at."

Stephen was about to reply, to make some incredibly witty remark that would doubtless both impress Aarti by demonstrating just how clever he was, and encapsulate the whole state of the pornographic world they lived in, when Kohan unfortunately cut him off.

Ignoring Aarti, Kohan began interrogating Yuri. "How did you get access to this data? Not everybody is allowed to have it, you know. We had to sign a huge document to even be allowed to look at this stuff . . . " Kohan was territorial, almost outright jealous.

Stephen and Aarti decided to find the nearest barista, leaving Yuri and Kohan alone to discuss the finer points of who should and shouldn't be allowed to look at Ubatoo's data. All while the LCD screens graciously kept displaying a moment-by-moment update of people's interests, desires, and fetishes, as if the screens themselves had their own desire—that someone would just look at them. Soon, many people would.

-EPISODES-

Stephen's daydreams didn't wander to things he didn't possess or conquests he hadn't yet made. Instead, he imagined himself on a TV show replete with a prime-time audience scrutinizing his every move, and wondered, what would they think? Would they need a narrator to understand him or would his actions say enough? Now, in particular, he questioned how even a narrator could justify the last two and a half wasted years. What could possibly be said, except that he had been tired. Exhausted. Burned out.

He came into the GreeneSmart-years spent, and in his time there, the weariness didn't subside. The closing of SteelXchanges took every last modicum of what he could give. And now it was clear that every facet of his choices for SteelXchanges had been monumentally flawed. What did he know about steel anyway? It wasn't as if his lack of knowledge was offset by his love of the metal. He had never given it a second thought before he joined the company. There wasn't a single reason to believe he could do something revolutionary with SteelXchanges. Transform the steel industry? Please. This shouldn't have been something he could have been duped by. But clarity had been elusive.

Nobody in the steel industry had paid attention to them for months. That should have been a glaring clue of things to come. And when they finally granted a meeting, it was all too apparent that they didn't want, or as it was spun, simply weren't ready, for doing things the SteelXchanges way. But he and his team were far too intoxicated with their dreams to see the obvious. Instead, the pieces of his plan were thought and then re-thought and endlessly tweaked, so much so that eventually they were so meticulously and intricately crafted that any possibility of them not being realized simply couldn't be fathomed. The idea lived beyond him; it no longer needed him to survive, though the same could not be said for him. Then, in a period far too short to rationalize even now, it went from a future too vibrantly alive with possibilities—to absolutely nothing.

Two years and six months after that state of nothing was reached, still no life directions had revealed themselves. But then came Molly. At GreeneSmart.

He returned again to the thought of what a narrator might convey about the last two and a half years. Though he could hear how the narrator might speak, in uneven tones and eclectic nuances to keep the listener attentive, the words she spoke eluded him. Would the narrator only see someone who had been wasting time? Would she understand how altogether drained he had been? Would he be put into some category of underachiever, to be conveniently classified and so easily forgotten?

No, that needn't be the case. There were better explanations. On the screen, the audience would watch as an image of Stephen came into focus and a distant minor chord was heard. Over this scene's opening shots, the narrator would start simply: "Molly," and then say nothing for an adequately sustained moment of stillness as the thoughtful notes faded—as if thinking of what other pertinent details need be conveyed.

The narrator would have to find the words to deftly express how unlikely it was that Molly and Stephen would ever find each other. It was as unlikely in GreeneSmart as it was anywhere else. Everything about them and their lives was so perfectly divergent that the possibilities of ever meeting should have been virtually nonexistent. The narrator would need to then underscore how well the two of them fit together, and that it was not long until Stephen would realize that this was the first time in years he had found someone whose life he wanted inexorably intertwined with his own. A good narrator would be remiss in not giving some explanation for all of this. Perhaps it would suffice to simply defer to the authority of felicitous timing. Perhaps that would be enough.

Some advice to the narrator: The narrator would be served well to shy away from all-too-common four-letter words of affection or trite clichés. Would it matter that neither Stephen nor Molly had put forth such words yet? Maybe they would in time, but that was reaching too far, too quickly. It wasn't to be in this episode, and so the viewer must wait. And as the camera panned back in the all-too-familiar slow dramatic retreat from Stephen's close-up to reveal an expansive panorama that somehow encapsulated Stephen's life, the audience would be left with an image of Stephen alone. The shot must be carefully selected to ensure the audience is not-so-subtly reminded of Stephen's life without Molly. They should have no recourse other than to believe she should have been in the scene with him, and that any other outcome must surely be a mistake.

Then the start of the close: The narrator should say what ought to be already clear: "Two and a half years. The time had amounted to this: both being where they needed to be at the right time." A slow fade to black, and the narrator's final words until the next episode: "It felt like something real and worthy, and that was enough for Molly. That it felt at all was enough for Stephen. And that it was so much more for both, well, that was simply the cherry on top."

-LIBERAL FOOD AND EVEN MORE LIBERAL ACTIVISM-

July 9, 2009.

The Touchpoints group grew steadily under the auspices of Atiq and Jaan. In the months since Stephen had entered the intern programming contest, nine new scientists had been hired onto the team—an astounding number for any group in such a short time. Atiq had taken Xiao's admonitions to heart. He wouldn't face them again.

The team of Atiq and Jaan was well known in academic circles and was the envy of what few competitors Ubatoo had. Almost every university professor and their students were vying for a chance to join Ubatoo, and in particular its data-mining team. Xiao, using his connections, had the duo of Atiq and Jaan interviewed in both *Forbes* and *The New York Times*—and had their articles appear the same week. As Xiao had instructed, Atiq sold the vision and Jaan sold the technical brilliance. It was rare for modern-day number crunchers to receive such a large amount of press coverage. It was no surprise that following the interviews over 390 doctoral-level candidates applied to work with Atiq and Jaan.

Only a tiny fraction of the candidates would see Ubatoo, however. A minuscule one out of every thirty-six Ph.D.s who submitted their resumes was even given the opportunity to interview in person with the Touchpoints group. For the interviewee, the process was a grueling full ten hours. The morning of the interview day was primarily spent giving a prepared talk about the research the candidate had done, his publications that he thought were the most interesting, and what research he planned to do if hired. The topics spanned the spectrum of computer science, from applications to system design to theory. Talk titles included the well-attended "Improving the Ability to Advertise Through Tracking: A Machine Learning Approach to Incorporating Weak Signals," to the not-so-well-attended "Theoretical Limits on Data Privacy." Of course, none of the incoming Ph.D.s had ever tried their approaches on the amount of user data Ubatoo had, despite being utterly confident that any amount could be handled by their, as yet largely untested, theories. The unwarranted confidence was excused by the interviewers. More data was gathered here in a single hour than any incoming candidate had ever dealt with. Had this particular hubris not been forgiven, it was quite likely no candidates would ever have been hired.

After forty-five minutes of questions following the candidate's presentation, the candidate was escorted to lunch by various members of the data-mining group. On those occasions when there weren't enough people to accompany the candidate to lunch, interns were sometimes invited.

Depending on which set of people had lunch with the interviewee, lunch could easily be the most relaxed part of the day, or the most dreaded. If the interviewee was fortunate enough to meet with the people who were not new hires (those at Ubatoo for more than six months), the members of the lunch crowd usually did well in ensuring that absolutely nothing about the presentation, or even work, was discussed. Likely, they'd already decided whether they would vote for the person to be hired, and now they wanted to know the person on a more informal level. The topic of conversation usually revolved around all the perks available, the food they were eating, how much the company had changed in just the last six months (the old days), and how the candidate would unquestionably regret not joining, if given an offer.

However, because the majority of those in the Touchpoints group had been at Ubatoo only a short time, lunches often took on a very different character. Regularly, the interviewee was taken to lunch by interviewers who had been at Ubatoo under a month and who were still trying to prove themselves worthy of being there. In these cases, lunch was usually an exercise in academic one-upsmanship, or as Stephen liked to refer to it, mental masturbation: a fun, all-too-frequent diversion that in the end led to a minute of satisfaction and a mess to deal with.

The game went as follows. The instant the meal was started, the interviewers would delve into a minuscule technical aspect of the work presented in the talk, which in some, usually non-obvious, way related to their own work. Of course, on that topic, only the interviewer himself could be the world's foremost expert. The real trouble started when the interviewee would try to interject an opinion that diverged from utter amazement at the obvious display of technical wizardry that the interviewer exhibited by being astute enough to find the small parallel to his/her own work. When such a diversion occurred, it was most commonly met with a Lord of the Flies–like ruthless barrage of questions designed to teach the interviewee that the only right response was sheer reverence. The sooner the interviewee realized the appropriate appeasement, the sooner the pain for the interviewee stopped.

There did exist, however tiny in number, a few lunches that began like this, but in which the interviewee addressed the challenge of one-upsmanship head on and proved himself able to stand his own ground. It was with complete surprise that Stephen noted that the interviewee was not berated or vindictively voted against in the hiring meetings. Instead, the interviewers usually passionately fought to ensure that any interviewee who could hold his ground would receive an offer. Nobody, despite any bruised egos, wanted to lose such a person to a competitor.

When the interviewee finished the lunchtime interview interrogation, usually thirty to forty minutes into the lunch—whether by acquiescing to the brilliance displayed before him or by displaying his own brilliance that outshined the others at the table, the conversation invariably turned toward the food they were eating. The free food was a perennial source of amazement for those who visited Ubatoo, and a genuine source of pride, and immense calories, for those who worked there.

Because it was quite rare for the interns to be able to contribute much to the conversation at these lunches, the interns had found other ways to keep amused. Out of such boredom was created the following classification system of the various types of interviewees, based solely on their discussion of the food they were eating.

> A *people manager* would start by saying: "It's an absolutely brilliant idea to have this quality of food. It keeps people on the grounds and working and thinking about Ubatoo. No wasted time going out. Very nice."

> A *salesperson* would start by saying: "All of this is free? Every day? That's awesome. I can't wait to try all of the cafeterias. I really can't wait to tell my co-workers back where I work. They're going to be *so* jealous."

> A *marketing person* would start by saying: "If I ate this food every day I would gain fifteen pounds my first year. It's like the freshman fifteen, like being an undergrad again. You guys should try to be more green, though. Green I could really sell."

> A *young engineer/scientist* would start by saying: "This food is much better than the other companies where I'm interviewing. How late are the cafeterias open? Do they serve all this food in the middle of the night, too?"

> An *experienced engineer/scientist* would start by saying: "This is as good as all my friends who came here said it was. You guys should really think about delivering this food to desks as well, especially for those days when things get busy. If we had perks like this where I am now, I bet people wouldn't be in such a hurry to find their way here."

Regardless of the position and the background, there was little chance that an interviewee didn't leave impressed. At least the food always provided a nice upbeat end to the lunch—whether the person would get an offer or, more likely, would not.

It was in the midst of one of the interview lunches that Stephen was interrupted with a call forwarded to his cell phone from his office line. A voice he couldn't quite recognize was speaking on the other end,

"Stephen, I hope you remember me. We met a while ago at the Ubatoo party. My name is Sebastin Munthe. Atiq introduced us. I hope that now is a good time to talk." It wasn't, but the invocation of Atiq's name was enough to motivate Stephen to excuse himself from the table, despite being in the middle of a debate about an equation that the latest interviewee had shown on slide three of his sixty-seven-slide talk.

As he scurried past the cafeteria's maître d', he rushed to find an empty conference room for a moment of quiet. He found *Pinocchio* and jumped in. "Hi, Sebastin. Great to hear from you again. It's been a long time." Stephen still hadn't the faintest clue who Sebastin was.

"Thank you so much for taking my call, Stephen," Sebastin continued in a vaguely familiar voice, the accent overly refined. "Normally, I would sit down with you and explain my group's background and goals, to make sure you're comfortable helping us. But in the interest of time, Atiq suggested I call you directly and, well, plead for your help. He mentioned you would be the one who would be fastest at the analyses I need."

"Of course, I'd be glad to help. I'm flattered Atiq mentioned me." Stephen was surprised Atiq still even remembered his name. "Are you tracking an advertisement campaign, or do you need some kind of demographic analysis done? I can help you with that as soon as I get back to my desk."

"No, no. Nothing like that, Stephen." A protracted pause arose before the conversation resumed. "I imagine it's best to quickly give you a bit of background on my group. I head the American Coalition for Civil Liberties, ACCL for short. We're a small but vocal group in Silicon Valley. We began by working on a number of pet social causes that we wanted to impact in our local communities. The ones we all coalesced around were those that as tech entrepreneurs we cared about tremendously, and, frankly, actually understood. Now, we're focused on only one primary area—we need to ensure that our fundamental rights of free speech, free information flow, and non-censorship are upheld. You'd think we lived in China or Cold War Russia if you knew the extent of information censorship and the ever-increasing invasions of privacy we all must endure. I don't suppose you're familiar with our group, are you, Stephen?"

Now it came back to Stephen. "The moral conscience of Silicon Valley!" he blurted out as he recalled Atiq's introduction of Sebastin at the party. These paranoid discourses on the evils of the U.S. government helped tremendously to narrow down the list of people who it could be. "Of course I'd be happy to help you in any way possible. I'd imagine that anyone at Ubatoo would help if they could."

"Excellent, Stephen. Yes, your company has been remarkably receptive; I think our mission fits well with yours. But, lofty goals aside, I need your help urgently, I fear our resources are far less than yours."

"No problem. What can I do?"

"I've just sent you an e-mail containing the titles of 960 books. I was hoping you could do a really, quite rudimentary, analysis of any activity surrounding them—if there are any particular geographies in which your partners are selling the books more than others, what the demographic makeup is of the buyers, and any other information you think would be interesting about the people buying or even discussing the books. Raw sales numbers, we already have. What we don't have is the ability to look across the Web and put some of the facts together."

"I can do it. But why are you doing this? Is there anything I should know about these books?" Sebastin's request wasn't difficult. Stephen had already mentally constructed the procedures to access the data he needed by the time he finished speaking.

"The books are a strange mix. They range from international cookbooks to government history to guides on how to sell collectible stamps. Most of them, from the titles that I can see, are fairly mundane. To be frank, we're not really sure why, but we suspect that all of them have made it onto some 'list of interest' in Washington, DC. This means that people who are buying the books are probably finding their way onto some 'watch list,' too. Obviously, as ACCL, and as Americans, we believe we should be able to read any book we want, and that tagging a person as a 'person of interest' just because of what they read is a ridiculous thing to do. But that's DC for you. I don't know how to find all those people who might be unwittingly putting themselves on government lists by just reading a book. I fear that without some more information, we're just poking around in the dark trying to help people we can't find."

"I can probably get the names of those who are buying the books or talking about them online. Can you use that?"

"That would be perfect."

Another long pause followed before Stephen continued. "What are you going to do with the names? Are you going to contact all of them or go public with this information?"

"I like the way you think, Stephen. But, first things first. Until we have enough evidence of what's taking place, it'd be premature to talk about this publicly. Assuming we find the right information, we would like to warn all those who are directly affected. Imagine if you knew that buying some book would put you on a list, wouldn't you want to know? People can do whatever they want with the information, use it, ignore it, either is fine with me. I just firmly believe they should be told."

"Of course. But it doesn't make sense. Tracking cookbooks? I have a hard time believing that would be useful. But if you think that this little bit of information will help, I'll be glad to get it for you."

Sebastin responded quickly but offered no further explanation. "Thanks. It will be a great deal of help. I'll certainly be sure to tell Atiq the next time I talk to him how helpful you've been. By the way, Stephen, not to beat a dead horse, but you know that last I heard, over a million people were now on at least one of the watch lists in the U.S. A million, just imagine that! 'Persons of interest'—all that means is that it's okay to tap your telephone, monitor your e-mail, watch where you go, and everything else you keep hearing about on the news."

"It's scary, I agree," Stephen said, hoping to divert Sebastin before he continued. But Sebastin wasn't done yet. He had plenty more to say about his conspiracy theories.

"And how do you think these people got on the watch list?" Sebastin asked excitedly. "Maybe it wasn't just reading some cookbook or calling the wrong family member or watching the wrong TV show. What if someone happened to read the wrong book *and* called the wrong family member? Or what if they watched the wrong TV show *and* happened to order one of these books from Amazon? God forbid you should also take a flight that same week. You know, that's truly all it takes. We just need to head this off and expose it for what it is."

"I can help—I'm happy to do it. I'm not even sure which list you're talking about, or whether these lists really exist, but we can talk more about that later. In the meantime, I'll start working on the list of books you sent to me."

"Fantastic. As you can tell, I always get a tad carried away. I hear it's a common trait for us bleeding-heart types, no? One last thing, though: the lists are real; they exist. And you're lucky not to have had any encounters with them." He finally took a breath. "Why don't we talk about the results in a week? We'd like to contact the people you find as soon as possible. I'll be sure to tell Atiq you were just the right person for this project."

Although Stephen might have been a bit unsure whether Sebastin really knew what he was talking about, and even whether he was a crackpot or visionary, Sebastin's intentions were in the right place. The more people who knew about these lists, assuming they existed, the better off the world would be.

Stephen had hoped he would do something worthwhile at Ubatoo, though he never could have imagined this. It was time to do something other than finding gullible masses to buy more expensive diet pills. He was doing well here—now it was time for him to be doing good, also.

-SUBJECTS-

July 10, 2009.

All told, since starting pre-kindergarten at the age of four, Molly had been in school for twenty-four years (minus the all-too-brief stint in the Peace Corps) of her twenty-seven-year existence. But none of her coursework in anthropology and political science had prepared her for this. Molly needed to create a web site.

As with any task she undertook, Molly had done more than her share of planning and homework before she began. Her first step in finding subjects to observe for her thesis was to ensure that she found all the right tools to create a web site for them to visit. Fortunately, the tools to create a basic web site were readily available online, with discussion forums, voting widgets, and chat gadgets already incorporated. The color palette for Molly's site was chosen from the standard set, "Serious Grey." Nothing flashy or neon was needed here. Anybody with a few days of patience and the perseverance of a pit bull could get a site running and customized and even look reasonably good. In less than a week, her web site, *EasternDiscussions.com*, was born.

Having constructed a simple, but entirely empty, web site, her primary task turned to finding the motivating content with which to populate it. If she managed to lure users to visit, she needed to entice them to stay, interact with others, and come back often. She had to create a place where users wanted to linger for hours, discussing politics, religion and whatever other contentious topics they could. Her research depended, first and foremost, on having subjects to study.

Like anyone else on a quest for information, she had started with the listings appearing at the top of the search results pages from Ubatoo. She searched for terms such as "Islamic support groups," "Middle East discussion forums," "Muslim news," and slowly made her way down the hundreds of links returned. She had originally intended to spend only a few hours looking for the content. However, it wasn't long before she was so immersed in the world she had unearthed that even she had to allow her schedule to take a backseat to her curiosity. On her first day of exploration, she skimmed months of postings on dozens of online discussion forums. Though she had started the day by taking diligent notes, they too had soon been abandoned so she could swiftly feed her voracious curiosity.

▼ ▼ ▼

"You ready for bed?" Stephen asked again from the sofa. It was 3:15 a.m., and Stephen had been home almost two hours, sitting in virtual silence, while Molly tried her best to reach a stopping point. He had returned early to spend a little time with her, but things weren't going as planned.

"Just a few more minutes," she begged from her desk.

"You've been working for hours without moving. You're going to burn yourself out being this intense all the time." Pot, Kettle, Black. He quietly walked over to where she was sitting and ran his hand lightly through her long brown hair. She didn't respond.

"You sure you can't do this tomorrow? I've been waiting all night to see you," he said, moving closer.

Her eyes stayed on the screen.

He took hold of one of her hands, and quietly invited, "Come on."

He tugged her hand a little harder, and might have sighed a bit when she didn't give in to the coaxing. Unfortunately, sighs have a propensity of being interpreted in unintended ways.

Enough. She snapped her hand back, "Stop. I told you, I have to finish. I don't hassle you when you have to work."

"Why do I bother coming home?" he blurted.

Exasperated. "I don't know. Why do you?"

"I should just leave." Resentful.

Frustrated. "Yes. You should. Just go back to your office and leave me alone."

▼ ▼ ▼

That shouldn't have happened. She knew it the moment Stephen stormed out the door. But today was not a good day. She was sorely disappointed. What she had found in her search had not been what she expected.

But that wasn't what had disappointed her. She was disappointed in herself for being surprised at what she had found. As a graduate student years into her studies, her reaction to what she found on the message boards made it blatantly evident just how unworldly she was, and for a would-be anthropologist, this was an appalling fact to face.

She had come to the message boards to find extremists, dissidents, terrorists, calls to arms, and calls for unification. What she found, instead, was a place where young Muslims faced the issues that mattered to them every day. She had read hundreds of posts talking about how to deal with teasing and bigotry. How to deal with wearing a *burqa* or even a *hijab*? How many messages asked if it was okay to date a member of the opposite sex without telling their parents? What were the limitations while still remaining devout? How many posts were written simply as support for someone whose circle of friends only knew about Islam from the urgent newsbreaks on TV? How many posts had she read about both young men and women feeling unsafe every time a news story came out about terrorist activity in Europe or in the Philippines that was as far removed from their lives as missions to Mars? There were far too many to remember.

And the worst part of it all was that she genuinely liked and sympathized with the people she read about. She followed their stories, like soap-operas in fast-forward, by reading through months of their lives posted over numerous messages and discussions in only a few minutes. How could anyone read so many personal stories and not be touched? It was natural to think about Cameroon again, about Sandrine, and about Francis. This was the kind of support that Sandrine had needed. Muslim, Christian, Hindu, Jewish, whatever. At a fundamental level, the support on these groups helped, and she wished that Sandrine had gotten that help, too—someone to talk to about what was okay to do with her, *to her*, and what wasn't.

How could Molly have known what she would find? But it was her job to know, at least to have an intelligent guess. The people she found were not the caricatures she had imagined—the imaginary lives she had based her thesis plans on. If people posting on the forums were not the angry mob she envisioned, there would be little point in her thesis. Understanding a young boy's decision about whether he could be friends with an American girl, or understanding a girl's thoughts on acceptable garments to wear, as important as both may be, were a lot less likely to impress her thesis committee than insights into the role the Internet was playing on Middle Eastern peoples' perceptions of the U.S.

▼ ▼ ▼

It was 3:55 a.m. when Stephen made his way back onto Ubatoo's grounds. There were only a few lights still on—more security guards than workers. He had spent the full day at Ubatoo, working harder than usual so he could make it home early. He would have rather been anywhere other than back on grounds, but where else was he supposed to go?

He didn't walk to Building 11, resolving not to let himself do any more work. Instead, he walked along the brick pathway past the usual concrete buildings, toward the gurgling fountains and the manicured lawns. All paths seemed to eventually end at Xiao's Ballroom. The lights were on inside. He went in, hoping someone would be playing games like they had after the internship contest, or hoping to at least find something to distract himself with for a few minutes.

Aarti was in the room, sitting at one of the many elaborately decorated tables that had been readied for some press function taking place the next day. She had a stack of papers piled high next to her and was thoroughly engrossed in her reading. She hadn't heard him, and he hadn't planned on interrupting her. But when she glanced up, she waved. Tonight, it was enough of an invitation.

She smiled when he approached. "Come here often, stranger?"

"Couldn't sleep. Just out taking a walk. How about you? You're up late."

"I come here to read sometimes—to get out of my office and out of my apartment." She looked a bit tired, but just as stunning as she had the first night at the party. Jeans and a white shirt were as flattering on her as what she had been wearing that night.

"What are you reading?"

Her cheeks flushed, and she smiled sheepishly as she looked away. Her hair, normally twisted close to her neck, was loose, and fell across one eye when she moved. "See all those papers right there?" She pointed to the stack of academic papers next to her. "Well, I'm not reading those." She lifted a novel from her lap and held it up for Stephen to see. "Much more interesting, especially alone at night." As soon as she remembered the salacious cover, though, she quickly put it back down, hoping he hadn't had time to let it register.

"Romance novels? You? I wouldn't have guessed."

She shrugged her shoulder ever so slightly. "Ever since I was fifteen—read about one a week."

"And do all of them have covers like that one?"

She held the book in her hand, now plainly visible for both of them to see, a bare-chested hulking man ripping off the flimsy, barely laced bodice of a forlorn maiden. Aarti responded in her characteristic drawl, this time made all the more alluring with the slight whisper of sleepiness. "Not all of them—just the ones I read."

And the conversation continued—talking a little about a lot. It probably would have continued until breakfast was served, but Stephen's phone chirped, and a message from Molly interrupted them.

> Am truly sorry.
> I am waiting up for you.
> Won't you please come home?

-NEWSWORTHY-

July 11, 2009.

What makes a young boy living in London care about Americans in Iraq? Most kids don't watch the news, don't care about politics, and probably couldn't find Iraq on a map. But on a message forum discussing America's involvement in the Middle East, a boy, who went by the alias **truthAndDare28**, typed the following message on his cell phone because he did not have access to a computer; he was fifteen years old at the time:

> Posted By: truthAndDare28
> Posted: Jun 18 2:23 am
> Location: London
>
> they wont move because they stuff their fat faces with lard and hot dogs and feces all day they cant fight because they are a bunch of limp pricks, i pray that the day will come. let us all pray that it is soon. brothers pray together that we crush these disgusting vile military crusaders give us the power to overcome. i am ranting i know but really worked up about all this today i will post again when I have the picture to show and not before then. in two days if willing

Though Molly never found out how the boy had come to have such a hatred toward America, within minutes of reading further, her curiosity about the pictures he wanted to show was no more. In posts dated two days later, others told of **truthAndDare28**'s outcome. He had died thirty-seven hours after his post, on his sixteenth birthday. There was violence. At least it was quick.

▼ ▼ ▼

As typical with Molly, the disappointment she felt because of the findings on her first day of searching made her more industrious over the next days. The initial indiscriminate exploratory investigations she had begun with were superseded by meticulous, deep searches. She methodically worked her way through the extensive list of results returned by Ubatoo. She had only needed to stumble upon the more obscure web sites, those that appeared far past the first few pages of Ubatoo's search listings, for her perseverance to be rewarded.

The pages she encountered in these seldom seen web sites contained posts from **truthAndDare28**, and far worse—the same hatred, the same urgency, but with deliberate wishful plans, clarity of thought, and explicit visions of cruelty. Each link she clicked led her deeper into the realm of questioning, hate, and the promised violence that every pressing news report had assured existed. For every post that expressed radicalism from one side, it was matched by dozens of posts that expressed it from the other.

This world she had uncovered was enormous. She pursued the connections from page to page, until she found herself at private sites that she was not allowed to access, or were written in a language she did not understand. So many links she found eventually led straight to MySpace pages, Facebook profiles, and YouTube videos, each serving as little enticements and open invitations for the too curious to delve further.

These web sites provided Molly with a wealth of content to populate her web site, EasternDiscussions. Although some of these web sites devoted part of their offerings to everyday discussions like shopping, dating, and support, unlike her first sample, none shied away from encouraging debates on religion and law, often supporting, and other times vilifying, extremist viewpoints and politics.

These were the posts that made the headlines. These were the posts that immediately sprung to mind when anyone spoke of fear, when anyone spoke of terrorism. These were the messages that would make it into her thesis; everything else was too pedestrian to be interesting.

The more she read, the more convinced she became that she was on the right track with her thesis topic. As more people came online in the Middle East, the more the need existed to ensure that what they saw wasn't just an echo of the hate for America that already surrounded them. How much did the views of a few vocal individuals, or a few violent posts, dictate the eventual perceptions of all the readers? If she could quantify the effect, her thesis would be complete.

Still, she had to ask herself, what's the difference between doing such a passive analysis and doing nothing at all? Unless she knew how to *change* the opinions of the readers and posters of a message board, why bother to study them? If she wasn't going to be in the villages help-ing people, she reminded herself, the impact she needed to have must be just as long lasting, just as real, and even bigger.

Could she systematically influence the readers and posters on mes-sage boards? Instead of just studying the influence of extremist individu-als, could she limit their impact? Maybe it would be as simple as making sure the messages that espoused the "right" ideas always bubbled to the top so readers saw them first. Maybe it was creating a credible authority, or set of authorities, to agree on a viewpoint and then expound on it. Or maybe it was much simpler. What about studying and controlling how long messages were—did shorter or longer messages have a bigger impact? How many calls to action should be included? How many ref-erences to prayer, to power, to God? Maybe it was even easier than that. Maybe it was just about presenting the "right" messages to the readers over and over again.

All of these things had to have some impact—if she could just quantify the amount and document it, not only would her thesis be more impressive, but it would also be useful. No thesis committee could possibly question its significance. In fact, Gale would be overjoyed. This went far beyond simply measuring information effects from discussion forums. It explored how to covertly control them.

What she needed right now, though, were subjects. She needed to have a web site where people were posting daily so she could run her experiments and study the effects they had on the evolution of opin-ions. How else could she test whether her methods of influence and control worked?

▼ ▼ ▼

Without visitors, as nice looking as it was, EasternDiscussions was worthless. However, attracting visitors was difficult. When people typed in relevant search terms on any search engine, including Ubatoo, her web site normally appeared in the fourth page of results or later, if it appeared at all. This meant almost nobody saw it. She was convinced that no search engine would put her web site high enough on their results pages until it became more popular. But to get popular, it either required a huge advertising budget or a lot of users. Neither of which she had. At the time, only six people had posted on the site. Of these six posters, two were real and four were pseudonyms that Molly used herself.

To take matters into her own hands, under a variety of names, she posted on other discussion forums about any and all relevant topics. In her messages, she always placed a link to a similar discussion she had fabricated on EasternDiscussions. She hoped that at least a few people would click these links and be sufficiently enticed to stay and post their own messages on her web site.

Her first post was made under the moniker *Sahim Galab*. She modeled her voice and tone after the more well thought out posts she had seen. Not only did this style come more naturally to her, but she also was drawn to those posts in her own explorations. Besides, she couldn't bring herself to compose a post like **truthAndDare28**'s. The deceit of appearing so passionate about things she didn't believe, especially in light of the boy's grim fate, was too much. As it was, she already felt guilty for her excitement in wondering if anyone would take her seriously.

A conference inviting Mustafa Kawlia, an extremist supporter who was not allowed in the U.S. because of his use of video messages that encouraged aggressive actions in the U.S. and Europe, had been announced. Numerous online discussion forums were teeming with fervent posts supporting the right for Mustafa to speak, as well as the opposite—soliciting violence against him if he actually stepped onto American soil. She needed all of these people on her own web site if she was going to get enough subjects for her study. In three forums on popular web sites discussing Mustafa Kawlia, this was what she posted:

Dear Brothers,

The right for Mustafa to speak must be respected. Anything less will only lead to more distrust from both sides. I do not understand why so many insist on trying to stop Mustafa from coming. Do you believe that as Muslims we cannot judge for ourselves whether he speaks for us? What do you take us for? You can see for yourself what he has said in the past (**video1**, **video2**). His words are severe, yet he has never told anyone to act violently. With or without him, it must be up to us to decide the actions, whether violent or not, we will take. To remove that choice from our hands is unacceptable, and I fear that it plainly forces us to one course of action over the other.

—Sahim

The advertisement for EasternDiscussions was subtle—it had to be in order to be effective. The links **video1** and **video2** went to pages on her web site that discussed the videos. She had created these fictional discussions between Sahim and other, more fanatical, imagined characters. Though the actual links to the videos were included on her pages, she hoped the discussion that users would first encounter would convince them to join in the fray and post their own arguments.

The idea worked, but only a little. Within a few days, she had twelve more real visitors to her site. But there were still few, if any, postings. Who would bother to write something if there was no one to read it? But she was patient. Within a week, there were forty-eight people on her message board who had posted more than eighteen messages in a single day. She was excited. It was small now, but this could be the first sign that traction was building. She eagerly shared the news with Stephen. But for someone who routinely dealt with hundreds of millions of users at Ubatoo, it was difficult to be enthusiastic about her forty-eight. Nonetheless, it was because of this exchange that the discussion with Andrew would arise a few days later, and a path to obtain Molly's users would present itself. So, perhaps, it was worth this temporary disappointment.

-PATIENCE-

July 20, 2009.

Judging from the flashing lights, news cameras, and roar of the crowd, the event could easily have been mistaken for a Hollywood movie premiere. The first sign that it wasn't such frivolity was the abundance of police officers in full protective gear. The second was the color of the skin of the people waiting in line to enter. The 1,500 tickets to tonight's event had been sold out since they went on sale two months ago, even before Mustafa Kawlia was given permission to enter the U.S.

Only a single entrance of UCLA's Royce Hall Auditorium was in use. The flow of people in and out of the auditorium was carefully monitored. All the news stories had warned against attending the event. But being there, amidst the crowd, waiting in line and watching and feeling the spectacle, with all of the energy skirting so close to violence, made even the most hyperbolic warnings sedate in comparison. The shouts from surrounding crowds and the yells in response from those in line were deafening.

Earlier this morning, Mohammad still had not decided whether he would bring his son, Adam. By the afternoon, watching the news reports showing the growing crowds of protesters, he had decided that Adam wasn't ready for this yet. Perhaps Mohammad was just being overly protective. But what father of a six-year-old son wouldn't be? Looking at the chaos surrounding him now, he was happy he had left his son at home. Maybe in a few years he could handle all this, but right now this was no place for him.

Mohammad had been waiting in line for over an hour, and the line behind him still stretched further back than he could see. He hadn't even planned on being here. Kawlia was well known, and the subject of his appearance a public controversy, but Kawlia was not the only one who spoke honestly. No, many already believed everything Kawlia would say tonight. Kawlia spoke openly and without fear, but the words he said were echoed by thousands every day. Being here, to show support in such a public place, was an empty gesture. Had Mohammad's imam not brought these tickets to Mohammad himself, he would not have come. But he had insisted, and now Mohammad stood in line, being jostled and herded like all the rest.

Only a few feet away from where he stood, among the shields and vests and clubs and guns, the barely recognizable bodies of the police officers stood joined, holding back a sea of protesters who threatened more violence than any of those standing in line. Over 8,000 protesters were expected on the lawn that night, more than five times the number of guests attending.

The line moved slowly. The entrance to the red brick building that held the auditorium was only thirty feet away, situated between the two imposing towers of Royce Hall on either side. When he was finally close enough to see inside the entrance doors, he noticed metal detectors had been set up. He saw the desks at which everyone's ID was being recorded, checked, and rechecked; saw the policemen searching every person entering—roughly handling every man and boy; saw the short bald man in a police uniform laying his hands on the few women who wanted entrance, mindlessly feeling for any weapons they might be hiding. He said nothing, but when he followed the gazes of those in front of him, he discovered them watching as carefully as he was. One wrong step, one accidental slip of this bald man's hand, and there would be immediate retribution. It wouldn't take much.

Throughout, the screaming and yelling continued around him. A young Muslim girl in yellow shorts on the shoulders of another Muslim boy directed her yells straight to Mohammad, imploring him not to go in. The sign she held simply stated, "This is not Islam." No, Mohammad thought, it is not. Amidst the pulsating sea of signs and posters, hers was not unique. Dozens of girls and boys clutched the same poster, declaring to the world through the news cameras busily scanning the crowds that they were not part of what Kawlia was saying—distancing themselves from the words spoken here. They were losing themselves,

Mohammad understood. They wanted to be lost and not to be found again.

The coolness of the inside air, and the escape from the crowds and the overwhelming noise, eased the tension in Mohammad's body. He relaxed a moment; even let himself be moved by the crowd. Soon, he would be seated, and the disgraceful yelling and noise would just be a memory. The metal detector was beeping and the overhead red light was flashing. A guard standing to the left of the detector roughly pushed him to the side. "Pay attention," the guard barked. "Can't you see it's red!" he shouted, angrily thumping the flashing light above him as though Mohammad were a child. "Take off your belt and shoes and give the man in the blue shirt any metal objects you're carrying."

He did as he was told.

"Send that one through again!" yelled the blue shirt.

And he went through the metal detector again. The guard who had spoken harshly earlier watched him closely. The light blinked green. Mohammad kept his face forward, never turning his head to face the guard, though as he passed only a few inches from the guard's eyes, he was sure the guard was still watching his every move.

Slam! The guard hit him hard on the neck with an open palm as he made his way past. The crisp clap of skin on skin hushed the room as everyone stopped to see what would happen next. "Don't forget your stuff over there," he said, pointing with his now red hand at Mohammad's shoes. "Wouldn't want you to leave them here by accident."

Mohammad walked over to collect his belongings from the now laughing man in the blue shirt. The line behind him started moving again. The cacophony of the room resumed. The cool air overtook the memory of the hit. There would be plenty of time later to deal with the guard, with the man in the blue shirt, and with those outside. Mohammad was patient.

-HYPERGROWTH-

November, 2008.

Academic aspirations took a backseat to Xiao's desire for fame and wealth. He never found the need to hide his ambitions; rather, he made them known at every available opportunity. In his interview with *Forbes* magazine, when for the first time he entered the ranks of the Forbes World's Wealthiest 400 people, among the questions the interviewer asked him was, "What is your biggest regret?" Xiao answered, without missing a beat, that it was being interviewed for an article about the World's Wealthiest 400 people and not the World's Wealthiest 100. And the executive board members of Ubatoo fell in love with him all over again. He was living proof that capitalism was honorable if enough public relations and money were behind it.

Xiao exemplified the Silicon Valley success story. He was a large, fast-talking man whose family had emigrated from Hong Kong in the 1970s. In stark contrast to Ubatoo's erudite research environment, his lack of academic credentials made him a controversial choice for the position of Ubatoo's CEO. Nevertheless, his experience, unabashed brashness and vision for the company had resonated with the company's board, and an offer had been extended. Now, after seven years of being the very public front man of Ubatoo, his academic credentials, or lack thereof, were long forgotten. The sole purpose of his one degree, from high school, was to serve as a dusty decoration in his father's home library.

Despite six years of working with Xiao, Atiq dreaded setting foot into Xiao's office. The supple leather office seats placed in front of his desk had been specially crafted to sink deeply with the slightest weight. At Xiao's insistence, all visitors were offered only these seats. When Xiao sat in his own chair, behind an imposing, oversized, hand-carved desk of dark wood imported from India, the pecking order in the room was firmly established. If Xiao was in a good mood, he would kindly move the unmistakably too expensive, and exceedingly gaudy, trinkets at the edge of the desk that obstructed any seated visitor's view of him. Were he not in such a charitable mood, the infrequent sight of his eyes when he leaned forward to peer over the clutter would be all that the visitor was granted.

"Atiq, you've had an incredible quarter here," Xiao said with a smile. He started moving the trinkets. "Your new group is on track to account for more than $220 million in revenues this year. That's a great beginning for your Touchpoints project."

"Thanks, Xiao. We're excited about the results, too. And there's so much more that we have planned for this quarter. We've already started—"

"That's what I wanted to talk to you about, Atiq," Xiao said as he interrupted Atiq in mid-sentence. Here it comes. "Just imagine how much more you would have accomplished had you been able to meet your hiring goals. Your group has some of the highest margin dollars for our company; we make more for every dollar spent on you and your projects than any other research group here. And, when you don't make your hiring goals, per person, you lose more than any group here. What happened?"

Atiq wasn't sure if he should defend himself, point out the flaws in Xiao's logic, or whether it was a rhetorical question. Probably all of the above. "Xiao, there were a lot of moving pieces that had to fall into place to get where we are. We'll make up the hiring this quarter at the very latest . . ."

"Atiq, I'm not really looking for excuses. You know better than that. It's a tough project. I get it. I just want to know if you think you can manage this responsibility and growth by yourself? This is a hypergrowth environment we're in right now. It's like 1999 all over again. But this time, we've got it right and we're on the proverbial rocket ship. Hiring is the single most important thing we do. It's like Sun Tzu said,

'Although there is stupid haste in war, winning has never been reached with long delays.' We need to be firing on all cylinders. Do you understand what I'm saying?"

The "Art of War" quote had come out. That was Xiao's signature way of ending a conversation, as if quoting (or if history serves as a guide, more likely misquoting) from a sacred text that contained irrefutable, and somehow universally applicable, arguments.

Years of working with Xiao hadn't eased the awkwardness of this moment. Eventually Xiao would start talking. It was just a matter of waiting and fidgeting like a scolded child until he did.

"Atiq, I want to help you succeed. Why don't you take over the internship contest that Lynn is setting up this year? It usually yields a few good interns who convert to full-timers."

"Xiao, I think Lynn will be disappointed. She's been working on organizing this intern thing for weeks." The last thing Atiq wanted was to be in charge of the intern process. There were so many mediocre candidates to cull through.

"Yes, but she's doing fine in her hiring, Atiq. It's your group I'm worried about. I think it's best if you handle it."

Acquiesce to the punishment. "I'll talk to Lynn today."

"Thanks, Atiq. One more thing before you go. It's time for your quarterly bonus. What do you think would be appropriate for this quarter? It'll be long overdue by the time I finally get to it, if we don't figure it out right now."

Well, this was certainly new. Usually bonuses arrived in a sealed envelope and were never spoken about. "I don't know, Xiao. I think that it was a pretty good quarter, all in all. Touchpoints is ahead of schedule."

"Come on, Atiq. Just a number," Xiao said as he typed a few strokes on his keyboard. "I have the spreadsheet loaded on my screen. Just tell me how much you need to keep you going so maybe next quarter you can actually meet your hiring goals."

These little repeated jabs were a lovely characteristic of Xiao that Atiq tried his best to overlook. Unlike Xiao, who had embraced Capitalism as a religion wholeheartedly, for Atiq, it was difficult to talk about money so brazenly. Never had money been talked about so openly while growing up or even now in his own household. Though his parents were not religious, perhaps the one thing they took to heart and tried to pass on to their children from their mild Islamic upbringing was that money was to be shared, not hoarded. It would be good to pass that on to his children, too, assuming it was still possible. But, alas, he wasn't at home, and Xiao wasn't going to wait much longer. With Xiao, shyness and modesty got you nowhere. "Well, last quarter was $400,000, and this quarter was really quite good. Despite the hiring, everything about Touchpoints is going amazingly well, including more revenue than expected already. I leave it to you, of course, but how about $450,000?"

"Got it. Thanks, Atiq. Don't forget to talk to Lynn today."

Atiq smiled. At least there was a silver lining. He offered his hand to shake, which Xiao firmly did, with a large genuine smile. Without another word, Atiq walked out the door. As he left, Xiao typed in $399,999 and submitted the form.

-LITTLE PINK HOUSES-

July 12, 2009.

Yuri was a rock star. That's the only way to describe his meteoric rise in status among the interns just five days after first showing his demo. News of his tying in the real-time activities of what Ubatoo's users were doing with the strikingly high-resolution images of people's homes and apartments spread like wildfire. Interns waxed poetically, presumably as close as they ever came to being English majors, about the beauty of what Yuri had done, and even delved a bit into philosophical discourses about the future devious and deviant possibilities.

It had become a favorite pastime for interns to use Yuri's system to investigate each other's residences and see what one another had been doing the previous night. Their embarrassment was literally magnified when the findings were, for fun, projected on one of the many walls of LCD panels linked together for simultaneous presentations across Ubatoo's buildings. Then there was no hiding, anywhere on the grounds at least, about what it was that "someone in the house" was doing to make the house glow pink.

For Yuri, his quiet nature was both an asset and a liability. Had Yuri told his sponsor about his project, it would have earned him nothing but unbridled accolades. First, he would be complimented for his computer vision work, the excellent use of the imagery and satellite data that formed the core of the demo (and was his forte). Then, kudos would also be given for the use of data from a different group that normally had few interactions with the computer vision group. On top of everything else, he would also be praised by even the most persnickety of engineers at Ubatoo who only cared about how the system was designed and programmed, because Yuri's design was elegant by any standard.

Yuri, who had studied computer science for twelve years by the time he arrived at Ubatoo, spent the first of those in Krakow, Poland, where he "programmed" a computer without ever having access to even the most basic machine. He wrote his programs on a piece of paper and handed them in to his teachers who graded them by hand. It was this dearth of resources that made his systems compact, easy to understand, and easy to add to: elegant, in the parlance of computer scientists. Yuri was on his way to becoming one of the many prototypical Scientist-From-Another-Country-Comes-To-America-To-Follow-His-Dreams-And-Achieves-Amazing-Success stories. The only thing holding him back was his quiet nature. Eventually news of this system had to emerge in order for the honors to begin.

Yuri's lack of interest in achieving stardom at Ubatoo was what freed the project to move forward at a lightning pace without the usual encumbrances of office politics and pandering for praise. Every night when the system was projected on the larger-than-life walls of LCD panels, more interns watched the show. Even the most cynical of them found it difficult not to be a bit awed by the sheer beauty of the high-resolution virtual strolls and flyovers through their own neighborhoods, and the not-so-subtly voyeuristic glow of the houses they encountered. The project was left to grow with Yuri as the de-facto leader, and with numerous other interns providing new appendages to the project.

It is interesting to recall that the research was being conducted by people who were adequately shielded from the truth that Ubatoo was a money-making machine and not simply a tech playground. Therefore, the most lucrative avenue of research, the green houses indicating that money had been recently spent or was in the process of being spent at one of Ubatoo's merchants, was summarily ignored. Instead, the only color that held any attention was the one that was the most fun to delve into—pink.

Sometime in the middle of the night of the fifth day after its disclosure, five interns working on the project, Yuri, Stephen, Kohan, Andrew (a returning intern who last year had worked in the search engine/

ranking group, and now worked in the e-mail group), and Rob (an intern from the user interface group), decided that the name "JENNY" should be adopted for the project.

▼ ▼ ▼

The story of how the name JENNY came to be starts out much like any story, whether from Shakespeare or modern romance novels—being wronged by a lover, finding new and intricate ways to take revenge, and in the process coming to understand, or at least partake in, all the unforeseen events that transpire along the way.

When Rob first saw the demo, four other interns with various expertise were present. Yuri, of course, Andrew, and Stephen and Kohan, who had carte-blanche access to the warehouses of data that Ubatoo collected. As part of the Touchpoints group, by their very job description, they were supposed to be drawing connections and insights by analyzing vast amounts of data. Andrew, who happened to be in the room while Rob was getting the demo spiel from Yuri, did what almost 80 percent of the interns at Ubatoo did—designed automated ways to analyze web pages and e-mails to find out what they were about. As for Rob himself, he was part of the group that made sure everything at Ubatoo not only looked aesthetically pleasing, but was also easy to use. Rob's main contribution to the project, besides making the demo look even more dazzling, was the raw emotional turmoil and associated angst he provided.

"Yuri, can you do me a favor?" Rob asked immediately after seeing the demo. "Do you have Los Gatos covered in your map yet?"

"Sure," Yuri replied. He moved the view on the screen away from Ubatoo's surrounding neighborhood and dragged the cursor south, toward Los Gatos. "Here you go. Want to look up a particular address?"

"Give me the mouse for a second?" Rob asked.

Yuri scooted over as Rob grabbed the mouse and rapidly made what looked like a series of twitching movements back and forth. Then, he quickly moved and zoomed into a neighborhood lit up in a variety of colors. He kept adjusting the view until he found what he was looking for. "It's a friend's house," he explained. "Looks like she's still awake. Her house is green—what does that mean again?"

"Oh, that's nothing too interesting. She's just buying something online."

"Really? Isn't it a bit late to be buying something? It's almost 1:45 in the morning. What is she buying now?" Rob asked.

"Sorry. I do not know. I just record that money was transferred and with which store. Stephen or Kohan might know." Yuri replied.

"What's the address?" A voice called from across the room. It was Kohan.

"89 Sunfire Avenue," Rob said as he straightened up from looking at Yuri's monitor to talk with Kohan.

"Okay. Just give me a sec."

"Oh, never mind that, Kohan," Yuri said. "Her house just turned blue. She's chatting with someone online now."

"It was nothing, anyway," Kohan replied. "Her name is Jennifer R. Briend from what it looks like here," he said tapping his screen. "She just bought some wine online. Want to know the vintage?" Kohan said smugly.

"Yep, Jenny, that's her. And that's okay about the vintage," Rob said. "I don't suppose you can tell me who she's chatting with now though, can you?"

"Yep, but it'll cost you."

"What? Really? How much?" replied Rob, annoyed.

"I'm just kidding. Hold on a second."

"Don't bother, Kohan," Stephen interjected. "Already got it. And this information is on the house, no charge at all. Looks like she's chatting online with someone named Ben Cappiello. Does that name mean anything to you?"

Rob was gritting his teeth. Any suspicions the group had that she was more than a friend were incontrovertibly verified.

"Look," Yuri interjected as he projected the image on the LCD monitor closest to Rob. Rob spun around to watch as Yuri clicked on Ben's house and a bubble appeared above it with images of porn and bits of chat messages with Jenny intermingled. "He's chatting with her while looking for porn."

"Rob, it gets worse. Check out Ben's e-mails to Jenny," Andrew added. "I'll pop it up on the screen; I'm not about to read that one out loud." The remaining LCDs crisply displayed their raunchy e-mails for all to see. "The next one, too—and these are just the first few e-mails I found between them."

"What the hell?" Rob almost screamed, surrounded by images of Jenny and Ben and their e-mails. Then, just as fast as the yell had come, all traces of anger were gone.

"Thanks," he resumed calmly. "That's about it for me for tonight. I've got to go. Nice demo, Yuri."

Before Rob walked out of the room, Stephen called out, "You okay, Rob?"

"I'm fine." But on his way out, he called back to those within earshot, "Anybody want to get a drink?"

A moment of confusion at the prospect of leaving the grounds flashed its way across their faces. Ultimately, though, watching Jenny, Ben, and Rob was enough to convince them that a drink was definitely in order. The night started at the Rose and Crown Pub, progressed to the always bustling Nola's, and ended next door at the Old Pro. Rob had a lot of misery to share.

-TRUTH, LIES,
AND ALGORITHMS-

July 13, 2009.

Whether it be for "show and tell" day at your local kindergarten, finding just the right caterer for your daughter's wedding, or the going rate of enriched uranium in the underworld of Russia's black markets, Ubatoo was the right place to find answers. Search for anything, find the best results the Web has to offer, see some ads, maybe click them, and then repeat, every day, many times a day.

Through the years, almost 87 percent of all the searches in the U.S. and over 49 percent of them worldwide flowed through Ubatoo in exactly the manner just described. And the amazing fact was that nobody—without exaggerating—nobody, at Ubatoo could have guessed the breadth of queries that would eventually be asked, and the insatiable appetite the world had for information.

Over the years, the common queries that everyone typed at some point in their web-searching lives, "Money," "Houses," "Sex," "Adult Pictures," "Politics," "Music," were handled extremely well at Ubatoo, as they were at every web search engine. What set Ubatoo apart, and imbedded Ubatoo firmly in everyone's daily routine, was the absolutely brilliant job it did when those common queries were discarded in favor of those that held more personal meaning. At that point, users joined what was mathematically known as the "long tail."

The queries in the tail are those that aren't asked very often. The reason it's often called the "long tail" is that the majority of queries submitted to Ubatoo aren't common. They are simply what make you, you.

They are what make you unique to Ubatoo. Everyone queries for "sex," and everyone queries for "money." In contrast, all those requests for information that you, and only a few others in the entire world would think of querying, such as "did Freddie Krueger's gloves have four blades or five," are what distinguish you from the rest of Ubatoo's users. These are things you care about.

The moment you discovered that even a few of these queries could be answered well, a vital seed was planted. This was a place to turn to whenever information was needed—no matter how strange the topic. Without knowing what information you would eventually search for, Ubatoo, seemingly magically, was able to find an answer, blazing through tens of thousands of machines, all sorting and sifting through the unfathomably monumental number of words ever written. If you asked anybody at Ubatoo how they did it, or how they possibly figured out what ads to show you when you asked such esoteric queries, the answer was always, it's the intelligence built into our Algorithms. More precisely, but perhaps with less marketability, it was all about "ranking"—how one result was chosen to appear above another. How one web page was more about what you wanted to see than some other.

Many, many companies (on the order of hundreds), people (on the order of tens of thousands), and dollars (on the order of billions) were devoted, and continue to be devoted, to ranking. Ubatoo's army of Ph.D.s working on just this problem, who were versed in everything from computer science, mathematics, statistics, linguistics, cognition, perception, and psychology, kept Ubatoo on the cutting edge of this problem. These people were affectionately called "*Tinkers*" within Ubatoo. Their sole job was to tinker with the ranking procedures in small ways that kept improving the order in which you saw the results. This excruciatingly tightly focused attention to ranking was crucial to Ubatoo's success. When this was married with Ubatoo's already huge head start and foresight into building enormous computational resources into its computing cloud, the combination ensured that Ubatoo kept, at the very least, decades ahead of their nearest competition.

Every infinitesimal change to the ranking mixture was tested with thousands of users. Every click, word typed, query entered, was tracked to decide whether you were just a tiny bit more satisfied with the changes. Of course, this could never be done for the majority of "long tail" queries; too many of them existed. Instead, Ubatoo relied on the fact that if their algorithms and ranking functions worked well on the queries they tested, they would also work well for the queries that were important to you. That assumption was dead-on accurate. These ranking procedures were never adjusted without extensive testing; too many errors arose when humans were allowed to use their intuition. It also made sure nobody was able to bias the results to benefit any web site that was their personal favorite.

It was because of this dogma that getting more people to Molly's site, EasternDiscussions.com, was a terribly daunting task—even for someone who worked at Ubatoo. Nonetheless, this was precisely what Stephen needed to do. He needed to ensure that Molly's web site appeared as close as possible to the top of the search results when someone typed anything related to politics and religion in the Middle East. The higher her web site appeared, the more people would see it, the more people would visit her site, the more people would contribute to its discussion forms, and the more chances Molly would have of gathering enough subjects for her thesis. The problem was, of course, that at least dogmatically, there should be no way to make this happen.

▼ ▼ ▼

Molly had rarely been able to make it to Ubatoo to join Stephen for lunch. The shifts she worked at GreeneSmart and the interviews and lunch meetings Stephen often had to attend made lunchtime get-togethers almost impossible. Because of this, in the few instances when lunch did happen, they attempted to sit by themselves. Besides, Stephen didn't relish the prospect of having to keep the conversation interesting to both his work friends, who would invariably talk about work, and Molly, who would understandably be bored to tears. Occasionally, when someone didn't get the hint that the couple didn't want to be social, circumstances and politeness left little choice. On one of the rare days when Molly met Stephen for lunch, Andrew was at the Asiatique Café in line immediately behind them. The amiable conversation in line hadn't ended with an invitation for him to join them, but when Stephen and Molly went to find a seat, Andrew hurriedly followed them to their table.

Before either Andrew or Molly had a chance to go beyond introducing themselves, Stephen plunged into a conversation that had a chance of interesting everyone at the table. He described Molly's predicament, getting subjects onto her web site, and admitted he was lost on how to help her.

"If you could get your web site to appear in the top ten results for even just a few popular queries, that would drive enough users to you, I'd imagine," said Andrew, talking directly to Molly.

"I think the question is how I do that. I don't have any budget and I need to have this happen sooner rather than later. I just need traffic, even if it's for a little while, just long enough for me to finish my experiments."

"Do you know anyone in the ranking group? They might have some insights," Andrew replied, this time talking directly to Stephen.

"I don't think they would help though, do you? I figure that with all the religion we have here on never hand-tuning results, and being purely algorithm-driven . . . blah, blah, blah," Stephen said with exasperation. "Nothing is hand-tuned, right? I think it's pretty unlikely they would help."

"I've done it before, though, for a friend's site. I mean it was last year, when I was an intern in the Tinkers group, so things might have changed since then. I'm not even sure it could be done again," Andrew said.

"No, no. What I'm trying to do is to move just her site up a few notches. You couldn't have done that, right?" Stephen asked.

"It wasn't really anything big. When I was an intern last year, we were encouraged to run some test users through some tweaks to the ranking system. We ran the experiments from start to finish, and then presented the results to the ranking team."

"So you made up results to help your friend? Really?"

"The results weren't really *that* made up. I didn't just lie about them. I might have slightly enhanced the changes that boosted my friend's site higher and presented only those, though," Andrew reasoned, with a grin.

"Nobody noticed?"

"Oh, relax, Stephen. It was just for a week or so. I'm sure that if anybody noticed it was probably put down to a statistical anomaly. Things like that happen. And it sounds like that's what Molly needs, anyway."

Andrew was using off-hand comments about statistics with this crowd? "No, Andrew, *actually*, things like that don't just happen. Andrew, the kind of statistical errors you're talking about are so many standard deviations away from the expected that the chances are negligible, you should know that." Stephen was only willing to suspend disbelief for so long.

"Fine. Maybe it was put down to 'stupid intern can't do anything right.' Whatever, it worked. Ubatoo's fine, my friend's site got more traffic—he's fine, and I'm fine. It's all fine," Andrew replied defensively.

"What does your friend do, anyway?"

"It's really just a friend of my parents. My family is into buying houses and the whole real estate thing. This guy has been our real estate agent for years. The only thing I did was make sure his name popped up higher in the results. Now he gives us early access to his properties, foreclosures, whatever else, before he tells others. It's paid off."

"Unbelievable. The whole thing is unbelievable," Stephen was starting to rant. "We literally decide who gets to see what and when, and with all the religion we have here on being fair . . . and you bend all our rules for a real estate agent? It's a pretty massive letdown, don't you think? I could think of a few good reasons to bend our rules, orchestrating world peace, solving world hunger, but for a real estate agent?" Underneath the table, Molly's silent kicks had been growing increasingly more violent for the last few minutes, trying to get him to end this outburst. Andrew, meanwhile, hadn't said anything.

Stephen opened his mouth to speak, but Molly sharply pinched the back of his neck to silence him. "Can someone help me do the same thing for EasternDiscussions?" she asked hopefully.

Andrew didn't say anything at first, finishing off his Coke and moving onto the coffee that was getting cold. He made a show of the long breath he exhaled. "If it's still possible to do, I suppose that I could try," he said finally. "But, listen, do me a favor, okay?" Andrew cautiously asked Stephen.

"What?"

"If you come up with something decent when you're working on the Touchpoints project, make sure my name is attached to it, okay? Just say I gave you some ideas for the e-mail part if there is one, or make something up. Every little bit of goodwill helps. I really want to get an offer here this year. Otherwise, I'm on the job market again, at the end of the summer . . . "

Stephen flashed back to the time when he was heading his own group at SteelXchanges, and he thought about how lucky he was to never have gone through this tit-for-tat negotiating there. He and Arthur had been cofounders; there wasn't this trading of misdemeanors. He wondered whether his team had played these games, too. He had never seen it, but now, he doubted they would have been any different. Here, at Ubatoo, he was just as much a part of the reality show–like alliances as Andrew was. "If there are any breakthroughs, I'll bring you in."

"Thanks, Stephen," Andrew replied without looking at him. "Just get me the details later today. I can't control when the next tests are, but it shouldn't be more than a week or two."

"I thought you said you weren't even sure it worked the same way as last year," Stephen challenged, only half joking. Molly kicked him again.

▼ ▼ ▼

Hand in hand, Stephen walked Molly back to her car from the Asiatique Café. Lunch had been productive, but it was hard not to feel cheated out of their time together. "Play hooky with me?" Molly urged.

"I'd like to, but I can't. I've got too much to do today. Can I take a rain check?"

"Come on," she pleaded, still holding on to his hand. "Nobody cares when you're here and when you're not. Nobody's even going to notice. Besides, even if they did notice, who knows, they might actually think you're human if you take an afternoon off sometime."

"Don't you have to work at GreeneSmart today?"

"I took the day off to work at home. Tell you what, I'll give you a few options of what we can do, and I'll let you decide which one you want."

"I'm listening."

"We could go into San Francisco and ride the cable cars and then spend the rest of the day at the art museums. That's option one. Second, maybe a leisurely drive up the coast on 101—and take the next few days off and stay at bed-and-breakfasts we find along the way. Third, we could go outlet mall shopping. What do you think?"

"Really, all fascinating choices. But I'm still going to have to—"

"Or," she interrupted him, "we could go to a movie and watch the most brainless, gory, horror movie we can find and gorge ourselves on a bucket of popcorn. There's always that option, too."

She had him. If they hadn't met at GreeneSmart, the only other place they ever might have had even the smallest chance of meeting—if the stars aligned just right—was at an otherwise completely empty B-rate horror movie. Anything and everything that looked like it might be scary, campy, bloody, over the top, they watched—from aliens to demonic possessions to chainsaws.

Before he could agree, even though it was already abundantly clear by his expression that he would, she sweetened the deal. "I'll even throw in a quickie back at home. You know, just in case you still aren't sure."

It's good to be a tough negotiator.

-NEGOTIATIONS AND
HERDING CATS-

July 13, 2009.

"How are you enjoying being a manager, Jaan?" Atiq asked over a boiling cup of milky *Teh Tarik*—pulled, frothy, black tea—made by special request for Atiq by one of Ubatoo's sous-chefs from Malaysia.

With the countless recruiting trips and press interviews, it had been several weeks since Jaan and Atiq had a chance for their usual one-on-one meetings. "Managing is not for me, Atiq. I don't know how you do it. Personally, I'd rather be left alone. I've been working on my new project for a month now, but being a manager is really slowing it down," Jaan replied.

"What project is this? Completing Touchpoints, I hope?"

"Nope, it's brand new. I've been thinking about where our next breakthrough will come from. The more I think about it, the more I realize Ubatoo already has a massive amount of information about people who are online. I want to see how much we can find out about people *not* online." Jaan bounced up to the whiteboard and grabbed a marker, ready to write the moment the need arose. "My mom—she never touches a computer. In fact, she's afraid of them. Normally, you'd think that Ubatoo couldn't get any information about her, right?"

"Sure," Atiq shrugged.

"But I, and my brothers and sisters, write e-mails about my mom and my parents all the time. In fact, the pictures we upload, quite a few have her in them. It's too easy. Atiq, I don't know why we haven't done this before." Jaan was drawing stick figures in rectangles representing photographs on the board with labels of "Me," "Brothers," "Mom." He continued, excitedly, "Try this, just go to any photo sharing site, ours or any of the others, look at how many pictures have labels on them like 'Me and mom,' 'My mom,' or even 'Mom and grandma.'" Another stick figure of grandma. "You'll get hundreds of thousands of images. If we recognize the woman in a few pictures that I uploaded with this label, voilà, we've got her." A bull's-eye drawn over the figure of "Mom." "We know what she looks like, who she's with in the picture, and what her relation is to the person who uploaded the picture—me. We know she's my mom. If we know something about me, then we know something about her, too. If we know something about my brothers and sisters, which we do, then that tells us even more about her. With just a little bit more work with the data we already have, we already know a lot about my mom. We just have to put it together."

"Why would we, though?" Atiq asked skeptically.

But Jaan wasn't listening. "It's not even that hard. When I buy a present for my mom, what do I do? I buy it online and have it shipped to her. Sometimes I even attach a note, like 'Happy Birthday' or 'Hope you feel better,' or 'Thought you could use this.' Think how much information Ubatoo has on my mom. Birthdays, illnesses, her likes and dislikes, her address, hobbies, her kids—and never once did she touch a computer."

Atiq hopped out of his chair and grabbed the marker from Jaan's hand. He drew a few more boxes with "father" and "classmates" written in them, and arrows pointing haphazardly around the board. "It's not just you and your brothers and sisters. If your mom's friends, old classmates, or even your father, for that matter, are online and they talk about your mom or buy her presents, we have all of their profiles to use as well. With all your mom's relationships, we'd certainly be able to profile her. There are old class rosters and yearbooks online, too; they must have information to mine as well." Atiq darkened the circles of the bull's-eye centered on "Mom." "Very nice, Jaan. We should have done this earlier. It's so obvious."

Jaan smiled a very satisfied smile.

Atiq stared at the whiteboard a moment longer, imagining connections drawn between the hundreds of stick figures that would eventually be connected to "grandma," new sources of information being brought online from the mass of photos their users had uploaded, and profiles being created on people who had never touched any of their products. "That's clever, Jaan. I'll take it upon myself to find some people to work with you on this," Atiq promised. Then he added, "Might want to keep it quiet until we give our PR department a chance to develop a positive spin on this before news of it leaks, though, okay?"

Focus, he had to remind himself, focus. "But listen, Jaan, I really need you to wrap up Touchpoints, too. I'm counting on you for that. We need to deploy it across the company, and it's not going to happen without you."

"Don't worry so much. I've got an eye on it. The interns are already using the system every day, and the new hires are creating additional features. It'll be done and fully deployed this summer. I don't need to supervise it as closely anymore."

Struggling not to let his frustration show, Atiq replied, "Jaan, you're in charge of it. Keep a close eye on it, okay?" Good scientists don't always make good managers, Atiq thought to himself. He'd have to remember to get someone to take over Jaan's management responsibilities soon.

"How are the interns doing, by the way?" Atiq asked. This was the first time they had spoken about them since the conference call about Aarti and William on the second day of intern season.

"They're fine. I don't talk to them much—I've been so engrossed in my new project. I usually just e-mail the interns and the new hires when a new project comes in for them to work on. So far, they've finished the projects quickly, so I imagine everything's going well. Don't worry, I'm working them hard," Jaan replied with a grin.

"I hope you're not burning them out. When's the last time you met with them?"

"Atiq, they're interns. Don't worry about them. We can always get a new batch," Jaan joked.

Atiq wasn't smiling.

"I worked with them for a week when they first arrived. They're up to speed," Jaan continued more seriously.

"Jaan, maybe you could meet with them more? It might be a good idea to suggest a few more interesting projects, too. I don't want them getting bored and doing something pointless for their summer."

"Okay, I'll try to find out what they're working on. Just let me get a bit further on my project, and I'll set up regular meetings with them."

Management by negotiation—this was all the pushing Atiq could do. Hire the brightest minds and herd them like cats. Push too hard and they'll leave the company. Ubatoo's competitors would happily entice them before their resignation letters finished printing. Ubatoo's culture would never allow for a more direct order to be given, unless, of course, it was from Xiao.

-THE JENNY DISCOVERY-

July 15, 2009.

Within days of the now infamous "JENNY Discovery," a bulletin board was erected in Jenny's honor (this bulletin board was real, physical, and tacked to the wall). Although easily misconstrued as inhumane torture for Rob, it was actually created by the other interns to serve as Rob's public, cathartic, emotional therapy. Its initial incarnation was simply a place for push-pinning printouts of all of Jenny's e-mail that had even the hint of being, or being misconstrued as, sexy. However, within hours of it being put up in the intern pit, and every intern having read the e-mails, nobody seemed interested in it anymore.

Kohan, who had taken charge of the board, wasn't about to let its life end without a fight. Fortunately, scrutinizing Jenny's buying habits proved to be another source of interest. Even if some of the purchases were innocent enough (dog collar, leash, scarf, leather belt), when seen in the context of the e-mails, they were incontrovertible evidence of a deviant lifestyle.

In an ironic twist, the only one who was left out of all the ensuing fun was Yuri. Though it was his demo that started this race to discover "The Real Jenny," the one indisputable fact was that Jenny didn't search the Web for porn. Her house, despite constant monitoring, never turned pink. For Yuri, the fact that his demo was no longer the center of the action put him in an even quieter mood than pre-disclosure of his project.

Throughout, Yuri was working on the next "breakthrough." Just because Jenny's house didn't turn pink, didn't mean that Ben Cappiello, the recipient of Jenny's attentions, wasn't a consumer of all manner of lurid pornographic content—and not just the usual mild-mannered bits that were Cinemax worthy, nor even the material that some might try to cover as a business expense in pay-per-view hotel rooms. Ben's forte was material that could solely be found on the Internet; the legality of it was questionable in parts of Europe, and it was certainly illegal in the United States. But that was just the start.

When Yuri returned to the intern pit, he did so with trepidation. He walked straight to Rob. "Rob, I think you should see something." Immediately, Rob, Andrew, Kohan, and Stephen looked up from their computers. "I just sent you a few e-mails I found in Ben's account that you might want to take a look at."

Rob turned on the LCD panels next to him as he opened his e-mail. All eyes turned toward the screen as the image blinked to life. "Whoa!" he shouted as folds of deep pink were projected for everyone to see. As soon as recognition struck, he shut down the monitor as fast as his hand could move. "Maybe you guys could just look at it on my screen," he said quickly as he scooted away from the desk to make room for everyone.

"Is that Jenny?" Kohan asked Rob. Rob just glared back.

"No," replied Yuri. "Ben sent this e-mail to someone else—Claudine."

Rob scrolled past the dozens of pictures—amateurish images of messy, messy close-ups.

From: BenP101@ubamail.com
To: ClaudineRR@ubamail.com

Subject: Pictures

Claudine, check out your pictures (I attached the best 20). I don't know what you were shy about . . . they turned out beautifully. You look awesome.

And don't worry. I won't show them to anyone, as long as you don't either! I can't wait for our next session (maybe video next?)

See you tonight,
Ben

"Wow, I agree with Ben. She had no reason to be shy. She's really hot," Andrew stated matter-of-factly.

"Yuri, why would you want me to look at this?" Rob asked.

"Keep going. Read the next e-mail I sent you," Yuri replied.

From: BenP101@ubamail.com
To: JPeters22@ubamail.com,
         Eddie.Miter@ubamail.com,
         ASingh@ubamail.com

Subject: Number 14!

Check out our usual picts page (**Here's the _link_**). Claudine makes 14. I'm tied with you Eddie. Still working her for a video. What's up with you Singh—3? Hah.

THE MAN,
Ben

Rob followed the link in the e-mail to a private photo sharing page created on one of Ubatoo's partner properties. It was configured to only allow the four users, BenP101, JPeters22, Eddie.Miter, and ASingh, to enter. Sure enough, Ben's fourteen girls, Debra, Karen P., Lisa, Monica, Cynthia, Karen S., Jessica, Alison, Chloe, Amanda, Rachel, Leah, Claire, and of course, Claudine, lay splayed for everyone to see. Eddie.Miter had his own list of fourteen, with many more videos. Only Monica appeared in both Ben's and Eddie's catalogs. JPeters and ASingh had their section of conquests too, but with only a paltry seven and three girls for themselves—far outpaced by the prowess of the other two.

Stephen was the first to leave Rob's desk. Yuri second. Then Kohan, and finally after some not so subtle convincing, Andrew. Long after the crowd had gone, Rob continued to scan the images posted by the four men, as well as anxiously watch all of Eddie's videos. He needed to make sure his Jenny was nowhere on this site yet.

A fit of passive aggressive jealousy? A warning to Jenny to see what her friend, Ben, was really like? Or just needing to do something—Rob's reasons weren't clear. He reconfigured the settings on which the pictures of the girls appeared. Instead of limiting access to only the four, he made the page publicly accessible. For good measure, he added a few words to each image's captions and tags as well. Now, when people searched for nude pictures, sex, teens, porn, sluts, they would easily find this page waiting to answer their queries. Twenty-seven people were searching for some combination of those words the very minute Rob made the change. All of them were given a brand new set of girls to ogle over that they had never seen before and who had no idea how their images were being used. That hour, 302 more people. That day, 6,236 in total. Only a few of the 6,236 knew Claudine personally, and only a few of those would eventually forward her pictures to her friends.

▼ ▼ ▼

Stephen could already feel his heart starting to skip a few beats. It wasn't just an expression this time. It was the days and nights of no sleep, of barely moving from his seat, and the fact he had just consumed two shots of espresso.

"Gilroy is only forty-five minutes away from here. I say we go down and check them out," Andrew continued. He had been on this train of thought for the last ten minutes. It started when he did more "investigative research" on Claudine and Monica, two of "Ben's women." They lived only an hour away from Palo Alto, in Gilroy, CA. "Aren't you guys curious to see them in person?"

"Andrew, you've got to calm down. Besides, they're probably already asleep. It'll be a total waste of time," Stephen said, rolling his eyes. What he had wanted to say was "Andrew, get a life," but it probably wouldn't hold much weight coming from someone who had voluntarily stayed up all hours of the night reading other people's e-mails and casually perusing their exploits—all for a colleague he barely knew.

"It'll be a waste of a trip, for sure," Yuri replied. "But they are not asleep," Yuri popped up a map of JENNY on an LCD panel on the wall, showing two houses colored blue. Looks like they are both awake and chatting online."

Andrew smiled triumphantly, "Anything else, Stephen?"

"Andrew, think about what you're saying. You want to go see them? Think they'll invite you in? Maybe go to Claudine's room, have some drinks, take out a camera, or what?"

"What are you doing that's so important? You're sitting here with us, too, you know. Besides, it'll be fun just to get out of the office for a bit and do something."

"He's right. I'm in, Andrew. I'll go," Kohan said. "Besides, it really would be nice to get out of here for one night."

"This is the best you can come up with? Just leave the poor girls alone," Stephen replied.

"Your loss. Anybody know where I can get a pair of binoculars or something?" Kohan asked.

"I'll come, too," Rob announced. "Maybe it'll be a perfect night, and we'll see Ben and Jenny there, too. Stephen, Yuri, coming?"

"Well, I can come," Yuri said. "If you would like, maybe we can take one of Ubatoo's street-scanning vans. They have a nice set of zoom lenses and cameras on them for the high-resolution pictures we're gathering. If there's anything that can be seen from the outside, we'll broadcast it back through our internal network so you can watch it, Stephen."

"Thanks, Yuri, but no. I think I've seen enough of Claudine and Monica. There's not much more of them to see."

"We can take the van?" Andrew asked excitedly.

"Of course. I use one all the time for my research. Besides, we've never really tested its capabilities in nighttime conditions," Yuri said. "Who knows, maybe I'll publish a paper on its performance at night." Yuri might have been kidding, but it wasn't clear.

"I'm ready!" Andrew exclaimed, getting out of his chair fast enough to startle poor Yuri who happened to be standing in front of him. Kohan grabbed his cowboy hat and was already out the door. The rest soon followed the bobbing hat in the distance.

"Good luck, I guess," Stephen murmured to himself as he rose from his seat to go back to the café to get something to drink. He needed to start on his project for Sebastin, but desperately wanted another coffee. Then he remembered his heartbeats, especially the skipped ones. "I think I've had enough," he said out loud, but there was nobody left to hear him.

-I DREAM OF JENNY-

July 15, 2009.

Skipped heartbeats or not, the decision not to get more coffee was a bad one. Despite his best intentions to complete his work, the lack of company and the many sleepless nights proved too worthy an adversary. After an hour, Stephen gave up trying to work and decided to call it a night. He stumbled home in a daze, his body still jittery from the fading caffeine, and his head defiantly drooping low, ready for sleep. With each step, his feet fumbled as they found every pebble that had made its way onto the sidewalk.

When he finally walked through the door of the apartment, Molly was wide awake. She was seated where she always was, at her computer, oblivious to the world around her. He could tell by the way she was sitting, with one hand cupping her chin and the other poised ready to click the mouse, that she was doing what she did for far too many hours each day—repeatedly hitting refresh on her browser, waiting for the next message to be posted to one of EasternDiscussions message forums.

As he came closer, she started telling him excitedly about a message that had been posted earlier in the day. Andrew's changes to the ranking hadn't taken effect yet, so each message posted was still an exciting event. She stopped talking in mid-sentence when she saw Stephen's already wobbly stance giving way under the weight of his own body. "Come on, sleepy, let's get you to bed."

"I can't sleep yet, Molly. I have so much to do for tomorrow. One of Atiq's friends is calling me tomorrow for some project I was supposed to have already done. I haven't even started it yet."

"Can't you ask Kohan to do it for you tonight?"

"He's out tonight. I'll tell you about it later. That's a whole other mess with Kohan and Andrew . . ."

"Why don't you get a few hours sleep? I'll wake you in a couple of hours when I come to bed. Come on, I'll lay with you for a while."

He wrapped his hands clumsily around her head and pulled her toward him. "Thank you," he said, with his eyes and head already sinking.

"Alright, alright. Come here." With that, she led him to the bedroom. There, they laid in the dark, curled tightly into each other.

And in the haze that sometimes precedes sleep and passes like an eternity between the final brief moments of awareness and the oblivious comfort of rest, deep and peaceful, he watched idly as his thoughts interweaved with his days, and took shape as dreams.

Stephen's eyes blinked open to unfamiliar sounds from outside the bedroom. Molly was still with him, he could still feel her rhythmic breathing softly on the back of his neck. "Wake up, Molly." He put his hand on her bare leg, gently trying to shake her awake. "There's someone in here."

Skipped heartbeat. "Molly, wake up. I think someone is in our apartment." She didn't move.

Under the closed door of their bedroom, a flickering blue light made its way into his wide open eyes. The voices from outside grew louder. Just the TV. Nothing to worry about.

Out of bed. To the door. He pulled it open and stepped into the next room.

He fumbled for a light switch he couldn't find. The white flash of a camera. Molly? Another flash. Molly draped with a thin blanket, in a bed, awake, terrified. "What are you doing, Molly? I thought you were asleep in the other room."

She didn't turn her gaze to face him. Another flash of a camera.

"That's perfect." A voice called from the darkness. "Now take off the blanket." She did as she was told. Hot white skin on cool white sheets. "Molly, stop being so shy." The voice was familiar. "Come on, Molly, you look great." She did look great. The voice—it was Andrew's.

"Ready," a voice yelled out. Flash. Flash. "Perfect. Now that is something beautiful," Yuri was saying.

"What are you doing?" Stephen thought, or maybe said aloud.

"Shhh. Stephen." Molly called to him from the bed. "Come lay with me." No. No. Another flash. "Yuri is going to turn on the video camera. Come here, with me."

Stephen sunk further back into the corner. His hands feeling the empty wall. Where was the light switch?

"Don't be afraid," Molly called soothingly. "They promised not to show them to anyone. These are just for you and me. I thought you'd like them."

"Just for you two," Andrew affirmed. Flash. Teeth gleaming. Damaged grin.

Four imperfect crescents welled with red in his palm; nails piercing through the skin. "That's enough," Stephen ordered in a burst of confidence. The flashes stopped.

Around him, three LCD panels glowed a dim grey. "Try searching for the pictures, Stephen. Let's make sure this works." He found the letters on a keyboard, M-O-L-L-Y. Total: 10,522 results returned in 0.0003 seconds. The center LCD scrolled through message forums probing Molly in depth. Users posting, chatting, and sharing—all about Yuri's pictures. With a loud click of a mouse, the photographs revealed themselves on the second LCD. Click, videos sputtered to life on the third.

"The video cameras work well at night," Yuri exclaimed. The grainy shaky images, taken with an inexperienced yet all-too-willing hand, conveyed their message clearly enough.

"Stephen. These are your friends. Take the pictures down. Make them stop," Molly pleaded as she hid beneath the blanket.

The last few steps flew beneath him as he found Andrew. "Take them down. Delete them all. Right now."

"Of course." Andrew pressed a few buttons on the keyboard. The LCDs turned off. The room went black. "All gone."

Molly fell back into her pillow.

"I think you should look at this." It was Yuri talking.

A map of the JENNY system, centered on their apartment, slowly appeared on the center LCD. It was black, there was no activity happening online. "It looks good," Stephen called out. "Thank you."

Yuri pulled the mouse back toward him, zooming the map out. The two LCDs on either side of the first, presented the adjacent neighborhoods. With tiny, barely audible clicks, one by one, each house turned from black, green, blue, and any other color—to pink. A narrator with a quirky voice and uneven tone, kindly explained, "Molly found her way to the hearts and homes of all her neighbors."

Yuri pulled his mouse back further. Dozens of LCDs covered the walls, extending the map in every direction. Snakes of pink, like flowing water, emanated from each encountered house, branched and divided, until all of the LCDs shone brightly with only one color. The bright pink from the LCDs exposed Molly—still covered only with a thin diaphanous blanket, staring intently at the screens all around; exposed Andrew's face, inspecting Molly; exposed Yuri, with camera in hand.

The narrator continued as this episode faded, but the words were lost in the light.

Andrew motioned to Yuri. Yuri tossed the camera to Andrew.

"One more picture, just for me," Andrew explained. Flash. A room filled with harsh white light. The blanket did nothing to hide the body underneath.

Stephen fell into a quiet, unadorned, sleep. He held on a bit too tightly to Molly, so that when it came time for her to get up and press reload, she didn't bother to move. It could wait.

His breathing had finally calmed down, and she didn't want to wake him. They both could use the sleep. Just like every other night, she would face her own set of dreams in a few minutes, and it would be good to know that someone was there with her. They slept for a full five hours, the longest they had been with each other in days, holding on to each other through a pall of altogether too vivid dreams, nightmares, and complete and utter exhaustion.

-A FIVE-STEP PROGRAM-

Hallucinations and Archetypes

July 16, 2009.

Stephen woke to an empty apartment dappled with morning light. A note was waiting next to him, instead of Molly.

> Some really nice results just this morning! Looks like traf-
> fic is finally picking up. Thanks for all your help. Whatever
> Andrew did worked! More traffic and people posting on my
> site than I could have imagined. Let's try to talk tonight.
> There's so much to tell you about. We haven't talked in
> days.
>
> Love, Molly

He held the note in his hand for a few seconds. If his imagined television audience could have seen the intensity of expression in those moments, they would have suspected nothing short of a man on the brink of foretelling the fate of humanity.

The reality, though, was less dramatic. Molly had never written a real physical note to him. Come to think of it, he couldn't recall the last time anyone had handwritten a note to him. Molly had written plenty of e-mails, but they were short and to the point. She had never signed it with "love," or anything else for that matter.

But here was a physical piece of paper in his hand, more than half of which talked about work. What was wrong with him? Just like the first night in this apartment, setting up Molly's computer, this was too much thought about too little. For all he knew, it was probably how she signed all her notes. This was unquestionably the first and surest sign he was growing older, and becoming feeble-minded. But even more probable, he suspected, was that this overly long, and entirely unwarranted, pause for introspection was due to his overwhelming exhaustion. Likely, he may well have found a handwritten breakfast menu equally intriguing in his current state.

But then again, things were going well. After a four-year-long interruption, he was finally enraptured with his research again. All of this was heightened by Molly—someone who felt the same way about her own work. Who else would not only understand, but also experience, this kind of consuming drive? Perhaps, as he reconsidered it again, the breakfast menu really wouldn't have been an adequate replacement.

Despite all of these thoughts and Molly's request to talk that night, there was still a good chance he wouldn't make it back in time. He had an enormous amount to do today before his meeting with Sebastin (it had been seven days since he had last spoken to him), and there was a company-wide meeting that he should attend as well. Last but not least, his curiosity about Kohan's night was hard to contain.

▼ ▼ ▼

Stephen had promised nothing specific to Sebastin. Nevertheless, he wanted to impress. He had always lived by the motto of under-promising and over-delivering. Plus, there was the chance that Sebastin might remember to put in a good word with Atiq. And the fact that Atiq clearly thought highly of Sebastin wasn't far from his thoughts.

With a hot cappuccino on the desk, and two handmade chocolate croissants from the pastry cart ready to go, he opened the attachments in the e-mail that Sebastin had sent a week ago. He quickly scrolled through the list of 960 books on his screen. Just as Sebastin had indicated on the phone, there was no discernible pattern. The list contained cookbooks, textbooks, fiction, non-fiction, history books, agriculture, literature, philosophy, engineering, religion, mathematics, and more.

Normally, this in itself would be an interesting puzzle: How did all these books make it onto the same list? Maybe if he hadn't delayed this project until the last minute by working so much on JENNY, there would have been time to figure it out.

Time for work.

Like their public-facing search engine that brought Ubatoo to such fame, there was an equally powerful, but never publicized, search engine for everyone's e-mail that was available only to Ubatoo's data-mining group. People outside Ubatoo were able to search their own e-mail, of course, and the data-mining group searched everyone's e-mail. He typed the first book's title, "World Survey on the Role of Women in Economic Development," and submitted the query.

Instantaneously, several hundred e-mails came up that contained the full phrase. He had to choose "Sort by sender," "Sort by recipient," or "Sort by date." He sorted by the sender—only a dozen or so unique senders had composed e-mails containing that book's title in the past year. He clicked over to the "instant message" tab to see if anyone had sent any instant messages containing the title of the book. Only two people had, but that was just for this one book.

> Step 1: Set up a program to send all the titles of the books through the internal e-mail and instant message search engine and gather the names of the people who had ever used the titles in any of their correspondences, and also note how often they had used them.

The time to write the program was far longer than the time it took to run it. After writing the program in about twenty minutes, within a few seconds of starting, it ended. A bit anticlimactic. But now any e-mail or instant message that contained the titles of any of the 960 books was accounted for. There were 73,291 people who had mentioned the books at least once in their correspondence.

> Step 2: Let's figure out who bought these books. The purchasing records of stores that used Ubatoo's credit card and transaction processing systems were the easy ones to access. There were only some tens of thousands of those stores to look at. Those would take only a few minutes to scan through once started.

Within a few minutes, at least several hundred machines somewhere in Ubatoo's cloud were dutifully scanning records from the past year trying to uncover all the people who bought any of the 960 books in the last year. Only 29,084 people bought any of the books listed, a terribly small number for that many books. These were clearly not bestsellers. That analysis was far too easy. "Okay, Sebastin, watch what we can do now," he said aloud.

The problem with a number like 73,291, or 29,084 for that matter, was that, although it was good to know, it was way too large to be useful. Hopefully, ACCL wouldn't send out a warning e-mail to all of these people and scare them unnecessarily.

He needed to narrow it down. In quick succession, he tried a few guesses to prune the number down to something more manageable. The one that worked well was to just look at the people who had purchased more than one book from the list. That made sense, since if they had bought only one, it may be just a coincidence. There were only 2,602 people who had bought two or more books. That's a better number.

So 2,602 people bought at least two different books from the list. How many of them had actually sent an e-mail or instant message about them, too? That list had been created in step 1 and was waiting to be used.

> Step 3: Find the people who appeared both on list-1 and on list-2 and merge the lists. These are the people who wrote about the books AND bought at least two. That's probably the set of people who are most into the books.

The set of 2,602 that he found earlier only reduced to 2,423 after step 3 was completed. Not much of a reduction, which meant that if someone bought two of the books on the list, he was likely to talk about them, too. Nonetheless, this was definitely the set of people to concentrate on—buyers who cared enough about the content to discuss it. If Sebastin was going to contact anyone, this was a good set of people to start with.

But books? Why books?

It felt stupid. Who looks at book reading patterns and thinks they know everything there is to know about someone? No, that doesn't make sense. The fact they bought these books was an indication of something else. The U.S. government, no matter how paranoid or ridiculous they seemed, couldn't really care that someone just bought a book, could they? What they cared about was that if the person was the *type* to buy one of these books, then that person was the *type* to do something more dangerous, something actually worthy of being watched. But why not just find out what that is—Ubatoo had the data. Let's figure out what *type* of people these people actually were.

To do this, he needed to look beyond books and see what else the 2,423 had in common. If these people really participated in activities that put them on a watch list, there were probably a myriad of other patterns to discover from the things they did online. Back to Ubatoo's repositories to find all of their recorded actions for years past.

There wasn't enough time to do this nearly as comprehensively as Stephen would have liked. He selected just four from the hundreds of things Ubatoo knew about its users, and looked for patterns in them. For each of the 2,423 people, he examined:

1. What web sites they had visited in the last two years.
2. What they searched for on Ubatoo.
3. What products they most often bought using Ubatoo's credit cards.
4. Where they had traveled to, as inferred by Ubatoo's records of 1–3 above.

All of these were already conveniently stored in the profiles of the 2,423 people that had been diligently created over years. This information was ready, patiently waiting to be used.

What he found was that, of the 2,423 people, many consistently went to Mideast news and entertainment sites, but also to political and religious discussion boards, sites about lectures given by people he had never heard of who spoke of religious points he had never encountered, and even some private sites that he would have liked to look at in depth, but just didn't have the time. That's just attribute #1. The other attributes, #2–#4, held patterns, too—there were dozens of common searches performed by the 2,423, many out-of-the-ordinary products they had all purchased, and many places in common to which they had traveled. These patterns were just as important, if not more important, than the books they read.

He would have liked to have systematically matched all of Ubatoo's 200 million users in the U.S. to each of the profiles of the 2,423 people. This would have uncovered whether other users existed out there like one from the set of 2,423. But time—time was running out . . . He had promised Sebastin something today, and doing this would take far too much time.

Instead of comparing all of Ubatoo's users to 2,423 profiles, he created a new hypothetical profile—a single archetype from the 2,423: Stephen called her *Lucy*. Lucy would be constructed through synthesizing all the patterns he had just uncovered. If most of the 2,423 had visited *Aljazeera.net* many times, then Lucy had too. If most of them had traveled to countries in the Mideast, then Lucy had as well. Whatever the 2,423 most commonly had searched for—that's what Lucy had searched for. Lucy was the epitome of the patterns Stephen had found. He made this computer hallucination in the likeness of what the 2,423 would be, if they were just one person.

> Step 4 (for fun) [Controlled Hallucinations]: Create a new profile that is the synthesis of the common patterns in the 2,423. Label this profile "Lucy."

With only 2,423 people to examine, Lucy was created, and she developed all her web-surfing and traveling habits faster than the time it took for him to type his name.

Lucy wasn't some outlandish artificial-intelligence dream come to life in a futuristic movie. She wasn't a sentient being in the making, hell-bent on eliminating the human race. No, far from it. She was just a list of a few words and numbers in the form of a profile, like all the other profiles that sat in Ubatoo's repositories. But Lucy had a bigger job to do than just exist as a computer hallucination that Stephen had fashioned.

Though Stephen didn't have time to check which of Ubatoo's users matched each of the 2,423 people individually, he did have time to see if they matched one profile: Lucy's profile.

> Step 5 (for even more fun): Find other people who may or may not be on the original list of 2,423 who match Lucy's profile. These are the people who should probably be on the ACCL list, too, but may not have been uncovered by only looking at their book buying and reading patterns.

Thanks to Jaan's system, the last question, which would normally take days to answer, would be completed in just a few hours. He set a high priority for the job—over 6,000 computers somewhere in Ubatoo's cloud obediently aborted whatever project they were working on, and immediately started on Stephen's.

Stephen helplessly watched as the progress bar made its excruciatingly slow crawl to 1% . . . 2% . . . 3% . . . 4% . . . 5% . . . 6% . . . Finally, at 6% he convinced himself that it would be okay to leave the computer—at least long enough to grab some lunch and bring it back to his desk to watch its climb to 100%. He returned in time to see 28% . . . 29% . . .

Hopefully it would be done soon. There was so much more he could do.

-OVER-DELIVER-

July 16, 2009.

"Stephen! How are you? Give me a second. Let me clear out my office. I was just finishing up a meeting," Sebastin said enthusiastically as soon as he recognized the caller.

"I can call back later . . . ," Stephen said. As he was accustomed to at this point, nobody stuck around to hear his last words. He was talking to himself again.

About a minute later, Sebastin returned to the phone after ushering the others out of the room. "Alright, the room's empty. I have the files you e-mailed me open on my screen. So what have you found?"

"First things first," Stephen replied. "Let me tell you what I did. I started by doing exactly what we talked about, finding everyone who bought one of the books. The procedure I used was to . . ." and he continued his monologue for three minutes. He knew it was unlikely Sebastin was interested, but he had also learned from working with all the other advertisers in the past few weeks that his results never seemed as impressive to them as when they were derived in some mostly unintelligible manner that suitably confused them. ". . . so, in the first file I sent you, are all the people who purchased a book from your list within the last year."

"That file looks huge. How many people did you find?"

"29,084. I also included their e-mail addresses. I thought you would probably want those."

"Wonderful, this is truly wonderful," Sebastin said.

"That's just the beginning," Stephen said happily. "That number was too big, of course. So, first, I found all the people who bought at least two books. Then I went ahead and checked which ones of those wrote about the books in their e-mails or instant messages. These people are the high-priority ones. Warn them first. They're the most likely to be talking about the books in public, writing messages about them, and so on."

"You scanned through all of their e-mails? Really?"

"Just the ones who used our own e-mail service. Fortunately, from what I remember, that's most of them. Anyway, I found 2,423 people. The entire processing took less than two minutes." It was always fun to boast about Ubatoo's massive computing resources. A couple years ago, nobody wanted to hear about how many machines were used or how long the processing took. It was just in the past year that the number of machines grew so astronomically large that even the average advertising client, or charity client in this case, cared.

"Amazing. Just amazing."

"Yeah. It really is. But, wait, there's more!" he said. He always used this line in his presentations to advertisers. It was a bit cheesy, a bit too much like he was selling a set of knives in an infomercial, but if the advertiser liked the results already, this only endeared them further to the presentation.

"Alright. I'm all ears."

"Now, this is something I didn't quite understand, but I checked it a bunch of times to make sure it was right. In the process of doing this analysis, I had to cluster the buyers and books." Without Sebastin's expression to judge, Stephen couldn't be sure whether Sebastin had any idea what clustering meant. "I mean, I grouped the results together so I could find correlations between the books by using the people who bought them as signals. Basically, I created a bipartite graph and propagated the signals originating from each node . . ." Too much again. He stopped talking there, realizing all this was probably far more gibberish than Sebastin had bargained for.

"What I'm trying to say is that if I look just at the people who bought more than one book on your list, almost all of them only bought books from a tiny set of sixty books. Doesn't that seem strange?" Stephen waited for Sebastin to digest this.

Sebastin didn't respond, so Stephen tried to explain it one last time, "*Out of the 960 books, 900 of them were random*—they had nothing to do with that tiny set of 60. In other words, 900 books were just a distraction. It was almost like someone in your group just stuck them in there to make this task more challenging for me. Does that sound plausible?"

More silence on the other end of the phone. Stephen waited patiently, but when a minute had passed without a sound, he had to say something. "Sebastin? You still there?"

"Yes, yes. I'm here. Sorry, just thinking. That is very strange. I have no explanation for why that is." Some typing started in the background. "That is the small list of books in your third attachment? I'll look into that. Let me think . . ."

Another long pause arose before Sebastin spoke again. "This is certainly a lot of information for me to absorb." He sounded distant.

Stephen feared he was losing Sebastin, so he quickly went on before Sebastin had time to make an excuse about having to leave, or being called into a different meeting. Most advertisers resorted to any number of excuses the moment the analyses started getting too hairy.

But Sebastin had no intention of cutting the call short before he understood absolutely everything Stephen had to say. He was quiet only because he was trying his best to make sure he could follow every step. Sebastin was thankful for the conversations he had endured with the engineers at his old company, iJenix—otherwise, he'd be struggling far more than he was right now.

Stephen launched into a discussion of Lucy, profiles, and hallucinations and archetypes. These were all words that Sebastin thought he knew the meaning of, but certainly not in this context. It was only when Stephen started winding down that Sebastin could begin to understand again.

"Remember when I said that I thought books were a . . . well, ridiculous thing to look at that didn't make sense to me? This is my way of getting around that. Sebastin, this is really important. *This is what you should have been asking me for* . . ."

Stephen finally paused for a breath before the final push. "I found people like Lucy. The list of books that Lucy read is just one of her attributes. But she's more complex than that. There are other attributes about her that are just as important—what she bought, which web sites she visited, what she was interested in—what she searched for, and where she traveled . . . Even if some of the people who are like Lucy didn't read the same books, so what? Many of the people I found are just like her in other ways, I mean dead-on, exact, matches—and some have read the books, some haven't. That's not really what's important. What do you think?"

"I gave you a list of books—and this is what you came up with?"

Stephen couldn't tell if Sebastin was angry or happy. He didn't know what to say.

Sebastin continued, "That's incredible. I'm speechless."

"Exactly right. Me and my girl, Lucy," Stephen said, delighted.

Sebastin, though, had one more question to ask before he was ready to share fully in the happiness, "How many people are on this list?"

"5,000."

Stephen explained further, "What I mean is that I just gave you the top 5,000 people to keep it simple. They're all pretty good matches, but it is sorted. The people on top are the ones who matched Lucy the most closely; the people toward the bottom matched less. So, if you're going to go after the highest-risk people on this list, start at the top."

If Stephen could have seen Sebastin, he would have found a man in a state of excitement that went beyond the surprise witnessed by wide-open eyes and a mouth agape. The emotion for Sebastin was a combination of stunned, contented, aware, done. "5,000 people—this, this is really a lot to digest so fast, Stephen. This has really surpassed all my expectations. Thank you."

"It's my pleasure. Hope that it does you some good."

"It will. I'm sure of it. Listen, Stephen, let me take you out to lunch to thank you in person . . ." They set a time and exchanged pleasant well wishes.

Stephen was ecstatic. Someone had made it through all of his analyses, and even though he wasn't sure Sebastin had completely understood, he seemed to genuinely appreciate it.

It was approaching 4 p.m. Finally, Stephen's to-do list for the day was empty. The company-wide "rally the troops" meeting was getting ready to begin; he gladly would have skipped it to hear about Kohan's night. But, alas, Kohan and the rest were still nowhere to be found.

-A LIFE CHANGED IN FOUR
PHONE CALLS-

July 16, 2009.

Five thousand people. This was far more than Sebastin had anticipated, and 4,000 more than he needed. One thousand would have met
his expectations just fine.

This assignment was thankfully coming to a close. It had taken
months to get the information—much longer than he had predicted.
Soon, he would hand over the list to Rajive, get paid, and be done.
Then, he could go back and concentrate on what ACCL was really
about, ensuring the right to free speech, to a free Internet across all de-
mographics, conquering the "digital divide," and things that he and the
other founders—Mark, Elizabeth, and Nate—actually knew something
about.

So how did he get away with telling Stephen the story he had told
him? He had two things going for him: First, the lies he had told Stephen had been vague enough to be plausible if Stephen were to do any
research on ACCL. It was true they were interested in free speech and
privacy, and their web site said as much. It never mentioned watch
lists, but then what site would? Second, with Ubatoo's reputation for
how hard they work their interns, he was confident Stephen wouldn't
bother to do any research on him or on watch lists; he was far too busy.
And if Sebastin were pressed to give yet another, third, reason, it would
be that he was a salesman, and a good one at that, at least when it came
to selling inside Silicon Valley. Selling an intern on a childlike vision
of the idealism that surrounded him daily? If he couldn't do that, shame
on him.

Still, Sebastin couldn't help but think it would be easier not to live this duplicitous life. He had to hide what he was doing from everyone at ACCL. And despite their ups and downs when they sold iJenix, he had tried his best to come to terms with how much richer they were than he. They would immediately know that something was amiss if they found out he was having meetings at Ubatoo that they weren't privy to. Besides, all this hassle wasn't worth the small amount of money Rajive had offered him. It wouldn't even begin to get him close to what Mark had made years ago.

He was curious, though . . . How good were the names on the list? Were these really people who should be on a watch list? If they were, shouldn't this list be worth a lot more than what he was being paid? If what Stephen promised wasn't too good to be true, the list was worth significantly more. It would at least be interesting to know.

He would have picked up the phone immediately and called some of the people on the list, but he wasn't prepared yet. What would he say? He had to come up with a good script. Otherwise, he would just wind up scaring them for no reason. He knew better than to call in the midst of his excitement right now.

He would give himself until tomorrow to think about it. He had waited this long; he could wait one more day.

▼ ▼ ▼

Sorted. The 5,000 names on the list were *sorted*. The boy, Stephen, had given him the list ordered; the persons on the very top of the list were the ones that were most likely being watched. So, to start with, Sebastin chose a name at random from the very last of the over one hundred pages of names and contact information, *Muratt Merdin*. If he could verify that this person, from the back of the list, would be a good candidate to put on a watch list, then anybody who Stephen had found who ranked higher, would surely be a good candidate, too.

Sebastin waited anxiously as the ringing on the other end of the phone heightened his anticipation, like the clicking of a roller coaster before the freefall.

"Hello?"

"My name is Sebastin. I'm calling on behalf of the American Coalition for Civil Liberties. May I speak with Muratt Merdin?"

"Speaking."

"Mr. Merdin, this isn't an easy topic to bring up. You might want to sit down. ACCL is a non-profit group located in California. Our goal is to preserve people's rights. We are not a government organization, and we are not saying you are in any trouble. But we do have reason to believe that your rights are being violated."

"What are you talking about?"

"Some of the actions you have taken online or offline may have put you on a government watch list. Please understand. We are only trying to make sure your rights are not violated. We are not affiliated with any government agency in any way."

"I didn't do anything. Am I in some kind of trouble? Are you a cop?" Mr. Merdin was already approaching hysteria.

Twenty minutes into the conversation, he had finally calmed Mr. Merdin enough to go through a list of possible reasons why he may have made it onto the list. "Mr. Merdin, I'm trying to help you. If we know why you're on the list, ACCL can use all of its resources to get you off the list. Let's start with the basics. Have you flown out of the country recently?"

"No. Not recently." A clearing of the throat. "I flew to Turkey last September," he admitted. "But I have family there," he quickly added.

"Anywhere else?"

"No. I didn't fly anywhere else." But there was hesitation in his voice when he said this—a weakness that any attentive salesman would catch.

"Mr. Merdin, if you're not honest with me, I can't help you. Did you travel anywhere else?"

"I have friends and family in the area." He paused as if trying to stop himself before saying something more.

"Where? And for how long? I'm trying to help, Mr. Merdin."

"All around there. Turkey, Iraq, Syria—my family is there. I went for two months. Am I not supposed to visit them?"

"Of course you are, Mr. Merdin. That all sounds perfectly normal. May I ask what it is you do, Mr. Merdin?"

"I am sure you already know that I'm a civil and structural engineer—for seven years now. Is there something wrong with that? Why are you asking me these questions?"

"I'm just trying to gather enough information to help you. Tell me, did you visit any web sites that might be considered controversial? Sometimes that causes problems, too. Especially in conjunction with travel."

"I always search for any news around the world . . . about home."

"Certainly. Who doesn't search for news about home? Anything else that I should know about?" Next time, Sebastin thought, he would have to ask Stephen for the reason why each person was on the list. This guessing game wasn't making his life easy.

"Sometimes I don't even pay attention to what I click on or what I read . . . I just click sometimes . . ."

Sebastin interrupted him, "You haven't found yourself on any controversial political sites or any web sites that someone might consider radical or extremist, have you? Even just out of curiosity, or even by accident. So many times that's what triggers these alarms."

"No, never. I would never . . . Maybe by accident I might have clicked on some link, I don't know . . ."

Closer. He was on the brink of getting something. Some admission, some sign—something to verify the list. Sebastin stayed quiet, hoping Merdin would continue.

Merdin was on the verge of hysteria when he did. "I would never . . . Who would even know? I can't be in trouble for accidentally seeing some web site. That's impossible. This is not right."

"I agree with you completely. But I'm not the one who put you on the list. I'm trying to be the one who gets you taken off. Mr. Merdin, if I look up all of your searches in the last two years, are you sure I won't find something that might at least appear suspicious? I'd be happy to go through the list with you. I'm trying to help you. Let's look up your searches in the past year. It'll just take a second for me to bring them up. Give me a second." Sebastin loudly struck a few keys on his keyboard. On Sebastin's screen, it brought up the game of Mine Sweeper. For Merdin, each key press moved him one step closer to divulging his curiosities.

"It's already loaded a few months," Sebastin confirmed after about fifteen seconds.

"Already? How did you—"

"It only takes a few minutes," Sebastin interrupted. "Let me look for the few months before you left on your trip—September last year you said it was. Okay, here we go, just a few more seconds." Sebastin tapped his fingers on the table loudly, making sure Merdin heard the taps, could hear time ticking away.

Another shot in the dark: "By the way, that's quite an interesting selection of books you've read."

Merdin didn't respond. If something was going to happen, it had better happen soon.

Tap, tap, click, click, tap, tap. Misstep—Mine Sweeper game over. "Okay, let's see. Let's start with June of last year. I've got it all loaded now."

The phone line went dead.

First one—verified. Innocent curiosity? I would have put this guy on a watch list myself. Nice job, Stephen. Just need to check a few more and we'll officially be done.

The second call, made to another name near the end of the list, proceeded like Merdin's, with the same level of anxiety. The third call was made to a person picked from the middle of the list. He had become enraged and hung up. Not the explicit verification that would have been ideal, but most likely a positive indication nonetheless. He would check a total of five. Two more to go.

Call number four, a random person, M. *Mohammad*, chosen from page 8—moving closer to the top of the list.

The phone rang twice and was picked up. "Hello?" It was a young boy's voice on the line.

"My name is Sebastin. May I speak with M. Mohammad?"

He heard the boy yell for his dad. "*Baba! Baba*, your phone."

In a moment, Sebastin could hear the father scolding his son, "Adam, how many times have I told you never to pick up this phone? Now leave this room."

He could hear the scuffling of feet as the boy ran out of the room.

"How did you get this number?" an angry voice demanded.

"My name is Sebastin. I'm calling on behalf of the American Coalition for Civil Liberties. Is this M. Mohammad?"

No answer. After a minute, a dial tone told him no one was on the other end.

Sebastin was flipping through the list, trying to decide who else to call, when his phone rang. The caller ID displayed the number he had just dialed.

"Now tell me, what is it you want?" the man on the other end of the line demanded.

"My name is Sebastin. I'm calling on behalf of the American Co-alition for Civil Liberties. Mr. Mohammad, this isn't an easy topic to bring up. You might want to sit down for it. ACCL is a non-profit group located in Silicon Valley. Our goal is to preserve people's rights. We are not a government organization, and we are not saying you are in any trouble. But we do have reason to believe that your rights are being violated."

"What do you want?"

"Nothing, sir. I wanted to tell you that some of the actions you have taken may have put you on a government watch list. Please un-derstand, we are only trying to make sure that your rights are not vio-lated. We are not affiliated with any government agency in any way."

"What list?"

"We've compiled our own list of people we suspect are being watched unfairly. As I said, I am part of ACCL. My goal is to verify that you are aware of what's happening to you."

"I am on *your* list?"

"Yes. That's why I am calling. I'm trying to warn you."

"Warn me? Who are you? Where are you?" the man on the other end of the phone demanded.

This time it was Sebastin who hung up the phone. No more veri-fication needed from Stephen's list. He just wanted to give the list to Rajive as fast as possible and be done with it. He shouldn't have used his name or his own phone. That was hasty. That was irresponsible.

Within two minutes, Sebastin's phone rang again.

"We should talk about your list, Sebastin Munthe of 192 Freyet Road, Los Altos, California. Shall we talk at your house or over the phone?"

-GIVING THANKS-

July 16, 2009.

The deep bass and blaring horns of swing music kept the noise level of Xiao's Ballroom high. Waiters and waitresses made their way speed-ily through the crowded room on roller skates, shuttling hors d'oeuvres and drinks to all the gathered engineers and salespeople.

Thankfully, Stephen found at least one familiar face in the crowded auditorium; Aarti was standing by herself watching the spectacle around them. Still on a high from his conversation with Sebastin, Ste-phen wasted no time in telling Aarti about his project and his results.

He spoke too fast and too loud. He hadn't even started in on any of the details when she pulled him closer to warn him "I'm not sure you should be talking about any of that here. It's probably best to keep it to ourselves, don't you think?"

Stephen was surprised. "Everybody here works for Ubatoo. I can't imagine that we can't tell them what we're doing." Then he kept going, undeterred, though now in an urgent whisper, just barely loud enough for Aarti to hear.

She didn't protest or warn him again, and though she listened to every word, she had little to say. "I'm boring you with this, aren't I?" Stephen asked. "I should probably just let you enjoy the food and take a break in the few minutes we have before the meeting starts."

"No, Stephen, of course you're not boring me. This is what we do," she said as she laid her hand on his folded arms. "No, it's not that at all. I'm just really surprised to hear about what you're doing. It doesn't sound like one of Jaan's usual requests." She stopped talking to stare at him, apparently trying to discern something in him that she herself wasn't ready to reveal. Whatever it was, she eventually decided to continue. "It's a hard problem to tackle. I've been—"

She never finished her sentence. The lights flashed off and on and the mad dash for the few remaining seats ensued. They soon lost each other in the rapidly moving streams of people. If she wanted to continue, Stephen figured, she would find him again afterward. Knowing her, she probably had some insight from one of her own projects that she thought might help him. She'd probably be right, and it'd probably be something he hadn't yet considered, but should have. She never continued, though, and he never brought it up again.

▼ ▼ ▼

Despite all the organizer's best efforts, the air of joviality that usually permeated the "rally the troops" meetings was missing. The domestic and worldwide economy had been deteriorating for months. Though Ubatoo seemed to be bucking the outside economic trends, and was still managing to produce revenue and profits at astonishing rates, the fear of the inevitable crisis hitting them was on everyone's mind. The fear, like everywhere else, wasn't some far away hypothetical concern—it was personal. The vast majority of the employees, especially the senior members of the staff, were far too disproportionately invested in Ubatoo. Their lofty compensations, as well as their enormous nest eggs, were dependent on the stock continuing to climb. Though nothing had been said regarding this financial crisis and its effects, rumors anticipated that it would be addressed today.

In contrast, all the summer interns were anxiously awaiting a different segment of the speech. Unencumbered by worry over stock options, they were just hoping their group would be mentioned. The more often their group was talked about (as long as it was in a positive light), the more the group would need to recruit to meet the inevitably increased expectations. This had the desired consequence of improving the interns' likelihood of receiving full-time offers. Surprisingly for this crowd, nobody had actually studied the correlation between the number of mentions and the number of job offers, but when the rationale for receiving such an anticipated reward was shrouded under such a glaring lack of transparency, there were many tempting straws to grasp.

By the time Xiao reached the podium at center stage, the music
had smoothly faded away. As usual, Xiao didn't waste time on pleasantries. The artificial lights dimmed, and Xiao's PowerPoint slideshow was
projected onto a forty-foot-high screen behind him, which bathed the
room in a cyan glow. Xiao shuffled back and forth in front of the projection screen, casting an intimidating larger-than-life shadow. Revenue
projections and web site traffic estimates flashed above his head, then
were gone within seconds. He didn't spend much time on the money;
the numbers were too large to hold any tangible meaning to anyone
in the room. It was enough to know the figures were enormous, and
growing.

Next, it was time to discuss the technological accomplishments
since the company's last meeting. Deeply liking and appreciating technology was what made Xiao so well suited for this company. Unlike
many other CEOs, Xiao wasn't afraid of technology or engineers, and
instead held a genuine interest in how things at Ubatoo were accomplished, not just the amount of money they brought in. Much to the
delight of the employees, the majority of his time was devoted to presenting new milestones attained. He always took advice about which
ones to present at these meetings, but the final decision was his, and
he chose those he personally found most fascinating. He left it to the
Vice Presidents below him to make certain those people who didn't get
mentioned were adequately reassured that their projects were of great
importance to the company as well.

"Before I get into what I had planned to say, I just learned that Ubatoo has reached another milestone in the number of servers we have
running across the world. The 3,700,000 mark was reached yesterday.
That's the good news—but that was yesterday. Today, I was informed
that even with all of these servers, we will face a severe shortage within
three years. Assuming we continue to grow as expected, we will need
to vastly increase the accumulation of machines just to keep up. Either
that, or you all will need to come up with more efficient algorithms to
search through all of our content. Think about this, all of you budding
stars, the best thing you can do for us is to make us scale upwards. We'll
have more data, more users, and more services than we can keep up
with unless we become more efficient. Keep that in mind! But now,

congratulate our team for building the world's most powerful computing cloud. Congratulations all around!"

The auditorium burst into a standing applause. The kudos were well deserved. Had the machines not been put online, the research and the development of new products would have been impossible. What type of scientific playground would it be if there weren't enough toys to play with?

"We have more good news. Despite immense pressure from our competitors domestically and abroad, we have gained market share in almost every market targeted this quarter. Most notably, I would like to congratulate our team in Beijing. They've far surpassed our projections and have handily made Ubatoo the most visited site in all of China." The screen cut over to a teleconference with the China office, a room packed with smiling employees—a sea of dark hair and neatly pressed white shirts. They waved and cheered gleefully into the camera.

When the polite applause subsided, Xiao continued, "One of the biggest new initiatives we've launched is through our London office. It's a partnership with the British Police." The faces of the happy employees in China were abruptly replaced by a scraggly group of engineers from the London office—all as equally cheerful and waving as the first group had been.

"After months of negotiations on every aspect of this deal, we have finally started receiving live video feeds from the security cameras placed at many intersections in London. As some of you may know, these cameras are recording day and night, and are being monitored, live, by individuals from within and outside of the police forces."

The screen now revealed sixteen video feeds.

"What you're looking at here are video feeds that we've archived, and which are being played back from our own servers. We've just secured a contract to provide data storage for the video for many of the cameras in London. But, much more importantly to us than the storage, is what we will be doing with this raw footage. We will be creating the tools to automatically analyze the videos. We are going to be launching a massive research initiative to apply the discoveries from our computer vision group to all of these videos. This will be one of the largest computer vision tasks ever undertaken. If all goes well, within three years, we will have access to all the video feeds and will be detecting suspicious actions and tracking criminals both when they are online and now even when they are offline—well, at least in London! If you know any colleagues looking for work in any aspect of computer vision, tell them to start applying here. We'll be growing this group aggressively. For now, though, I would like to personally give my thanks to the London team. You've opened up a brand new chapter for Ubatoo. Well done."

The standing ovation lasted a full minute. Then, Xiao continued more somberly, "We had hoped to have the same type of video feeds set up in airports across America as well. Unfortunately, that seems to be taking longer than expected. Hopefully we'll be back on track next quarter and will be providing the same type of services in the U.S. that we do abroad."

Atiq felt both relief and sadness. Relief, because unlike the last meeting, where he was chided for his slow recruiting, he thankfully was not on the "try harder next time" list today. He had escaped without mention. Sadness, because he knew the VP in charge of obtaining the video feeds from airports around America, and she was a hard worker. Ubatoo executed its part flawlessly, but these large endeavors simply took time. It was hard for their personnel to get a foothold inside U.S. government security agencies. Nonetheless, this would be little consolation to her. She would be feeling the pressure to deliver something that was completely out of her control. It was only a matter of time before Ubatoo worked with the U.S. security agencies, but Xiao also knew that lighting a fire under her would do no irreparable harm, and had the small possibility, in Xiao's mind at least, of doing some good.

Xiao continued his presentation, "With so many accomplishments, I don't want to end this meeting on a down note. Here, at Ubatoo, we've been lucky not to be caught up in the devastating economic turmoil taking place all around us. But clearly from the e-mails I have received, many of you are worried. Let me simply say this to you, we're doing fine. You've seen the numbers now, so you know we're actually doing better than fine. Our search, e-mail, phones, and all that we do, keep people coming back to us. In good times, people look to us to buy things for their entertainment and their hobbies, and simply to live their lives.

But even now, every day, more and more users are turning to us as things go bad in the economy. People need real information; people need the Internet to find answers. We provide it to them. Through all of your work on your own projects, keep in mind that we empower people. Sometimes, with the amazing amount we accomplish every day, it's easy to forget what we've accomplished overall."

With that, the slide on the massive screen changed, and simply had the words "Thank You" on it.

The lights didn't turn on yet. Xiao continued. "Oh, and I almost forgot. To thank you for your hard work, I'd like to give each of you a little economic stimulus of our own. We have bonuses for all of you— yes, that includes our interns and part-time workers—to thank each of you for the job you are doing. Congratulations to all. Enjoy the rest of your summer. We'll talk again in the fall. I'm sure we'll have amazing new updates to share then."

With that, the lights turned on and the swing music returned. The excitement and joviality came with it. Not only were things going well enough for everyone to get a bonus of $3,500, but Ubatoo was still hiring, was still focused on innovation, and was still making headway into new unexplored areas of research. Success in a time of surrounding failure; they were undeniably blessed.

-A DRIVE THROUGH
THE COUNTRY-

July 16, 2009.

The "rally the troops" meeting was over well in time for dinner. To-night, because Stephen was dining alone, there would be no negotiating or deciding by committee about where to eat. He selected the Delhi Café. It was a cafeteria he rarely went to since almost no one ever agreed to walk that far across grounds. But this evening he was in the mood to walk outside; last night's anxious sleep and the non-stop work today were taking their toll. Even more than the work, the phone call with Sebastin had taken a lot out of Stephen. Whenever he had to interact with customers, or any human in a professional capacity, he left the meeting worn out. He would much rather interact with the thousands of computers at Ubatoo. It was certainly simpler and less taxing.

People rarely ventured into the Delhi Café without a native Hindi speaker. The chef, who was recruited straight from Bukhara Restaurant in New Delhi, India, insisted that not only he, but all of his sous-chefs and all his wait staff be brought over, too. None of the frontline spoke English well. The aptly, if not creatively, named Delhi Café, had been informally rated by *Zagat's* reviewers, who attended the opening week celebrations via an invitation from Xiao himself. The rumor was that they had told him off the record they would have rated it a 29 (out of 30) for the food, lower on the decor (it was, after all, an office building), and much lower on the service (it was not served at your table). Nonetheless, the expense (free) would likely have been rated well, too.

As he entered the Delhi Café, the warm aromas of heady spices and the massive jumble of crowds in the waiting lines matched his impressions of what India must be like. He took his time trying to make sense of the enormous variety of unfamiliar and daunting food drenched in brilliant colors awaiting him. Eventually, he settled on slow-cooked lamb over saffron-infused rice, with an appetizer of jumbo prawns in a spicy masala from South India. He wasn't sure what the vegetables were, so he skipped them, much to the annoyance of the servers. Apparently only their Caucasian diners ever skipped the vegetables; everyone else who came took generous helpings of everything.

With dinner piled on his tray, and a sugary sweet bottled drink imported from a part of the world he wouldn't know how to find on a map, he sat alone and immersed himself in checking e-mail and surfing the Web on his Ubatoo-issued phone. Fifteen minutes later, the chairs surrounding him were taken all at once. With trays full of food, Kohan, Yuri, Andrew, and Rob claimed the empty seats.

Stephen looked up in surprise, "When did you get back?"

"We just got back on grounds a few minutes ago. We looked for you at your desk, but couldn't find you," Rob answered.

"So we tracked you on your phone," Yuri said. "Then went to the cafeteria nearest your location."

"Clever, eh? That's the first useful thing for this tracking stuff I've ever seen. We're just going to stalk you from now on," Rob interjected with a half smile.

"Alright, let's hear it. Any interesting stories, photographs, or videos to share?" Stephen began, but it was a tactical error to start off so obviously interested.

Nobody responded.

"Anyone going to tell me what happened?" Stephen asked again.

"You should've been there," Andrew said.

"The lamb is awesome," Kohan said, deliberately changing the subject. He wanted to ensure Stephen didn't get any details too fast.

"I like the prawns better myself," Andrew countered.

"No, no. All of you. If you ask me, the soup is best," Yuri chimed in, taking part in the annoy-Stephen game that was working infuriatingly well. The silly chatter about the food was just beginning.

"We should tell him about the party. Rob, why don't you tell the story? You're the star of the night," Kohan said.

Sigh. "Fine, fine. I'll wait," Stephen said, knowing that encouraging them with even the slightest bit of interest would do nothing but prolong the pain. This was his punishment for not going with them last night.

After they moved on to dessert, Stephen tried again. This time, he went straight for the weakest link, Yuri. "So, Yuri, at least maybe you can tell me what party you're talking about, and what Rob did to become the star of the night?"

Yuri thankfully showed some mercy. "Well, the first part I can tell you about. You'll have to ask Rob about the rest. We told you we were going to take one of Ubatoo's vans to Gilroy, right? I sat in back with the computers. I was just using JENNY to watch Monica and Claudine—to make sure they didn't decide to go to sleep before we got there. They started instant messaging about some party. It was good that I was watching them. Otherwise, they would have been gone by the time we arrived. I looked through their e-mails to find the party address. We went, too."

Then Andrew took up the story, "It was just after midnight when we got there. Our fearless leaders, Kohan and Rob, led the way. Nobody even noticed us when we walked in."

"Nobody noticed you? Did Kohan still have his cowboy hat on?" Stephen asked smiling.

"No, thank God. We finally got him to take it off by the time we made it to Gilroy," Rob replied.

Andrew continued his story, "Kohan went straight for the beer, *sans* hat, and we lost Yuri to a foosball table."

"Did any of you see either of those two women you were hunting down, Claudine or Monica?" Stephen asked.

"I found Monica," Kohan answered.

"What did she say when you introduced yourself as her very own honest-to-goodness deranged stalker? Did you bring up the photographs?"

"No, no. Come on, Stephen. What do you take me for? I just left the door open for her to bring it up herself."

"And did she?"

"Well, no. That would be a bit awkward, don't you think? How does one bring that up in casual conversation? We talked for about ten minutes before we were interrupted," Kohan paused as if waiting for a drum roll, "by Ben Cappiello, the one who started it all."

At the sound of Ben's name, Rob's Pavlovian response must have been triggered, as he abruptly dropped his spoon so he could repeatedly thrust out the middle fingers of both hands along with a torrent of obscenities.

"Precisely. Thank you, Rob," Kohan said as he nodded his head toward him. "Well, I think you're already getting an inkling of how the night went. I went to get Rob and Andrew."

Andrew took over. "The first thing Rob does, without hesitating for a second, he starts screaming like a banshee at this poor guy. 'You bastard! Great pictures of Monica and Claudine!'"

Andrew patted Rob on the back before continuing. "Ben is, of course, clueless as to what's going on. Then Rob had his shining moment. Rob, being as suave as we've all come to expect, tells the gathering crowd all about the pictures that Ben sent out—a blow by blow of the entire web page. I don't think they knew who created it, Rob or Ben, or why it was being brought up. So, there he was, this intoxicated idiot nobody knew, angrily recounting the pictures, the e-mails, the little contest they had."

At this point, Rob had a grin on his face and was nodding his head stupidly.

"Nice job," Stephen said. "Sounds like you made a nice new group of friends." Though he knew it was unfair of him, he had to wonder how Rob, or even Andrew, made it into Ubatoo. They might be brilliant at their jobs, but outside of work—unbelievable.

Kohan recounted the tale from there. "I think Ben was just shell-shocked that someone knew about his e-mails and videos. We had to take Rob outside before he started frothing at the mouth. I hope nobody there ever finds out who we were or how we got there."

"Well, I gave a few people my business card while I was there," said Yuri. The conversation halted.

"What? Why, Yuri?" asked Rob, incredulously.

"I told a couple of girls I worked at Ubatoo, also," Andrew volunteered.

"You thought telling them you were an intern at Ubatoo was going to impress them?" Rob asked maliciously.

The conversation continued for a few moments without Stephen. This, this right here, is what it was to be a brilliant intern . . . To pass all the rigorous entrance exams, to be one of the few allowed access to the brightest minds, with the unfathomable amounts of data and resources—and this is what their brain power was focused on. Was he getting too old for this? Maybe. But he wasn't positive that age had anything to do with it. He'd recruited and managed a group of people this young before. They may not have been as smart as these four, but he didn't recall hearing about these types of nights either. Would these four be the role models and icons that the next set of interns admired? Had any of the other scientists at Ubatoo had internships like these? He couldn't imagine they had, but then, there were a lot of things he couldn't have imagined before he started at Ubatoo. He wanted to go home.

The conversation was still in full swing. Rob turned to Yuri: "If anyone here ever finds out how we learned about the party, or worse, if Ben figures out who we are, he'll figure out how we knew about his e-mail . . . It won't be good for us." Rob glowered at Yuri. "What do you think, Stephen?"

Stephen fixed on Rob, trying not to glare. "It'd serve you right if he found out." That, apparently, wasn't what they wanted to hear. "Nothing you can do about it now anyway." With that, he started piling his dinner debris on his tray. The others followed.

As they were walking out, Yuri took Stephen aside, out of earshot of the others. "Do you have time to talk today, Stephen? Would you have time for a walk tonight? I must talk to you about something."

"How about tomorrow instead?" Though Stephen's curiosity was certainly piqued, tonight he just wanted to see Molly.

-CONTROL-

July 17, 2009.

"I have so much to tell you about," Stephen bellowed as he opened the door into the apartment at exactly 12:30 a.m., a full two hours earlier than usual. He had meant to get home even earlier, but as usual one thing led to another, and he wound up staying on grounds far later than he had anticipated. Not hearing anything, he asked with a slightly quieter squawk, "Molly, you still awake?"

He dropped his keys as he fumbled to extricate them from the lock. As groups of them tumbled out of the keychain, landing with noisy metallic clanks against the floor, Stephen muttered a few choice curse words as he bent down to gather them. Despite his well-intentioned attempt to be quiet, in case Molly was napping, he banged his head against the door knob on his way up from the floor. Given the barrage of further cursing, any chance of Molly, or the neighbors, being asleep was dashed.

Giving up any attempt at a hushed entrance, he let the door slam shut as soon as he managed to ineptly maneuver all of his body out of the way. He found her seated and wide awake in her usual position at the table, peering around her computer screen watching him intently.

"Smooth, Stephen. I'm a lucky girl," she said dryly.

He rolled his eyes and dropped his backpack as he walked toward her. In the less than ten seconds it took him to make it from the entrance hallway to Molly's desk, her eyes darted to the screen and back again to him. He couldn't help but be strangely proud of her. Until

Molly, he had thought there was no chance of anyone being geeky enough, and driven enough, to appreciate or even endure him. And she was really cute, too. He was lucky indeed.

"What do you have to tell me about?" she asked, eyebrows raised. Again, her eyes darted back to the screen before his answer began.

"Today was an incredibly strange day. Have I ever told you about Sebastin, the guy I'm working with at ACCL? You, the anthropology, sociology, political science, liberal do-gooder are going to love what he does, and since I'm helping him, you're going to love what I do by transitivity, you know? A couple of weeks ago . . ." He didn't bother to finish his sentence. Her eyes were staring at her screen, scanning someone's latest message post, no doubt. She wasn't even trying to hide the fact she wasn't paying attention anymore.

Stephen studied her for a moment, deciding how to proceed. Escalation would only lead to him walking back to Ubatoo alone again. "You know what?" he finally asked. "I'll tell you about this guy, Sebastin, later. Let's hear about your results—the ones you wrote about in the note you left me this morning. I'll get us something to drink."

"Sure," she replied without looking up. But when he exited the kitchen, she hadn't moved.

He poured two Cokes in glasses, grabbed a bottle of rum, then walked past Molly to the couch and plopped down noisily. He zealously mixed the drinks, ensuring the ice loudly clinked against the glass as many times as possible. Eventually Molly turned around to acknowledge, if not him, at least his attempts at creating an enticing racket. Her frown softened a bit when she saw the drink waiting for her. She walked over and sat beside him, taking the rum and Coke he held up for her before she reached the couch.

"So, Miss Molly, I got your note this morning. What's going on?"

Molly told of the events that had transpired over the last few weeks. It had been that long since they had spoken in any detail about her work. Not that it was all Stephen's fault—there was a lot to get done in a short amount of time, for both of them.

". . . whatever Andrew did to direct people to my site, it's working. I had 1,729 visitors just yesterday. There are a ton of posts in all of the discussion forums."

"I'll have to thank Andrew. Be ready, though. I don't think Andrew's little lie is going to last all that long. Someone's going to find out about it."

"I know, I know. That's why I'm going to start my experiments soon. Right now, depending on how you count them, there are almost fifteen debates on my site, and those are just the ones about politics. To be accurate, 'debates' is probably putting too positive a spin on it. There are at least fifteen conversation threads on which people are arguing or insulting each other. To start with, I thought I would leave three of them alone, like a control group."

"Sounds reasonable. What about the other twelve?"

"That's what I wanted to talk to you about. First, I'm just going to monitor the overall sentiment of the conversation—see if it's negative, positive, what they're all favoring, hating, etc. I want to record how often the overall sentiment changes and see if I can pick up any factors that initiate the change."

"You do know there are automated sentiment analyzers we use at Ubatoo to do exactly that?"

Molly looked a bit impatient. "Okay, but, I'm not Ubatoo, and that's not what my thesis is about. I can do that by hand when I need to. What I'm really going to try to do is see what it would take to *change* the prevalent sentiment. If the conversation has turned into an America-hate fest, how we're evil and the root of all the world's problems and that usual rant, then I'll see what it would take to tone that viewpoint down, or in the best of worlds, change it."

"You know, though, we probably are—" Stephen started to say, without putting much thought into his words.

"Really, you think so, do you?" Molly answered curtly before he could finish his sentence. "So, Mr. Computer Scientist Intern, what do you know about what's happening in the Middle East, or for that matter, in the U.S.?"

Ouch. Stephen backed down quickly. "Sorry. Go on. I'm listening." Apparently, this was not the time to try to make casual conversation. He should have known better.

"Sorry. But listen. I have a series of experiments planned for the other twelve conversations. I'd really like to run them by you to see what you think. Stephen, this is beyond anything I could have done before so I'm in a bit of uncharted territory. If you read what these people write, it just hits you over and over how important it is to know how to change their opinions. The more I watch them, the more I feel, I mean, I just know, that when the Internet reaches already unstable countries, we have a chance to make sure it doesn't make things worse and let violent or extremist thinking grow unchecked."

Quietly, she said, "Maybe I'm getting in over my head. I feel like I'm working in some psych-ops experiment, and that's not what I wanted when I started all this." She knew she was exaggerating her feelings in the moment. Nevertheless, it struck her just how far she had come from her initial goal of being an anthropologist helping migrants. When had any real anthropologist ever strived so determinedly to *change* the subjects she was studying? What happened to wanting to study them without influencing them? No, this was not anthropology like she had envisioned. Maybe it was more like psychology experiments, maybe worse—all thanks to her advisor, Gale.

"It's mesmerizing watching users and trying to figure out what makes them tick," Stephen justified. "What's great is that you're even taking it a step further than just watching and analyzing. You're trying to predict it, even control it. I don't know what this will eventually be used for, but personally, I think you should just join Ubatoo now and get it over with. They'd love you."

"Stephen, forget about Ubatoo for a few seconds. Think about all those madrasahs where kids who are brought up learning to read with only hate pamphlets and hate teachings. What do you think will happen when they get access to the Internet? Think they'll ever see both sides of a story? I doubt it. Access will be controlled in the same way everything else is. All the hate and the biases will be validated through yet another medium. Knowing how to transform opinions on the Internet seems like such an obvious thing to study."

"It is. You absolutely should be doing this study. If—no, when—it works, it'll get used, and it'll make a real difference. I don't see any way it isn't going to be useful." Even in graduate school, he had never had this much passion about his thesis. If he ever had the chance again, he would choose only projects that at least had the potential for making an impact, and the potential to be something he could stay passionate about.

"Could I see some of the postings on your site now? You probably have a bunch of interesting ones from all the new users," Stephen said, trying to cheer Molly up. The middle of thesis research was no time to be questioning the path she was on.

They both walked over to her computer, her leading slowly, still deep in thought. Her silence melted away as she read through the postings to find the perfect one to show Stephen. A day ago, she struggled to find a single interesting post. Now, there were dozens in just the single conversation thread she was inspecting. The postings were diverse in their style: some were well thought out treatises, some incoherent, some pleading, some demanding, many ranting. Most were simply by people who wanted to be heard, even if all they did was express passionate agreement with another's opinion. She stopped at a message from a user who went by the name GR.Zadeh and read it aloud. It was a particularly malicious rant about the police action in the 19th district in Paris, which had occurred just a few hours earlier. She scrolled down a few pages and selected a couple replies to show Stephen. He read them with detached interest. He was certainly happy for Molly, but he knew better than to pretend to know enough about the issues to make any insightful observations. Her web site was doing well—posters were responding and inciting each other, creating new topics to discuss, and most importantly, coming back to post again. Her subjects had arrived.

After reading a few more posts aloud to Stephen, she explained her next steps. "You remember that I post under the name Sahim Galab, right? Well, since this conversation thread obviously turns deeply negative, Sahim is going to post messages imploring patience until more is known. Sahim's character is ready to support a fight and any necessary actions, but only after he knows all the facts. Since this Paris news just came out, and nobody knows the details of what happened, this fits him well. In a few hours, I'll probably also post from my other character, M. Zakim—he's the prototypical inciter, ready to blame and see the worst at every opportunity. These two are going to verbally go at each other. Maybe I'll have a few more characters that I've been incubating weigh in for good measure. The whole point is that they'll debate Sahim, and in this instance, Sahim will come out victorious. We'll see what effect that has on other, real, participants."

She waited for it all to sink in before continuing. "I'm going to measure the effects of all the techniques I come up with to influence my users, quantify them, and make a detailed analysis on how to use them effectively. For all I know, it may have a decent chance of working just with Sahim, since he's already known from other discussion forums, and he has a bit of a reputation from the very first posts I made about the videos of Mustafa Kawlia. Remember those?"

"I remember Mustafa. And I get what you're doing. You're writing a handbook on how to manipulate public opinion on message boards," Stephen replied with a huge grin. "One thing does concern me, though."

He slowed down a bit to make sure he chose his words more carefully than earlier. She waited, anxiously looking at him, wondering if he would be as concerned as she was that maybe she was taking this study too far.

"How are you going to make this study scientific? I love the idea, but if your thesis committee sees it, they're going to want to know things like how you measured the results, how statistically significant your results were . . ."

She was relieved. He hadn't shown concern that she was doing something wrong or going too far. All his other concerns were easily addressed.

"Imagine if this does actually limit some extremist poster's influence. Imagine that for a thesis. I can feel it. I'm definitely getting closer," she said more confidently.

"Just make sure you don't get caught. That would be pretty hard to explain."

"Caught? By who?"

"By the real users on your site. I can't imagine they'd be too happy if they found out they were being—"

"Oh, I won't," Molly replied, cutting him off. She quickly changed topics. "Want to talk about other experiments I could run? I have a bunch of ideas."

"Good Lord. Sure, it's only 2:00 in the morning, plenty of time before the sun comes up."

Molly inhaled the remaining rum and Coke and bounded to the couch to get her notes. Stephen wearily followed, and sat next to her as she rattled off idea after idea to subtly manipulate the decisions and opinions on the message boards, such as "accidentally" lose some posts, artificially boost the rankings of some posts, create dozens of artificial personas to weigh in, cross-post to other forums, sound educated, sound passionate, pretend to be old, young, male, female, change the font color, size, and the list of tactics went on.

They worked together until nearly sunrise, diligently assessing the pros and cons of each variation. At 5:15 a.m., having been away from her computer for three hours, she was aching to see how many more posts had been made in that time. The moment she went to her computer, Stephen let his heavy head lead his descent onto the couch. His eyelids relaxed to a close, resting his stinging, thoroughly bloodshot, eyes. The distant tapping of the keyboard and the soft rustling of Molly's papers kept him company for the few moments before sleep overtook any possibility of staying awake. Besides, there was no chance he would see her for hours anyway.

-A TALE OF TWO TENURES-

February, 2004.

It is rare for an outsider to see the elaborate processes in place at a university to decide which of the next year's student candidates are worthy of acceptance. When talking about graduate students, this process takes on monumental importance. At the end of a graduate student's studies, she is forever a representative of the school. By bestowing that student with a piece of paper declaring her a Ph.D., the academic institution stands behind that person, and professes that the student is now worthy of being a peer to its own best and brightest faculty members. Given the gravity of such an implicit and explicit proclamation, it may be surprising to find that entrance decisions often devolve into games as ferociously fought (and with as equally short-lived rewards) as the king-of-the-hill games children play. Such was the case with Molly Byrne, and her entrance into the ivory towers of academia.

The problems arose when Molly's application arrived simultaneously on the desks of two committee members. The issue wasn't that two people were asked to review Molly; it was that the two were from different departments in the university.

Molly's application to the Ph.D. program at Brown University was for a dual-title Ph.D. in two departments, the Department of Political Science and the Department of Anthropology. This meant that, first and foremost, she was a masochist at heart, since she had to complete the requirements for two Ph.D.s simultaneously. Second, both departments had to accept her into their programs. But this had been her desire ever since she found out that Brown offered such a curriculum.

She wanted a real understanding of what migrants' needs were (the anthropology degree), and also the politics involved in getting migration reforms enacted into law (the political science degree).

Individually, to each department, she suspected she had a decent chance to make it through the admissions process. Her undergrad work, completed at the University of Virginia, was top notch, her recommendations stellar, and she had all the requisite extracurricular interests—all focused on independent research and publications, naturally. To cement her case, she had even gone so far as to contact the professors she wanted to work with in both departments. Molly didn't need to visit their web pages to learn about their interests. She was familiar with their research, having cited their work in her own publications, the first of which she'd written while a third-year undergraduate. She contacted one professor in each department, Dr. Patricia Norris in Anthropology and Dr. Gale Mitchell in Political Science.

When Molly's application packet landed with a very loud thud on both Mitchell's and Norris's desks, they both dreaded having to read through another voluminous package. Nevertheless, after looking it over, they both independently concluded she would be an ideal candidate for their respective groups. Neither gave it another thought until the admission meeting was held to discuss their applicant shortlists.

At the admission meeting, Dr. Patricia Norris, a tenured professor for twelve years, said she was willing to take on Molly as her student. The Department of Anthropology, which was notoriously laidback in its following of procedure, especially when compared to the normal exacting Brown standards, didn't require anything else. Dr. Gale Mitchell, a professor who was coming up for tenure consideration in the next two years also had glowing things to say about Molly, but insisted she be solely in the Political Science Department.

"You know, Gale, this candidate, Molly, would be better off in Anthropology. The only reason we're having this conversation is because she wants this dual-title program we've started. But, given her research interest—migration—it's obvious she's better suited to my department."

"Pat, of course I agree with you, but I just don't have time to take on half a student. It's half the credit, and you and I know it's really the same amount of work. Frankly, I don't see how this whole dual-title thing works."

A credit issue. Gale was coming up for tenure soon, and although it was virtually guaranteed (she had been told as much by the department head in confidence—with strict orders not to share that information), she wasn't about to take any chances. With Molly only half under her tutelage, it would be half less a graduate student on her resumé. More importantly, the list of authors on any paper Molly wrote would have to include Patricia, and Patricia being the senior of the two, it would be assumed she was the project leader. That certainly wouldn't impress a tenure committee and would never lead to an endowed chair, if she dared dream that big.

"And," Gale continued, "the last time we had a dual-title student, I believe he wound up giving up the dual-title track, and completed his studies entirely in your department. Remember?"

Patricia knew this was going to be forever a sore spot for Gale, since she had campaigned hard to keep that student in the Political Science Department but failed.

"I'll tell you what. Why don't you go ahead and take her? I can find another student," Gale said. This apparent capitulation was anything but.

"You know I can't financially support her alone. But I presume you do remember it's school policy that students can get dual-title degrees here, in both our departments, and that we can and should share the costs."

"Sorry, Pat. The school has its policies, and I have mine. I just don't have the time for partially advising a student. Tell you what, then, why don't I take Molly now? And if some of your funding comes through next year, we can reconsider her transferring to your group then."

And so it was settled.

It didn't make too much difference at the time that the funding Gale had earmarked for Molly was from a project with an entirely disjointed set of objectives from Molly's interests. The project Gale envisioned was focused on understanding the velocity of information flow through the Internet. Truth be told, this was quite distant from Gale's interests too, but funding for faculty in academia wasn't always easy to

come by. When the Department of Defense and now the overly anxious Department of Homeland Security began to allow liberal arts faculty members to drink from their immense funding well, it wasn't easy
to turn down money, even if it wasn't an ideal fit. No matter, thought
Gale, as Molly's new, and sole, advisor, at least for the formative years,
it would be easy enough to get her to pursue the right topics when she
arrived.

It was no secret what "understanding the velocity of information
flow through the Internet" really meant. The only reason anybody
from any government defense agency cared about such a topic was to
monitor and quantify the influence that extremist individuals had on
the Internet or through their online social networks—the people they
sent mail to, the people they chatted with, the people they befriended
online. This was a far cry from Molly's goal of helping migrants in
Africa.

Long after Molly had settled in with Gale (though she had managed
to revive the dual-title degree, at least in name), Gale still kept steering Molly toward her own agenda, and Molly continued to tenaciously
push back. Besides being a topic Molly wasn't interested in studying,
Molly fundamentally disapproved of taking money from anything associated with Defense for her thesis. Nothing linked with Defense could
be meshed with her left-leaning disposition. But she was also, much to
her own constant dismay, a pragmatist. The funding made it possible to
pursue her degree, and though it pained her immensely to accept the
particular funding that Gale offered, the reality was, after all, reality.

It was Gale who suggested that Molly study the role of the Internet
and online discussions in shaping the perceptions of the U.S. in the
Middle East. A compromise. Molly's work would have a use beyond
monitoring extremist individuals and Gale knew this was a perpetually
fundable research topic.

Molly, now in her third year of graduate school, was still more of
an idealist than Gale would have liked. Even if this topic wasn't what
Molly had hoped for when she started, she perceived it as nothing short
of a chance to further understand sources of misinformation and propaganda. It was a crucial first step to avoid a rise in unnecessary conflicts,
not only abroad, but also at home in the U.S. Gale was happy to go along

with that view; the results would be the same. Neither Gale, Molly, nor anyone in any defense agency could quibble with its importance.

For the first part of her research, Molly was going to California, not only for a change of scenery from Rhode Island, but also to be among technologists and "Internet people" to hopefully find someone to interview for the background chapters of her thesis.

Whatever unflattering comments could be made about Gale, nobody ever doubted her ability to get the best out of her students.

-PRELUDE TO PIE-

July 17, 2009

The rundown hotel room was even worse than Sebastin had imagined—the windows were barred shut, the air conditioner broken, and the stagnant air stifling. He sat waiting on its musty bed, motionless, the scorching sun baking the tiny room. Succumbing to the heat, Sebastin's imagination steadily incinerated his grasp on his surroundings. The smell of the hundreds of sticky grungy bodies that had doubtless occupied the room before him was permanently embedded in its walls. No amount of cleaning, if it had even been considered, would ever dissipate the stench.

Restless and agitated, Sebastin moved to the room's rusted iron table, which in some earlier age must have passed for acceptable furniture. Sitting lifeless in its battered chair, Sebastin relinquished control to his imagination far too easily.

He envisioned those countless bodies that had writhed together on the bed beside him or had drunk themselves into oblivion there. Each image was as vivid and real as the reflection of his pallid face in the mirror in front him.

Sweat trickled onto his lips. The engulfing foul air and the oppressive taste of fear was unbearable. Hell could be no worse.

When M. Mohammad strode in, he seemed to sense none of the bodies Sebastin saw, or if he did, it didn't bother him. Mohammad wore a dark suit with no tie, and was more American than Sebastin had envisioned from their two phone conversations. The reality of the impending meeting flooded Sebastin's thoughts, abruptly releasing him from the turmoil of his delusions.

Two men dressed entirely in white followed closely behind Mohammad. Sebastin hadn't known how many there would be. Had it just been these two or an army of men screaming of Jihad, he wouldn't have been surprised. The room was already small—with these three, it became unbearably claustrophobic.

Sebastin remained seated, unconsciously running his hands along the edge of the decrepit old table. Mohammad, in control of the room as soon as he entered, took a seat across from him. The two men in white stood silently at his back, positioned deliberately in front of the window. All three stared intensely at Sebastin. For a few torturous moments, nothing was said.

"Tell me all about this list of yours, Sebastin."

Even if he wanted to, how could he? Who would believe a story about a list of books and an intern? Who would believe how he got that list of books? None of this would make sense. None of this, he feared, would do anything to help him make it out of this room safely. Instead, he told Mohammad again what he had already told him on the phone twice. "It has 5,000 names on it. They are people who are on watch lists . . . I called a few to make sure it was real. That's how I contacted you. That's all I know."

"Why is my name on it?" It was the same question as before. How long before he just asked for the list?

"I don't know. I told you before. I don't know. The list doesn't say why you're on it. It just has your name. That's all I know. I don't know anything else."

The air was stifling. Sebastin opened the top buttons on his shirt. He seemed the only one in the room who noticed the heat—the only one uncomfortable.

"What other lists have my name on them?"

"I only have this one list. That's the only one. I don't have any others. It's—"

"Who gave you this list?"

This was the only question Sebastin had anticipated and the only one for which he had rehearsed a response. He needed to sound confident. "It was given to ACCL anonymously," he heard himself stammer. He thankfully switched to automatic as he continued, "That's how we get all of our information. We never know who gives it to us. That's the only way we can get so much." He sounded credible. He had to sound credible. The argument was logical. It made sense. But he wasn't talking to others who were like him. Were they paying attention to how logical his argument was or to how little he was saying?

Mohammad slammed his fist on the table, his ring clanging loudly on the iron. "Do you know anything?" Mohammad stood up to pace the tiny room. He came back and slammed his fist again. "Do you know anything I asked you?"

Sebastin cowered in his chair. "Are you going to kill me?" How had he come to this?

The two men behind Mohammad stood motionless, enshrouded in the streaming sunlight blazing through the window. If they were laughing at him, he couldn't tell.

Mohammad looked on impassively at Sebastin. "You have been watching too many movies, Sebastin. I have no intention of killing you, *insha'Allah*."

What he had in his pocket, or more precisely what he didn't have in his pocket was the only assurance of that, Sebastin reminded himself. He had torn out only a few pages of the list to bring with him. The rest of the list he had left on his desk at home, with Mohammad's name prominently highlighted. If anything happened, it would be found, eventually.

"Let us see the list."

That's what this meeting was for; that's what they had planned. Sebastin slowly moved his hand to his pocket and took hold of the two folded papers. He looked at the men in the sunlight, their faces obscured in shadow. He hoped they were watching how slowly he was moving; no sudden movements, nothing to worry about.

"What is this?" Mohammad asked.

"It's part of the list."

"Where is the rest?"

"It's not here."

A barely perceptible movement in Mohammad's eyes. Before Sebastin could register what was happening, one of the men in white leapt over the corner of the bed, found his way behind Sebastin, and swiftly kicked the chair Sebastin was sitting on. Sebastin folded onto himself as his forehead caught the edge of the table on his way to the floor.

"Next time, you bring the full list, yeah?"

He groaned a yes. As he tried to pick himself up, the man dug his foot deep into his shoulder. He wasn't going anywhere.

"What am I supposed to do with two pages, Sebastin?"

"Call them . . . just call them . . . you can see for yourself if the list is good or not. That's what you said you wanted to do on the phone."

The man's foot moved closer to his neck and started pressing down.

Mohammad handed the sheet to the one still standing in the sun by the window.

A few words were spoken that Sebastin couldn't understand. Mohammad looked down at Sebastin and translated. "It seems he thinks it might be better if we use your phone. Do you mind?"

Sebastin moved his free arm to his pocket to take the phone out, and held it up feebly for Mohammad. Mohammad stepped aside so the second man could reach over and take it from Sebastin's hand.

The only sound was the man in white making the phone calls. The other three waited in silence as the calls were placed, one after the other, down through the entire list. Words were spoken, but Sebastin understood none of it. He was dizzy. The sunlight was still blazing through the window, picking up specks of dust and debris in the room on its way to burn Sebastin's eyes. He could do nothing but look straight up, struggling to keep out of the blinding sunlight. It was only when he saw the iron table and the smear of the still-fresh blood trail that it registered that his head was still stinging and the wet in his hair might not be sweat.

There was nothing to do but wait. Wait for all the calls to be made. Wait to see if Stephen's list was as good as he thought it was. Wait to see what would happen next.

▼ ▼ ▼

Sebastin woke to the sound of the three talking hurriedly. He had blacked out—he didn't know for how long, but he suspected it wasn't more than a few minutes. Sitting up on the floor with his back to the bed, he moved a little, but not without an immense amount of pain. His head was still stinging hot, but he was cold and sweating, and his shoulder and neck where the man had pinned him down for who knows how long were throbbing.

He hesitantly touched his forehead. He winced as he felt the still warm blood. He gingerly slid his finger through his soaked hair to find the extent of the cut . . .

"Sebastin, good of you to come back to us."

"You are a lucky man. We will buy the list from you. We also want you to go back and ask your sources for more information for us."

What should he say? What could get him out of this alive? "I don't know how I can get more information. I told you, all of it was given to us anonymously." There, that was right.

"Find a way to get a message to them, Sebastin. I'm sure you'll find a way."

How much were they going to pay? How much is it worth to them? He started as high as he thought he could get away with, but how was he supposed to estimate the value of this list or how much they had access to? "I want five million." It was fifty times what he was getting paid by Rajive.

"Dollars? You were hoping for five million dollars? Why not fifty million, Sebastin? Stop the joking. Sebastin, you lie on this filthy floor in your own blood, afraid for your life, and yet you still beg for money. Maybe we should just check your home. You wouldn't have left the list there, would you? You're not that stupid, are you? We could give you nothing, Sebastin, and just take the list. What would you do then? I think, Sebastin, that you are in no position to ask for anything." Mohammad cast a slow pitying glance down at Sebastin before continuing, "But we'll be fair. You and I will do business again. We'll call you to tell you what we will pay."

A kick to the head and he almost blacked out again.

Another kick. And he did.

-THE YURI EFFECT-

July 17, 2009.

Stephen's eyes opened as the morning light began trickling into the darker corners of the room. His blurry eyes focused first on the dirty glass from the night before. It was partially filled with a forgotten mix of rum, coke, and melted ice water. He heard the familiar tap-tap of a keyboard nearby. As he drowsily willed himself to an upright position, he found himself still on the couch where he had fallen asleep a few hours earlier. "Did you sleep at all?" Stephen asked, spying a blurry Molly, still hunched over her keyboard in the same position as when he had fallen asleep.

She turned to look at him. "No, not yet. I'm going to sleep in a bit. Just got a few more things to do." Even in his state, he could see her eyes were puffy and must be throbbing from the sleepless hours. Most likely, she had forgotten to blink enough. That's what happens to all computer addicts. Her eyes would be searing for the rest of the day.

He lifted himself slowly from the sofa and walked to Molly. Leaning over her shoulder, he ran his fingers through her dark brown hair. "Aren't you working at GreeneSmart today?"

"Not for another four hours. I'll take a quick nap before then," she replied, taking his hand from her hair and holding it in her own.

They sat at the dining table together, the sun streaming in from one side, the computer monitor reflecting it from the other. A few cautionary words about overdoing it or about her need for sleep would have the same effect on her that they had on him. Despite that, he said the expected words—told her not to overdo it, caringly suggested she get some sleep, and wished her the best of luck. But the moment he left to take a shower, the tap-tap of the keyboard continued, just as it had before he started talking.

By the time he entered the main room again, Molly had replaced him on the couch and was fast asleep with an alarm clock propped beside her. He didn't wake her to say goodbye, but he did stop to look at her for a few seconds. She would have fit in so well with any of the groups he had relished working with in the past, at SteelXchanges, in grad school, even in college.

As he was leaving the apartment, he glanced back once more to assure himself he hadn't woken her up. He couldn't help but worry about the impact he had had on her. Would she have let herself be so carried away with her work if they hadn't met, or had they enabled each other's mutilation of balance? It wasn't clear there was a difference between work and life for them, though. The work was interesting; the reason that they worked this hard wasn't because they needed to.

▼ ▼ ▼

By the time he entered Building 11, it was already 10:30, much later than usual. He wanted to dive into his e-mail before he went to talk with Yuri. Even before his monitor could wake up, Kohan was standing next to him. "Had your cappuccino today?" Kohan asked.

"Not yet. Give me a second. Let me just check my e-mail to make sure nothing urgent has come up. Ten minutes, okay?"

"Oh, don't give me that. I saw you walking in, checking your e-mail on your phone. Nobody wrote you e-mail in the last fifteen seconds."

Stephen smiled. "I am connected, therefore I am."

"Okay, whatever. Come on, let's go. I have some news to tell you."

The minute they were outside, Kohan launched full speed into his spiel. "Guess what Yuri got yesterday?"

"I have no idea. I was going to talk to him this morn—" But Kohan didn't let him finish.

"He got an offer."

"What? Here? I didn't even know they were giving them out yet."

"They're not. He just got one. But here's the kicker. You know he's in the computer vision group, right? Well, thanks to JENNY, he's now going to be working in your group," Kohan said, touching his index finger to Stephen's chest. "My group," he continued, poking his own chest. "Our group," he concluded, twirling his finger as if mixing a drink. "He's working for Atiq and Jaan."

Stephen was silent.

"He got an offer in our group. What about us?" Kohan continued. "First Aarti and that whack-job William get an offer, and now Yuri? Come on. There's no way we're going to get offers if the positions keep getting filled."

With that, they entered the cafeteria and split up for a few moments as Kohan went to get a fresh-squeezed pineapple juice and Stephen went straight for the caffeine.

"Wow," Stephen said when they were both seated. The conversation resumed where it had left off.

"Yeah, I know. And get this, Yuri wasn't even trying for the offer. Some product manager in his group saw JENNY. This product manager mentioned it to his boss, who apparently asked Yuri for a demo. Atiq found out about it, and that was that. An offer. The worst part about it is that all our ideas are in that thing. We better get some credit."

"Come on, Kohan, you know that Yuri will share credit. It's Yuri. You know he will."

"Well, we'll see. JENNY is a nice piece of integration work, but there's nothing revolutionary there. I worked on that stuff for the last two summers. I'm telling you there's nothing new."

"Were you an intern here last summer? Why didn't you tell me?"

"No. I did a couple of internships before this where I worked on something similar."

"Really? Tracking porn usage on a house-by-house basis? Or was it the spying on unsuspecting women in Gilroy part? You did that before? Is this a pattern of yours?" Stephen said, trying to lighten up the mood. He wasn't eager to be depressed the rest of the day.

"It wasn't porn usage, smartass. And it wasn't at Ubatoo. But pretty much everything else in JENNY has been done."

"Where were you before this?" Stephen asked, now genuinely interested.

Kohan hesitated a moment before answering. But his resentment toward Yuri overcame any trepidation he might have had. "I did a couple of internships at the NSA. The first thing you do is show people's data on a map, just like JENNY, right? Who wouldn't?"

Stephen just looked at him puzzled. "Let me get this straight. You've been holding out about doing an internship at the NSA? First of all, why would they hire you? You're not exactly trustworthy. I know I wouldn't trust you," Stephen kidded. "Secondly, the NSA? Really? So you were tapping people's phones?"

Kohan took the bait and was willing to change topics from Yuri, if only for a few moments. "First, apparently, I am trustworthy. I think working there is proof enough of that. But I think anybody with a nice GPA who comes from the Midwest is a good candidate. They recruit from the heartland, you know."

Kohan, now getting more tickled with the conversation, continued. "Second, tapping people's phones? Is that really the best you can come up with?"

"You already admitted you were doing the same stuff we were doing, so *you* were really spying on people, weren't you?"

Kohan clicked his tongue in acknowledgment. "Of course we were. You don't think Ubatoo is the only one who wants this information, do you?"

"You were looking for terrorist types, right? Or just monitoring everything?"

"Obviously we were looking for terrorists. But you know how the world's Internet and telcos are hooked up—when someone in Canada calls someone in Pakistan or writes him e-mail, it can get routed through the servers or switches on American soil. We naturally had to monitor that traffic as it flowed through America, right? You can figure out the rest yourself."

"Wouldn't almost all e-mails and Internet traffic flow through those same switches? So, you were monitoring everything then! See, you're even worse than we are."

"I wasn't," he said, emphasizing the "I." "You'd have to talk to someone else to see what the extent was, but then I'm sure we'd monitor you too, of course. Besides, I wouldn't tell you, not being trustworthy yourself."

"Touché. So you've done this data mining before, and at Ubatoo's scale, too. Didn't think that such a thing existed. That's remarkable, Kohan."

Kohan tipped his hat at him. "Nothing is done at this scale, Stephen. Besides, when I do it here, it's all on the up-and-up, it's not a secret, and we get paid a lot more, at least I would if I got this job. Damn Yuri."

"Forget Yuri, Kohan. Internships here and at the NSA—that's really impressive."

Kohan did manage to forget Yuri again for a few moments, and replied a bit more contemplatively. "After you get a taste of what you can do there, this is the only other place that compares. But it's really better here. Ubatoo has the computational horsepower to put any other place to shame. And, besides, everybody just hands us their data. Think anybody would just hand their e-mails over to the NSA? I don't think so. Here, we give people a shiny new phone to use, offer them free phone calls and a half-off coupon for pizza, and there you go. All of a sudden, everyone hands over their information happily. You remember what we talked about the first week we were here?"

"About diet pills, you mean?"

"Yeah, and about how we should put everyone's medical records online so they can search them? We'll get them integrated before the NSA does. You ask me, the NSA and all these agencies just plain did it wrong. They shouldn't have taken any information. They should have just made it enticing enough for people to give it to them—offered a free appetizer at Applebee's or a 10-percent-off coupon on your grocery bill every month. It wouldn't take much."

"At least we don't do anything horrible with it. Just show you some ads," Stephen rationalized.

"True. *We* don't," Kohan said, putting a huge emphasis on the "we." "Though, I guess, now Yuri does." Thus triggering another lengthy rant featuring Yuri.

▼ ▼ ▼

"I thought you had forgotten about me," Yuri said as Stephen entered his cubicle.

"Sorry, sorry, sorry, Yuri. I was tied up this morning. Want to walk outside to talk?"

A few minutes into the walk, Yuri told him the same story Kohan had earlier. After spending the morning commiserating with Kohan, Stephen could barely muster the perfunctory congratulations that were due.

"I am not sure that I want the offer," Yuri confided.

If Stephen could have thrown his arms up in exasperation, he would have. Stephen was positive that hiring in the Touchpoints group was a zero-sum game: When someone wins, someone else has to lose. If Yuri received an offer, someone else wouldn't. Convincing Yuri to accept the offer was not a task Stephen wanted. In the long silence that followed while Stephen thought about what to say, Yuri waited patiently.

Finally, it was Yuri who broke the silence. "I can see you are not happy with all of this either. It was the same with Kohan. I do not know why. You all will get offers, too. I am certain of it."

"Maybe. Maybe we'll get offers. Maybe we won't. But, Yuri, I can't understand your not taking it. This is the place you want to be once you get your Ph.D., right? And they're offering you the opportunity even before you get it."

There were so many reasons not to push Yuri to take the offer. It would mean a higher chance of Stephen getting one himself. Yuri was less than a year away from completing his degree, and Stephen had himself made this exact same mistake before—leaving his graduate program to join a company. How had Stephen taken on the role of convincing Yuri to make the same mistake he had? And so it continued, more of the same words back and forth, with Stephen playing the part of any good Ubatoo devotee.

As they walked back to Building 11, Yuri tried his best to cheer up Stephen. "I'm meeting with Atiq today. I'll put in a good word for you, too," Yuri offered, trying to reassure him.

But it didn't reassure him. In fact, it stung just as much as anything else today. Needing Yuri to put in a good word for him wasn't where he expected to be right now. "Thanks, Yuri," Stephen mumbled without looking at him. Yuri was just trying to do the right thing. "Make sure to mention Kohan and Andrew, too. We all contributed to JENNY."

They parted at Building 11. Nothing had been accomplished today, and nothing would be. Yuri left the conversation without any of the advice he had hoped for, and Stephen departed more lost and desperate than any time since he had left SteelXchanges.

-APPLE PIE-

July 21, 2009.

"Thanks so much for meeting me. It's been a long time since we've met in person," Sebastin said to Stephen as they sat down at the "Pieces of Pi" restaurant in San Mateo, a half hour from the Ubatoo grounds. He hadn't seen him since the party, which seemed years ago. The bandage on Sebastin's forehead covered the stitches. He just hoped it didn't start leaking again. Even then, he thought to himself, it would be entertaining to see how Stephen handled the blood.

"It's great to see you again," Stephen stated automatically. Although he had agreed to the meeting on the phone, he had only given it a 50 percent probability of actually occurring. If he had his druthers, he would prefer all business communication first through e-mail, then maybe via phone, then, only if necessary, in person. But sitting down to talk informally was absolutely last on his list. There was too much social chatter, too many distractions, and not enough substance for his liking, at least nothing that couldn't be accomplished in just a few lines of e-mail.

As Sebastin bobbed his tea bag in and out of his steaming hot water, he gathered himself to play the role he needed to once again. Mustering all his strength, he opened the conversation cheerfully. *Make this work. This has to go well so I can get what Mohammad needs.* "Stephen, let me just say again, thanks for all the data you gave me. It was simply incredible and far more than I could have hoped for. I think your findings will help me enormously." *Perfect. That sounded like nothing's wrong.*

"Thanks. I hope you can use all the information. I know it was a lot."

"Oh, yes, yes. It was wonderful. As a matter of fact, let me ask you a question, and forgive me for my bluntness. I would really like you to work with me full-time." *Listen to my words, Stephen. Work with me. Not Ubatoo. Not ACCL. Come, work with me. Give me some sign, any sign, that you know what I'm saying. I can't ask you directly. Think carefully, Stephen. Think about what I said.*

Stephen was prepared for a lot of different conversations (primarily revolving around the many new and innovative ways people invented to extract more data and work out of him), but this, he hadn't seen coming. "I'm flattered, Sebastin, but I really don't know what more I can do to help right now. I'm not even sure I know enough about ACCL, or what ACCL does, to decide."

Sebastin's demeanor seemed to perceptibly change, as if he was grudgingly resolved to give a spiel he had hoped he wouldn't have to give. *It had been a long shot. Stephen was too naïve. There was no time to work on Stephen. What had he been thinking? He had known this when he started the conversation. Now, he just needed to keep up appearances enough to get what he needed and be done with it.*

Back to the original plan. "That's why I'm here, Stephen. I'll tell you all I can, and then I'll leave it in your hands. Our core team is just four people, who are now trying to do something worthwhile instead of simply making more money. You can check us on our web site. All of our bios are there. We're not looking to build a huge team, just a few people we can work with. You'd be the second person we've hired. But we have an army of volunteers and partners. I think we're making a real difference."

"You mean by contacting all the people you were talking about?"

"That's only part of it. It's not as trivial as you make it sound. You must keep in mind, Stephen, that our rights, I mean including yours and mine, are being eroded one by one, and no one is even cognizant of it happening. It's about preserving our privacy, our ability to access information and to have discussions about any topic without fear." Sebastin's voice was steadily getting louder with every word. "Just because I read or say something doesn't mean I should be on a government watch list. Who knows why someone will be taken in for questioning, or God forbid, tortured? A few years ago, it was called patriotism."

Stephen looked around the restaurant several times, hoping nobody he knew was within earshot of this conversation. He could only imagine what others would think about Sebastin; probably the same thing he was thinking.

That's right, Stephen, look around. See everybody watching? Getting self-conscious yet? This was too easy. Sebastin took a deep breath before going on. "The only way we stay ahead of this is by contacting people and gathering all the evidence we can through all our sources of data, including, of course, all that you and Atiq have generously provided. Let's start with some e-mails and see how far that takes us. The point is that people should know why they've made it onto some watch list. I guarantee that most people don't deserve to be on it."

Stephen spoke quietly, as if somehow trying to mitigate the effect of Sebastin's loud ranting. "I have to admit it sounds interesting—more interesting than targeting advertisements forever." He wasn't sure why the words were coming out of his mouth, or where he was going with his reply.

"Our 'silver bullet' is that we have access to the data that companies like Ubatoo and the half-dozen companies that surround you in the Valley have, and that they are willing to share it with us to help further our mission. No government, no organization, has this. The Valley is a do-gooder's Mecca, Stephen. Everyone here cares about preserving our rights, cares about free speech, and really wants to do the right thing. I believe we've assembled the right team to make a difference." *And you're just the final step, Stephen. What do you think, Stephen? Enamored with us yet?*

He said it with a confidence possible only from having done something remarkable in the Valley. Nevertheless, Stephen wished the would keep his voice down.

Sebastin now awaited a response. "I'm really glad ACCL is around doing what it's doing," Stephen said. "I think it's admirable, I honestly do. I still need to think about it more. I hope it's okay for me to say that." It was a strange turn—from computer scientist to political activist in only a few hours. Even though the thought of more diet pill advertising campaigns and the still-fresh sting of Yuri's offer plagued Stephen's mind, he needed to reflect carefully this time. He had made too many hasty career changes in the past.

"Look, everybody feels indignant about what's happening around them. But you're lucky: You have an opportunity to do something about it. I'll leave it at that."

Hopefully, he really would stop the hard sell there. Stephen relaxed for the first time since sitting down, and the conversation steadied for a few minutes to something less taxing. Sebastin was understandably passionate about his work, but it was challenging to keep up with his intensity.

When Sebastin spoke again, it was on a new topic. *Stephen would be receptive to anything now, anything as long as I ask without the impassioned ranting. First, appeal to his technical wizardry. I'd bet a year's salary he's going to solve this problem, without caring what I ask, before we leave this restaurant.* "Stephen, I'm not sure if you can even get this data, but for the 5,000 people's names you gave me last time, can you tell me which ones are doing well financially and which aren't? Is there any way you can figure out how to estimate that? I have a gut instinct that tells me there's probably a lot of income and spending level profiling that goes into deciding who gets put on watch lists."

As Stephen had anticipated from the start, Sebastin wanted more data. Figures he would mention a job offer first; nothing works better than flattery. At least, though, this was a conversation Stephen was comfortable having.

It took Stephen a few seconds to consider the request. "I could find a way to estimate it, but why do you want it?"

Sebastin was ready for that question. "Maybe the less income you have, the more susceptible you are to being enticed by extremist groups, especially if you already have proclivities leaning that way, like this group of 5,000 is suspected to have? If there are patterns we can easily find, maybe we can have a class-action lawsuit showing unfair targeting across lower income levels. It's just a shot in the dark, but can you imagine the amount of publicity it would garner?" *Play to his imagination. Imagine doing something really big, Stephen. Imagine the good you'll be doing. Just imagine the difference you'll make.*

"I can get that information. A lot of people check stocks and mutual funds; I can see what they've been looking at. Maybe that will find a few people. I could also just check how much people are spending through Ubatoo's credit card. That will get more. If that doesn't uncover enough people, I suppose I could see if they've started searching on foreclosures, loans, mortgages, bankruptcies, and so on. We can probably infer what we need to know."

Before Sebastin could respond, Stephen tacked on, "Oh, and by the way, I'm not sure if I mentioned it earlier, but there's an intern in the data-mining group who worked at the NSA? He might be a good person to contact, too. Maybe he would have some advice."

A startled look crossed Sebastin's face. *Think. Think. Is there any way to use this? It was too much to think about right now. No. Better to go with his first instinct.* "Really? Let's save talking to him until a bit later. I don't want to raise any red flags with anyone until we have all the information we need to make a strong legal case. I hope that doesn't put you in an awkward position, but if we're going to make a strong case, the fewer people who know what we're looking into, the better."

"I think he's trustworthy, but you're the boss. When you need his advice, let me know. I'd be happy to make the introductions."

"Thanks, Stephen. Sounds like a good person to have in reserve. Anyway, everything you said sounds great. One more thing, can you also flag for me the people who have lost the most financially recently, I mean just of the 5,000 on your list?"

"That's no problem. But, again, I don't know if that will really be indicative of much," Stephen said distantly. What Sebastin did with the data was only mildly interesting to Stephen. That was something Sebastin would have to figure out once he had the data. Stephen was already engrossed in thoughts of how to implement Sebastin's request.

"Well, if you can, let's just try it. I can only guess, but maybe people who suddenly experience an extreme downturn are the most susceptible to persuasion? If we have the data, we'll figure out what to do with it."

And with that, Sebastin picked at his pie and took a long sip of his now tepid tea. *I bet he's already working on the problem. That's enough for today; don't push too hard. Besides, if he's half as good as last time, who knows how many extra treats I'll wind up with.*

Stephen sat in the booth without saying a word. He would stay that way for the few minutes it took to figure out the exact commands required to obtain the data Sebastin needed. This awkward interaction was exactly why he hated having these informal meetings in person. His coffee was cold and his apple pie neglected, the latter a poor substitute for Ubatoo's handmade croissants.

-THOUGHTS LIKE BUTTERFLIES-

July 24, 2009.

With only a few weeks left before the official end of their internships, the overwhelming majority of interns were getting increasingly anxious about their prospects of receiving a full-time offer. Every meeting an intern had with their sponsor came with anticipation and a hopeful but nervous stomach full of butterflies. Every meeting was a chance to hear good news. In reality, though, this almost never happened, notwithstanding the summer's anomalies: Aarti, William, and Yuri.

Stephen was in a unique position among the crop of interns. He was the only one who had led a company from inception, through hiring and firing, through growth and decline, and had seen the cycle from every angle. Nevertheless, despite the advantage this gave him in recognizing the rat race with the other interns, Stephen was unabashedly caught up in it as well. His work had been solid this summer. He had mastered Jaan's system. He had crunched numbers and scoured through petabytes of data looking for patterns in users, and in doing so had made many advertisers (and one non-profit organization) extremely happy. Nevertheless, as far as Atiq or Jaan was concerned, he had been doing exactly what he was hired to do. But who wasn't doing that much? It was abundantly clear that only those who exceeded expectations had a chance of a job offer. That is what Yuri had done.

▼ ▼ ▼

When Aarti asked for Kohan and Stephen's help on an urgent project, there were many reasons that they were willing to offer their services in any way required. The project, with the three of them focused on it, only took a day to finish—they started at 1:00 p.m. and by 12:30 a.m. Kohan's part was completed. Aarti and Stephen finished an hour later. The day had been spent improving a light beer advertising campaign aimed explicitly at people earning less than $35,000 in both the Carolinas and Georgia. The experiments were set to run. In twenty-four hours, the results would be tabulated and the success or failure of their analyses and campaign refinements would be known. There was nothing more to be done for that project, and it was too late to start anything new.

"I was going to see if Kohan wants to get some coffee. You interested?" Stephen offered to Aarti.

She took a book out of her backpack and held it up, this time with her hand deliberately placed across any exposed skin on an otherwise hot pink and lavender book cover. "Not tonight. I've got some important reading to catch up on," she smiled.

They started to walk out of Aarti's office. Both stopped before making it past the threshold. It was the only appropriate reaction. The sight of a gyrating Kohan, in full regalia, would likely have made anyone stop in their tracks. The hat. The boots. The mustache. An enormous set of headphones covered his ears, and tethered him closely to his computer on his desk. Despite his bobbing backside, his head had to stay still and slightly bent to ensure the headphones didn't come unplugged. Though no music could be heard to anyone but him, Kohan's urgently whispered rendition of Kid Rock's "I'm a Cowboy" was probably music enough for the audience—which, as they discovered from glancing around the room, also included Yuri, who had been helplessly trying his hardest to ignore the spectacle.

"Sure you don't want to join us for coffee, Aarti?" Stephen asked again.

She shook her head no, and with that Aarti departed, on her way to finding a comfortable spot on Ubatoo's grounds to read for a few hours, and try her hardest to remove that last image of Kohan from her mind before sleep came.

▼ ▼ ▼

At 2:15 a.m., instead of going home, as both of them should have, Kohan and Stephen walked to an all night café and ordered lattes from the single barista on duty in the nearly empty room. Stephen guided Kohan away from her, a precaution even Kohan found a bit odd. "I think I've come up with a project we can hang our hats on," Stephen said.

"I'm in," Kohan replied, without hesitating.

"Let me tell you what it is first, *then* you can decide."

"Okay, but, really, I'm in. You know I don't have a project of my own yet."

"I've been working with this group, ACCL. Ever heard of them? Atiq introduced me to the head guy, Sebastin, at the first party we attended. They're a non-profit that warns people when they are likely to be mistakenly flagged by the NSA/CIA/FBI/Homeland Security, or whatever government group is now doing all the wiretapping, tortures, and whatever else they do. You know, all your old bosses. Anyway, the ACCL tries to warn them, and the public, that this type of thing happens."

"I'm not sure I believe that any group knows what the NSA, or any of those agencies you mentioned, looks for," Kohan interjected.

"They obviously have some source I don't know about. These guys are all well connected. Who knows who they talk to? They've certainly attracted the attention of Ubatoo and a bunch of the other big tech companies around here. I imagine they have the ear of plenty of people in Washington, too."

"Okay, I'm skeptical, but go on. What've you been doing for them?"

"The same things we do for any advertiser who comes to us: sift through all of our logs and data, the usual. I just hand them a list of people who match the criteria they think are being targeted. Then, it's up to them to contact the people. I think they're setting up some lawsuits, too. But you didn't hear that from me."

"And Atiq is okay with you doing this? We don't usually hand out specific people's names to advertisers. We just usually use that information ourselves, right?"

"Well, it was Atiq who introduced us, and he asked me to do whatever they needed. They're not an advertiser. It's for a good cause. Besides, in the end, it's going to save these people from a ton of trouble."

"I suppose it will, if ACCL is right. So, what's your idea?"

Truth be told, after hours of tortuous thought, Stephen hadn't yet thought about a concrete project. He had wanted to brainstorm something with Kohan, but the unfortunate decision to start talking about this after 2:00 a.m., coupled with Kohan's already clear skepticism, wasn't boding well for a productive brainstorming session. But now he needed to continue with it anyway.

Stephen turned to the usual standby that is inevitably applied to anything done manually at Ubatoo—make it automatic. "Maybe we could automate the work I did for ACCL? Wouldn't it be useful for anyone to be able to log on to Ubatoo and get a 'How likely am I to be monitored score?' We would look at what books you've bought, what products, medicines, lawn chemicals you've purchased, what web pages you've visited online, what queries you've sent us, where you've traveled, who you've communicated with, and everything else we can get our hands on. We'd just crunch all that information and give you a single score, 1–100 of how likely you are to make it onto some watch list. It would be like a credit score, except rather than looking to see if you pay off your bills on time, we would look at a bunch of warning signals, telling you that you should be careful."

Kohan's expression portended his sarcasm. "If I get a score of 1, I'm basically Mother Teresa, and if I get 100, I'm Osama Bin Laden? Got to admit, Stephen, didn't see this coming."

"Something like that. If you've really got nothing to hide, and your score is high, you might want to know that. I'd certainly want to know, wouldn't you?"

"You definitely think differently than most interns here. I could have easily imagined that you would come up with a self-serve product where advertisers can explore their own data and reconfigure their advertising spending. You know, automate the other 99 percent of the work that you and I do. But, instead, you come up with the *Terrorist-O-Meter.*"

"You're still in, right?" Stephen said, trying his hardest to grin along with Kohan.

"First things first, Stephen. Where does this ACCL actually get their information? How do they know what books terrorists read or what web sites they visit? I didn't know they had an official reading list."

"Oh, come on, Kohan, you and I both know that once we have a few known terrorist support sites, we can infer dozens of others. We can watch who visits them and what other sites they visit, and what products and books they eventually buy, who they send e-mail to. For that matter, we could look at what soft drink they buy most or what car they drive most. You know this."

"I do. We would have killed for that information at the NSA," Kohan said, serious for the first time in this conversation.

"We have it all here, available to us. We have the opportunity to finally do something good with it, and get the full-time offers we want," Stephen said, getting himself more excited about the project.

"Okay, it's interesting. But I just can't see it having the same impact that Yuri's project did . . . Let me play devil's advocate here. First, why would Ubatoo really care about the Terrorist-O-Meter? It doesn't make them money and puts them in the spotlight for having this data. Second, technologically, it's a nice, maybe even really nice, use of Jaan's system. On the other hand, it's just applying some new rules to the same type of data crunching we do every day, like you said. Third, who in the world is going to champion this inside Ubatoo? Who's going to stick their neck out for this? I don't know, Stephen."

"Kohan, this is the *right* thing to do. Look at what we just did. We just finished using the world's largest computation machine for micro-targeting crappy beer to destitute people in three Southern states so they can get drunk faster. Don't you want to do something more meaningful?"

Kohan didn't respond.

Stephen tried again. "If nothing else, it's better than any other plan we have right now. Together we have a much better chance for success and I could use your help."

Maybe he would say yes. Maybe Stephen had finally broken through.

But it was not to be.

"I think this one is going to be all you, Stephen. Having done an internship at the NSA, it might be a mistake for me to be too closely involved. You might want to think about it too, you know?"

In fact, Stephen did know. Despite trying to sound convinced in his ramblings, he was far from it. Kohan's hesitation and reluctance derailed Stephen for days. Thoughts and ideas fluttered in and out of his mind like butterflies. They had no rhyme or reason, and each fleeting flash of brilliance held his undivided attention—but only until the next moment, when it was lost and forgotten.

-CORE-RELATIONS-

Four days later, a rational justification of the idea remained elusive. Nonetheless, that hadn't stopped progress. First, he committed himself to the project, despite any lingering trepidation. Anything else he had considered was too small, too incremental. And hadn't he just promised himself to work only on projects that mattered, and that he could be passionate about? Second, the fact that the algorithms and programs required to make the idea a reality were within his grasp was a strong motivation to continue.

The full potential of what he was going to create was as exciting as the early days of SteelXchanges. The system, which Stephen codenamed *WatchList* (instead of the Terrorist-O-Meter that Kohan had called it), was now just a component of a much bigger plan. If Watch-List worked, it wasn't an unreasonable leap of faith to foresee a world where knowing your WatchList score was as common as knowing your credit score, or even how much money you had in your bank account. It would be a score that everyone would want to track. There would be groups of users who disagreed with their score—but that was good. This is where he would truthfully point out to them that the score is based on the evidence that Ubatoo knows about you. The more details about yourself that you volunteer, the more accurately Ubatoo could predict your score. The less information you give about yourself, the less accurate the score. And this would be Ubatoo's reason for supporting the project: it would be an incentive for users to provide even more information about themselves.

His grandiose plans didn't end there. Once the system was created, it wasn't hard to imagine it would be self-perpetuating. Not only would there be an active discussion community around it, but the possibilities for collaboration with other similarly minded non-profits were enormous. This had the chance of becoming a clearinghouse for all things related to rights preservation, everything that ACCL had hoped to do, but on a much bigger scale. And Stephen would help architect it from the beginning.

▼ ▼ ▼

The magic he and Ubatoo brought to this project was how these analyses would begin. All he needed to initialize the system were lists of "seeds." These were lists of any entities Ubatoo tracked—books, web sites, people, events, profiles, discussion groups—that were labeled as being "of interest" to any government agency, say the NSA. From this small set, he could "grow," algorithmically of course, these seeds into a full set of profiles and individuals that were at risk of being labeled as "interesting" as well.

Fortunately, his work with ACCL had previously provided the necessary seed set. From the book list, he had found the people who read them. From the people who read them, he had found the web sites they frequented and built out their complete profile: Lucy. Then, he simply identified a larger set of people who were like Lucy—the list of 5,000 people he had already given to Sebastin. Everything was connected.

In academic circles, similar problems arose in statistics and artificial intelligence literature at every turn, something that had been the basis of decades of research in universities across the globe: the problem of extrapolation. Extrapolation, simply put, was the prediction of outcomes outside the range of the available data. Think about chickens. When you see a chicken on the side of the road, you assume it wants to get to the other side because every other chicken you've known has wanted to get to the other side. It's a guess, just a hypothesis, but you can't know for sure because you don't know about this specific chicken, only of others that you think are like it.

So who cares about extrapolation? Warning sirens are tripped when it's applied to people. Applied to people, it invokes ugly terms like "stereotyping" and "racial profiling." Irrespective of the application area, however, the need for the tools to perform this analysis existed across all of Ubatoo, from advertising and tailored-searches to the recommendation of videos to watch and web pages to read, to how to organize your e-mail, and even what groups you might like to include in your social networks. It was an omnipresent form of analysis constantly being run, over and over, incorporating all the new information as it became available. The goal was to fill in holes in the knowledge about you by finding people who may be like you.

To start, Stephen had already created a list of 5,000 people who were likely targets to be placed on watch lists. He meticulously filled in the profiles of these 5,000 with every piece of information he could find about them: what they searched for, what time of day they searched, what they bought, which forums they read, who their friends were and when they called them, what entries they put on their calendars, what files they had stored, how old they were, and even what their e-mails contained. He knew these people.

But it was only 5,000 people. He needed to apply what he knew to the more than 200 million people online in the U.S. There were two facts to remember when figuring out what these 5,000 people had to say about 200 million others. First, the simple reality expressed in the statement that "no man is an island"—everybody and everything was defined by their connections. Second, the expression of being "just another cog in a machine" needed to be updated. A web of shared interests, shared friends, shared traits, shared patterns existed between all people. This web, or more precisely, this graph, and one's position in it, defines each person. Not cogs in a machine, just points in a graph.

Imagine yourself as a little black spot on an enormous blank sheet of white paper. Your mom is another little black circle, placed close to you. You call her. When you do, imagine that you've drawn a thin line between you and her. Next, you send her a photo attachment in your e-mail. Better make that line a bit thicker. Buy her a present online and have it shipped to her? Make that line thicker yet—maybe you should use a marker now.

She calls your Aunt Theresa in Florida who appears as another little black point on the piece of paper. A thin line between your mom's point and Theresa's point materializes. Theresa receives an e-mail from her son, Antonio, apologizing for not writing enough. He's in Spain, doing his semester abroad. The line between Antonio and his mom, Theresa, grows thicker. Antonio chats with his girlfriend, Sarah (another point), at the University of Maryland, over some instant messaging program; their line grows stronger between them every minute they are online together. His girlfriend tells him that Amber (another black point), her twin sister (a strong line appears between Amber and Sarah), has just gotten her acceptance letter from Dartmouth and is starting next year. Months from now, Amber enrolls in a political science course in her first semester. Her textbooks, ordered on the web, arrive on her doorstep. She had ordered all the required reading and the supplemental reading, too: five textbooks and dozens of essays and novels.

One of the novels happens to be on a government watch list; they want to keep tabs on who's reading such "radical" ideas. Wonder if she talked about the novels with her sister? Maybe. Maybe her sister talked to her boyfriend. Did it go further? Unlikely. It's even more unlikely that Antonio talked about it with his mom. Who would? But unlikely doesn't mean impossible. He might have discussed it with his mom, who then talked to your mom, who then talked about it with you in some passing comment. Unlikely—yes. Impossible—no.

If you have enough of these types of connections, eventually the probability that someone will talk to you about something they heard second, third, or fourth-hand approaches inevitability. You're connected.

Don't talk to people much? No problem. Your connections, and everyone else's, aren't just to people, they're to web sites, to products, to places. You don't need to talk to people, you just need to interact with something, anything, that Ubatoo tracks.

No man is an island. That's why Stephen's approach would work, and that's why the technology behind the WatchList project was never in question. It consisted of a large graph with almost 200 million black dots representing the people online in the U.S., and 5,000 red circles, the people who were being watched. Ubatoo's knowledge was represented succinctly in the connections. All he had to do was analyze the graph. Just radiate the "bad" influence along the connections, and see which of the black dots start turning red. The further away you were from a red circle, the safer you were. Connected to too many people who were connected to too many reds? Be careful.

The system wasn't perfect. It really would benefit from using the NSA's entire watch list as a seed set. If he knew all the people who were being watched (what did Sebastin say again, a million people?), then imagine a million red circles to initialize the system. Having the data would make all of this much more reliable. But for now, any seed set would do. He could still find people with too many questionable connections—too many to be considered just a coincidence.

-COLLIDE-

August 5, 2009.

A graph is a graph—a bunch of dots and a bunch of connections between them. How hard could this be? Stephen was days behind schedule. Creating the graph and finding the data to populate it was easy. Ubatoo had the infrastructure ready and the profiles and the right connections were easily extracted from its databases. But the problem was that Stephen wasn't versed in the latest algorithms to tackle such massive graphs. There were so many parameters, or virtual "knobs," to tweak: connectivity constraints, damping factors, evidence cutoff thresholds . . . and the list went on. With graphs of the size he envisioned, the effects of improperly setting any of the knobs would be horribly magnified, making the resulting assessments of "red" versus "black" labels garbage. In fact, until two days ago, when he had suffered a mild panic attack, fueled in equal parts by desperation, sleep deprivation, and caffeine, absolutely nothing was working.

There were probably dozens of people at Ubatoo who could have helped, but given Kohan's reaction to the project, he hesitated asking. Fortunately, he was far from alone in trying to understand the impact of connections and evidence in graphs. As far back as the early 1900s, demographers like Alfred Lotka and the husband and wife team of P. L. and E. M. Gross started exploring the basics of a field that became known as *bibliometrics*. Bibliometrics, the study of texts of information, included studying the impact of information by looking at how often it was referenced by others—how often it was found useful, how often connections were made to it. Within the last decade, the latest research coming out of the computer science schools at Cornell and Stanford took bibliometrics a step further, using it to measure the influence of web sites by looking at how many other sites linked to them. From this, ranking in all major search engines took their latest inspiration.

Within the past few years, a new round of research was emerging—applying the principles of graphs and connectivity to ranking and importance assessment in specialized domains. In the countless academic papers Stephen had hurriedly examined to find any hints on how to set the "knobs" for his algorithms, he found the research paper of Aore and Mikens from Georgia Tech particularly helpful. Though they were working in an entirely different domain than Stephen (they sought to personalize video and music recommendations), they were the most pedagogical in their writing. They spelled out the intuitions they used for setting the "knobs" for their domain. Building from these insights, it was only a few more days of non-stop trial-and-error before Stephen got things back on track.

Between the fourth and fifth coffees of the day, Stephen was ready to run his first trial experiment with *WatchList*. It was still too soon to try his approach on the full graph with 200 million people; instead, only a small fraction would be used initially. Less than 250,000 people were included in this experiment. It would take only a few minutes to start seeing the first results.

It was 10:55 a.m. The data and programs were loaded, ready to begin. Leaning back in his chair, he typed the command that would put the gears in motion, then let his finger hover over the Enter key, gliding back and forth across its surface, but not pressing hard enough for it to register. He wanted a moment to review all the tweaks he had just made—to reconsider whether he had forgotten anything. No, he didn't think so. "Please, please, please work this time," he pleaded under his breath.

He let his finger drop, and with that, dozens of computers somewhere in Ubatoo's cloud instantaneously sprang into action. The graph was realized, the points were colored black and red, and the influence of the red nodes traversed the millions of links connecting the points in the graph. Before he could finish his cappuccino, the progress bar closed, and the hopeful "Run Completed" message popped up.

Now it was time to check the results and make sure everything worked correctly. The task of examining 250,000 results was not an easy one. He randomly picked a few names and manually traced their connections to see how far they were from the red nodes. So far, so good; the results seemed reasonable. Things were finally looking up. This was further than he had gotten in the last eight days.

Next, he searched for a few specific names—he had added a number of people he knew from high school, SteelXchanges, and even Molly, Kohan, and Yuri to the list of 250,000 people used in this experiment. His high school classmates checked out just like he thought they would; no major surprises there—no one was a terrorist. Same with SteelXchanges.

Knowing the task at hand at both an intellectual and intuitive level, understanding thoroughly the work he had done for ACCL, and playing with the data for the past few weeks, why was it not evident to Stephen what was about to happen next?

When he found Molly's name, it was bright red. His first error, he thought. What was wrong now? Even if her name were a little red, that would be understandable, but why was it such a bright red? He checked a few of the people she was connected to—they were red, but nowhere nearly as bright. The further you looked from Molly, the less red the graph became. How could this be? From where, then, was she accumulating the red influence? Something didn't make sense. The only way her name could be *that* red was if she was actually on the original list herself, and so she was making her surrounding connections red—being the cause rather than the effect.

Before this, no reason had existed for him to look over the full list of 5,000 names. He was an intern; this was one of several dozen projects he had worked on over the summer, who could have expected him to look at each and every name in every attachment? But now he found himself hurriedly scrutinizing the list, scrolling through the pages, looking for Molly's name. It didn't take long to find. He stopped his scrolling at line #4,793: "Molly Byrne." His Molly.

There she was, along with all the rest of those who were being watched. She had made it onto the list that he had handed to ACCL. She was part of the red point set. She, along with 4,999 others, was the source of the troubles that propagated throughout the graph. She was part of the set that was casting doubt and suspicion on all those who knew her, causing even those with no reason other than just talking to her, to be suspicious, to be red.

It was now 11:30 a.m. He left his computer and bounded to his car. Never once did it occur to him that if the graph were ever completed, Molly and he would be connected with thick dark strokes, not small thin lines. Her influence, whether drawn or not, was more on him than on anyone else.

▼ ▼ ▼

"Molly's been telling me what you've been up to since you left, Stephen," Allison said as the three of them waited in line for a lunch of hotdogs and popcorn at GreeneSmart's café. Allison waited for some acknowledgment, but it didn't come.

"Stephen, you with us?" Molly said, as she tapped him for a second time, having failed to get his attention the first time.

"Oh. Sorry. I'm just lost in a problem I'm trying to figure out. The usual Ubatoo stuff. They keep you thinking about work all the time," Stephen lied.

"Figures. You spaced out when you worked here, too. Speaking of which, are they working you too hard to come by and visit us sometime?" Allison affectionately chided. It had been a long time since he'd heard her motherly tone.

"Allison, I'm really sorry. Today's just not been a great day. I'll invite you to lunch at our cafés before the end of the summer. That way you can see what all the fuss is about for yourself. It'll be worth it," he said, motioning his eyes over to the hotdogs on their trays. "I guarantee it."

"Sure, Stephen. Just don't forget that invitation." With that, the conversation thankfully ended. Stephen and Molly walked in silence to a table by themselves.

When they were seated in GreeneSmart's swivel chairs, Molly was the first to speak, "Okay, so what's going on with you? What's so urgent that we had to talk right now? Is everything okay?"

Stephen didn't waste any time, "Your name may be on a list it shouldn't be on."

"What are you talking about?"

"I've never really told you about what I've been doing at Ubatoo. I've tried a couple of times, but our schedules just haven't worked out that well. I've been helping out this organization called ACCL. Do you remember me ever talking about them?"

"I've heard about them. They're all over the news. And a bunch of people have been posting about them on EasternDiscussions. I don't know if we ever talked about them, though."

"The head guy there, Sebastin Munthe, and I have been working together. I mean, I've been doing some data mining for him to find out who's next to make it on the official watch lists."

"You've been doing this? Ubatoo does that?"

"We have so much data that it makes sense for us to help out ACCL. Anyway, I'm the person who's been doing it."

"Wow. That's really, really, cool, Stephen. All the people on EasternDiscussions would be really big fans of yours. They're really enamored with ACCL—well, at least the ones who aren't cynical about everything," she looked at Stephen almost adoringly.

There wasn't time to bask in the glow right now. "But there's a problem. The point is, Molly, I think you're on one of the lists, too. You . . . you fit the profile too well. You spend all your time posting messages to the right sites, talking to the right people, buying the right books, and just think about your e-mail conversations, who they're with and what they say. And I'm sure you've entered hundreds of search queries to Ubatoo with the exact right keywords. If I'm right about who's most likely going to make it onto a watch list, I mean if the ACCL is right, you're probably already on some watch list, or will be soon."

Molly thought for a few seconds before responding. "So, what's going to happen now?" There was no worry in her voice.

"I don't know. Sebastin told me a while ago that anyone who is on their list will get an e-mail or a phone call from the ACCL, and they'll tell you what you can do. Do you know if you've already been contacted by them?"

"No, I haven't. I don't recall having seen anything like that in my e-mail. No phone calls either. I would have told you."

"Are you sure about the e-mails? You should have received it a few days ago. You haven't seen anything out of the ordinary?"

"I get about a dozen out-of-the-ordinary e-mails a day. You know the stuff I write about on my message board; people are writing me all the time. Sometimes to my Sahim Galab account, or sometimes to my Zakim account, or any of the others, too. I haven't seen anything unusual."

"No, but anything besides that? Addressed to you, in particular, not to Galab or Zakim."

"No. Not that I can think of."

Stephen waited a second before continuing. He wasn't quite sure how to proceed at this point. "Yes, you have," he said quietly.

"What?"

"I checked your e-mail account before I came here. You've already gotten the e-mail. It's been sitting in your inbox for a few days now. There's a meeting tomorrow night. A few other people were also on the e-mail."

"What? How do you know all this? I never said you could do that. Are you always checking my e-mail accounts?" She pulled herself back as far away from Stephen as she could in one abrupt motion. "Is that what you do all day?"

"No, no. Remember, you gave me your password?" He leaned in closer toward her and whispered, "'Mollycoddle.' Remember, you told me that the first time I was at your apartment?" Of course, he didn't bother to explain that he wouldn't have needed the password, and that her guess was right: This was exactly the type of thing he did all day. There would be time enough for that later.

"I didn't even have this e-mail account then."

"Everyone uses the same password for all their accounts, Molly. It's not much of a secret," Stephen said.

She was teetering between two options: storming out now or trying her best to wait the anger out. "You still read it without my permission." She exhaled a long restrained breath but said nothing more. The scornful look on her face was enough. "This better be damn good," it screamed.

Stephen didn't wait. He needed any opportunity to continue. "The e-mail from ACCL said there was a meeting tomorrow night. Someone from ACCL will be coming to talk to you and, from what I could tell, a few other people in the area who made it onto the list as well. I've never been to any of these meetings, but I'm going to guess he'll review what's going on and tell you what you should do next. That's all I know. I would ask Sebastin for details, but he's out of town."

"This is a giant misunderstanding. I don't have to explain it to you, you understand that. I'm just studying the people who post on my web site. I'm not planning to join any group and I don't believe any of the stuff posted. You still think I should go?"

"I think that's why ACCL is around. I would imagine these mistaken cases are *exactly* what they want to resolve." Stephen waited a few seconds to let it sink in, "I don't think you have much of a choice. You need to find out as much as you can. I don't know enough about ACCL to tell you what they would say, but if everyone is as passionate about helping as Sebastin is, you'll be glad you went."

"You think I'm in some kind of trouble?"

"I don't think so. I'm sure it's going to be fine. But I'd rather be too cautious than not enough in this case."

Now Molly was angry with herself. "I can't believe I missed that e-mail. What if I hadn't seen it in time?"

"It happens. Just make sure you go."

"Thanks for finding me," she said with a very clear hesitation in her voice. "Sometime you should tell me more about what you do with ACCL."

Molly understood enough only to know that she didn't fully understand what was happening. She couldn't predict how dire her situation was. Even online shopping companies who supposedly watched her and her shopping habits couldn't recommend the music or books she cared about. If they couldn't do that, how much should she trust Stephen's analysis? Every tech person she had ever known was overly confident about his own work. And there was enough empirical evidence from all of her studies to indicate that all the computer models, no matter who developed them, never captured the full picture. After all, that was what Stephen had created—another computer model of what it takes to be on a watch list. Maybe his analysis was faulty. For that matter, how much should she trust ACCL? They couldn't have direct knowledge of what it took to get on any of these lists either. Moreover, what did it really mean to be on "a list"? If she believed the posts on EasternDiscussions, most of the members of the forums were likely to be on any number of such lists, but they went on posting and living their lives just fine.

Stephen, on the other hand, had reason to be more pessimistic. He couldn't help but worry that it was his analysis that would eventually put Molly on a watch list if she hadn't been on one already. The line between cause and effect was blurry. Rationally, he wasn't guilty; he had meant only to try to replicate the signals ACCL said were being used by the NSA. He wasn't the cause of Molly being on the list, was he? No, that wouldn't make any sense. Now, there was no going back. He couldn't just delete his e-mail and ask Sebastin to delete it as well and start over. What if Sebastin had forwarded it already? Besides, there was always a chance that somewhere in Ubatoo's network there was a backup of that file in which her name was listed. It was only a matter of time before someone stumbled across the list again with a fresh pair of eyes and figured out what the list was for.

But Stephen had to stop thinking that way. His analysis had to be right. Molly was likely already on some list. This was becoming all too real. The abstract mathematical problem he had addressed so blithely as another step toward getting the job offer he had wanted for months now had a face attached to it. It was one he should have known would be there.

-CONTROL, REVISITED-

August 6, 2009.

"They changed it," Stephen called out, panicked.

A few hours before its scheduled time at 7 p.m. in Palo Alto, the ACCL meeting was moved to 835 Parkstone Way in Milpitas. Though the new location was only twenty miles southeast of the original, the street was an enormous distance from the safe immaculately manicured lawns and stately homes of Palo Alto. The home at 835 Parkstone Way was a tiny single-level grey house on a street with other equally small houses, and more broken cars than kept lawns.

Stephen had driven Molly to the house early, but not as early as Stephen would have liked. The dashboard clock said 6:43. They decided to wait together in the car until 7:00, to watch for anyone coming or going. Though neither knew what to expect, both had grown increasingly uneasy as the appointed time approached.

Left alone, Molly would have handled the stress in her usual way, compartmentalized it, dealt with it, and moved on. She would have defiantly overcome any trepidation by convincing herself this too was just part of her research—just another chapter to add to the thesis. It was Stephen's anxiety that had worked both himself and Molly into their currently agitated state.

Stephen kept an eye on the clock as it slowly made its way to 7:00. It was only 6:52 and the two dots kept blinking mercilessly until a number finally changed, and began their synchronized march again. He figured he had another six or seven minutes with Molly before she walked into the house. So, when she opened the door before the clock even struck 6:54, he nearly jumped out of his seat. With just a quick peck on the cheek and a cool "I'll be back as soon as I can," she leapt out of the car and walked toward the door. He would have said something, had there been anything left to say.

The screen door to the house was closed, but the main door behind it was wide open—at least they weren't trying to hide anything. Molly rang the doorbell before she finished her last step. A woman with dark hair peeking from under a headscarf came to the door, flashed a huge smile, and motioned for Molly to come in. As Molly passed through the entrance, she abruptly stopped before putting both feet inside. Then she turned around and waved, a very large and exaggerated wave, to Stephen. Then she was gone—disappearing inside.

The wave would be replayed in Stephen's mind from the moment Molly left his sight. Was it a "come now, I need you" wave, a signal to the occupants of the house that someone was waiting for her who knew where she was, or her way of trying to reassure him that everything was okay? It was only 6:57, and the worry was mounting.

By the time 7:00 officially came and went, no one else had entered the house. Perhaps they had not been early enough. Perhaps someone from ACCL was going to talk with each person individually, and the next person would arrive only when Molly left. It was, after all, a very private subject.

At 7:13, the screen door slowly opened, and a dark skinned man smoking a cigarette emerged. He held the cigarette between his two middle fingers as he lifted his entire fist to his mouth to draw in a long drag of nicotine. He turned to look directly toward Stephen. Maybe the reflections on the windshield were working in his favor, blocking the man's view of him, but there was no way to be sure. His gaze didn't waver for an uncomfortable minute. The cigarette spent, the man rose to go back inside. He, too, stopped before walking through the doors and turned again to face Stephen.

At 7:35, Stephen decided to move the car. From its current position, he could only see the screen door, but nothing beyond it. He swung the car around in a wide U-turn at the end of the street and parked on the opposite side of the road, directly across from the still-open door. Nothing was visible inside. From his vantage point, the house appeared uninhabited.

I should be in there. I should have insisted. Stephen had repeatedly volunteered to accompany Molly into the meeting, but she wouldn't budge in her determination to go alone. She had sense enough to know that Stephen would be unlikely to make things better. Molly wanted to listen with as objective a mind as possible, and Stephen was being anything but objective.

At 7:45, the wave had been replayed in his mind dozens of times in the last five minutes. It had been a "come save me" wave, he was sure. Yet, he stayed in his car waiting. He'd give Molly until 8:01. The next sixteen minutes wouldn't pass quickly. There was too much to think about and even more to imagine.

With sixteen minutes to go, there was enough time to play back the wave, retrace the torturous path that had led him to be waiting in front of a stranger's house, and revisit all that precipitated this sequence of events. Try as he might, though, he could not escape the same worries he had earlier. He was not to blame. His list did not put her on a real watch list. The only thing he had really done was get her invited to this meeting. The real threat was her name's presence on a list that neither he, nor she, would ever see. But what if he was wrong? What if the ACCL was wrong? Then he had just managed to put her name on a list with people that nobody would want to be associated with.

It was 8:02. There was no movement in the house. "Fine, 8:10 then," he thought to himself resolutely. "Absolutely no later." He would go in then, no matter what happened. But he needed to prepare. He needed to carry something, something sharp, maybe something heavy. There was nothing in his car—he had his keys, but that was it. He wasn't ready for this.

-FABLES OF THE DECONSTRUCTION-

February, 1996.

An outspoken traditional Indian man owning a dusty store that supplied farm equipment and homemade curry mixes to local farmers in a tiny town outside of Grand Forks, North Dakota . . . Stories don't start out with less likely scenarios. But that was Rajive's father, a first-generation immigrant from Lucknow, India. Like any well-raised dutiful son, especially any dutiful only son, Rajive did not ever seriously consider going too far from his hometown—even when the acceptance letters from universities around the country arrived in his mailbox. The tuition was too much of a material burden, and the distance too much of an emotional one. As a student in the department of Computer Science and Electrical Engineering at the University of North Dakota, Rajive was all too aware of what he had given up when he turned down the bigger name schools to stay close to home.

Standing with his father inside his shop, Rajive's freedom came abruptly, with absolutely no warning, three months before graduation day from UND. "*Raju*, your mom and I are going back home to Lucknow." This was a lot to process. *Raju?* His father hadn't called him that since he was twelve. Going back to India? After twenty-four years in the U.S.? "We wanted to be here for you—for you to finish your education. Now that you are finishing, your mom and I can go back home."

He looked at his father for a few moments before saying anything. If Indian boys ever hugged their fathers, he would have hugged him then. He would have at least said "Thank you," and maybe even "You didn't need to do all that for me." But displays of emotion didn't come naturally. Instead, without looking at his father, he replied, "When are you leaving?"

"A few days after your graduation ceremonies," his father smiled proudly at him. "Your mom would never leave before that."

For the first time in years, maybe since he had last called him Raju, his father put his arm on Rajive's shoulder. He spoke quietly, almost in a whisper, "When we go home, you leave Grand Forks, leave North Dakota, and go use that brain of yours. It's time. All of this," he said pointing at the one aisle of curry powders, spiced mixes, and dried *daals*, and waving dismissively at the other eight aisles of assorted small farm supplies that for as long as Rajive could remember his father had spent hours each day meticulously choosing, arranging, and displaying to the best of his abilities, "is not for you."

▼ ▼ ▼

May, 2005.

At 5:30 a.m., an e-mail message popped up on Rajive's BlackBerry. Rajive had been up for an hour already, rehearsing his presentation.

From: AlanMayer@nctc.gov
Subject: Tysons Corner Meeting and Presentation

Don't forget the Starbucks coffee. Bring something to munch on too.

Be early. I've slotted you for the first presentation of the day.

—A

Years ago, after graduating from UND, Rajive accepted an offer he received from the FBI. The lure of a bigger city, the potential opportunity to get a Master's degree in one of Washington, DC's universities, and the fact that his closest friends were also recruited directly into the same program gave him three very compelling reasons to join.

Years passed, and unlike his colleagues who came to the FBI at the same time, he successfully obtained his Master's. But when it came to work, like his colleagues he followed to the FBI, he did his job well, but never let it consume him entirely. Then, on a day that started like any other, the world was shaken by the horrific events of September 11, 2001.

Suddenly, his ability to speak Urdu and Hindi was more in demand than ever before. Combined with his computer science background, his value to the group escalated exponentially. Like many others working in any branch of national security, he channeled the outrage toward the September tragedy into working harder. Before he knew it, opportunities to contribute and to excel were thrust upon him.

When a position opened in the newly formed NCTC, the National Counterterrorism Center, he was one of the first to request a transfer. That was where he met Alan Mayer, a still rising government-lifer who was a level GS-14, hoping to become a GS-15 as soon as possible. Alan Mayer, now a Deputy Senior Operations Officer, who had transferred into NCTC the same week as Rajive, was looking to make a name for himself doing what he did best, understanding and profiling the flow of information through the U.S. intelligence agencies. The flow of information to the NCTC came from all branches of foreign and domestic intelligence sources. It was the NCTC's mandate to ensure that any information about international terrorist threats was aggregated, analyzed, condensed, and presented to all those who needed it.

At the meeting in Tysons Corner, Virginia, one of Alan's bimonthly cross-functional, synergistic, multi-divisional, out-of-the-box, offsites, Rajive was slated to be the first speaker. This was the first time Alan had let one of his subordinates speak there. Normally, Alan restricted the meeting to only those who held pay grades equal, or preferably higher, to his own. It was his chance to impress.

Rajive stood at the head of the table, in his nicest suit and most conservative tie, ready to begin his presentation. He looked to Alan, as the head of the meeting, to call the meeting to order. But Alan was in no rush. Alan was enjoying the attention. "What's the special occasion, Alan?" someone in a blue suit asked from across the table. "Coffee, cheese Danish, *and* donuts? What do you need from us this time?" Of the nine people in the room, eight people enjoyed the small talk. Rajive just waited quietly, repeatedly rehearsing the first few slides in his head. There were thirty-eight slides total. If he could just make it through the first few, he would switch into automatic mode, and he would be just fine.

When the cups of coffee were all filled for the second time, and Alan had sufficiently played the part of host, offering more coffee and pastries than a new air hostess on crack, he began. "Gentlemen, I'd like to introduce you to Rajive. He's been working with me since my first day at NCTC. For the last sixteen months, I've had him work on a project to document outstanding issues with our external partner-ships." Then, Alan turned to Rajive. "Rajive, we're running a bit over because of the breakfast. Can we try to wrap this up in about twenty minutes?"

Thirty-eight slides in twenty minutes—the presentation was sup-posed to be fifty minutes long. Skip the introduction. Skip the jokes he had planned for weeks. Skip the background. Rajive uneasily untucked his tie that had gotten stuck inside the waistband of his pants, and started. His practice served him well; his words did nothing to convey his underlying nerves.

"Let's get right down to the heart of the problem. We, the NSA, NCTC, CIA, FBI, all of us, we outsource the majority of what we build. I've talked to eleven scientists at the NSA, and three supervisory in-telligence and information analysts each at the FBI and CIA, and not one of them, not a single one, could tell me what analyses take place once the conversations from recorded telephone calls enter our system. With respect to e-mails we capture, it's even worse. Gentlemen, we are very good at collecting information. But we are very bad at analyz-ing it—we outsource every bit of analysis. None of our scientists know what analysis is done, how the analysis is done, or to what extent it even should be done." There, he had summarized fifteen minutes of his talk in under a minute. He had tackled the "intelligence" of the intelligence communities, the NSA, CIA, and FBI—*how's that for an opener?* His eyes darted around the room, waiting for the onslaught of questions. A few of the eight were looking at him, some already had the same vapid expression, and others were still concentrating on their donuts. Maybe he had gone too fast. *Another jab perhaps?* "What's even more troubling is that the companies you outsource your analysis to have sales offices in the U.S., but almost always have their technical staff, their scientists, elsewhere. I don't want to understate the problem, but if news ever gets out about the locations and nationalities of the scientists who are developing our very own intelligence software, it will be little less than a political time bomb."

Finally, some reaction. All eight were looking up from their Black-Berrys, laptops, and glazed fingers. Maybe it was the mention of a bomb. "Second, if you look ahead in your presentation book, to page 21 . . ." he waited until two of them actually opened the book to look. "The second problem I've found is that every time we buy software from one of our trusted outsourcing companies, every time we sign up for a new 'value package,' every time we agree to try some new fancy algorithm they've come up with, we give away details about our own information." He waited to see if anyone looked perplexed by his last statement. They should be, it wasn't meant to be straightforward. Rajive focused on the man with the coffee stain on his shirt. At least he looked suitably confused. "Even if we're not handing out the raw data we've collected on suspects, you have to understand that by telling outside companies the type of analyses we're interested in, we're telling these companies too much about ourselves. We're telling them how we expect to track people, where we expect to find clues, what types of clues we're looking for." Coffee-stain man was watching him closely now. "Every time we buy a software package, every time we tell the vendor how much data we expect to pass through their system so they can bill us the appropriate amount, or set up the appropriate number of machines for us, every time we make a move, we give away pieces of our own intelligence gathering plans. Someone out there will piece it all together and know exactly what we do."

"Now wait a minute, Rajive," Alan piped in. "Let's not alarm people unnecessarily. No actual information is leaking. You're not saying that. It might be best to state exactly what it is that you're saying."

Thanks for the support, Alan. "Alan's right, of course. There's no direct information leak. That's not what I'm saying. I'm saying we have a much more subtle problem. By the very act of buying some software package, you're saying too much. If someone out there knows all the analyses we're doing, then they know how to circumvent those analyses, too."

"But no one knows all the analyses we're doing inside the NSA," the man with the coffee stain interjected. "Hell, just a minute ago, you said my team of scientists, or apparently at least eleven of them— *we* don't even know what we're doing. So, if I'm to understand you correctly, others know what we're doing, but we don't? Is that what you're saying, son?" Seven people in the room laughed. Alan was glaring—at Rajive. Rajive was considering his options. *North Dakota looked really good right now.*

"There are only a small number of companies from which we buy software. If they share information, which you can bet that they absolutely do, anyone who wants to put together our analysis procedures just has to ask them. And secondly, as for your scientists not knowing what they are doing, that's not what I meant. They know what they're doing; they're just not doing the right things."

Ten minutes into the talk. *Bridges were burning all around.* Alan's hands were clenched in fists. *So I guess I'm not going to be invited back to this meeting. Let's incinerate the rest of the bridges, too.* "And that brings us to the final problem." *You're going to love me for this one, Alan.* "We've outsourced everything. The knowledge that we should be building in-house, the expertise that we should be fostering and nurturing to create the single best data-mining and intelligence community is all but dead." He didn't look at Alan; didn't look directly at anyone. "I'm not as smart as all those Ph.D.s at the NSA, my MBA doesn't really hold a candle to what they do. But I'll tell you something I learned in business school: It's called the 'not-invented-here' syndrome. Nobody, especially engineers and scientists, trusts anything built by anyone else. And as managers, division heads, supervisors and the such, all of you have to fight that every day. But it's possible we've gone too far. We've outsourced our brain trust. We're too far removed from the data. Undoubtedly, there are plenty of cryptographers working on securing their own information and breaking other's security to get access to locked data. But once we have the data, what then? We feed it into 'black boxes,' supplied by some contractor, and magically out comes an answer. But an answer to what? This black box has some algorithm, created by some scientist we don't know, answering some question that probably isn't relevant anymore. What are our own scientists doing?"

The man with the stained shirt, the man who Alan had invited from the NSA, spoke. "Our scientists have their hands full. We have immediate concerns that need to be addressed. You suggest we forget about those?"

Of course, the man was right. The most rewarded scientists were those who chose to be immediately effective, and they accomplished this by helping integrate or evaluate outside technologies, at the peril of their own research. The few who had chosen an alternate path, to pursue their own longer-term research, were stowed away in a few small relatively obscure groups, and most were left to figure out for themselves how best to be relevant. These scientists lived in fear of their projects being cut because of few immediate results. As anticipated, this problem perpetuated itself—few scientists excited about their work meant that recruiting the next star scientists would be excruciatingly difficult. They were constantly losing the best and the brightest candidates to outside companies offering incentives, in terms of support, research freedom, and compensation, far beyond the offers any government agency could realistically make.

And that was that. The next line, which Rajive would hand them on a silver platter so everyone could get along the next day, was the one all nine in the room would rally around. "Exactly, right. What we need is more. We need more scientists. We need more people to not only satisfy our current needs but also to look forward and to rebuild the expertise in-house." What he really wanted to say was that they needed someone with the balls to reallocate people to prepare for the long term, to figure out how intelligent intelligence agencies are going to operate in five, ten, or even, gasp, twenty years. Had Rajive known about Ubatoo at the time, he might have tried using it as an example to strive toward in terms of how to balance innovation and immediate results. But at the time, Ubatoo was still young, and nobody could have known where their management techniques would take them. Instead, all the intelligence agencies emulated the large, and habitually

ineffectual, consulting companies they worked with, and thus the problem of where they were today.

By the end of his twenty-minute slot, which ended three minutes
early, Rajive had said all he needed to say. At the end of the meeting,
handshakes were offered, and even Alan had forgotten about the earlier bad feelings. Beyond the perfunctory pats on the back, the presentation on what was supposed to be the potential sources of leaks and
the intricate deconstruction of the complex processes and information
flows through the intelligence agencies were largely forgotten or more
likely never really heard. Instead, what was heard was the need for
more money—especially if they were to take on further reaching projects. This was not the group who would reconfigure the current plans,
not the group to cut projects and make the hard decisions. No, this
was the group that needed ammunition to ask for more. More of everything. And this was just the ammunition they needed.

Though Rajive was vociferous and persistent for years after the
meeting, he was not invited back. He had little success in convincing management to build almost anything internally instead of looking outward for faster, cheaper solutions. Repeated pleas to incubate
technologies in-house were ignored, but not for lack of trying. Rajive
became the champion for internal technology conceived, built, maintained, or, at the very least, supervised by their own people. Yet, as
situations became more urgent and desperate, long-term thinking was
harder to fathom. More outsourcing companies than ever, with ties to
Japan, China, and Israel to name a few, had their software installed
behind all of the agencies' secure walls.

Rajive's advice was never followed. However, thanks to Rajive's
investigations and Alan's maneuverings, both he and Alan received
commendations for their long-term strategies combined with their recognition of current issues. It was, as their manager proudly declared,
"Something that all employees should strive toward."

Given their project and its recognition, both Alan and Rajive were
internally thought of as excellent candidates for cultivating and managing collaborations between internal and external technologists and
scientists, as a first step toward reducing the hold of the large outsourcing companies. In time, through a number of department mergers, re-

organizations, and renamings, Alan and Rajive were catapulted into new positions created to do exactly that. Finally, Rajive was able to initiate some of his plans, even if he had to do them himself. It was through his own perseverance that the hushed but abundant interactions with ACCL, as well as similar exchanges with dozens of other scientists, companies, and Silicon Valley techies, were born.

-CONTROL, FOREGONE-

August 6, 2009.

Time: 8:04.

Stephen's right hand tightly clutched his keys, waiting for the clock to mark 8:10. He would go in the house then, no excuses, no more waiting. Repeatedly, he fingered the tips of each key, trying to distinguish the sharpest. With each, he pressed it savagely into his left arm until he was certain that any more pressure would draw too much blood. He had to find just the right one—the one that could plunge the deepest into someone's neck if it came to that. He *knew* it was all impossible. Molly was just in a meeting. This had to be all his imagination. Just a meeting—that's all it was. But what if it wasn't? He would go in, and then what? What would he do? What would he do with a key?

8:07 . . .

Stephen's phone chirped. It was a text message from Molly, "Out in ten. Be there."

Where else would he be? His hand loosened its grip and the keys dropped to the floor. But within a minute he recovered, turned on the car and made a sweeping U-turn to his original space in front of the grey house. It was 8:09, and Molly was already exiting the door. No one was with her.

"You okay?" Stephen asked as Molly climbed in the car.

"Yes. Let's go."

She smelled of smoke and spices. She reached her hand over; he let her pull his right hand away from the steering wheel. Their fingers were locked as the house became a speck in their rear-view mirror.

"You okay?" Stephen asked again.

"Yes."

He gave her a few seconds, as long as he could, then asked, "What happened? How many people were there? Were you the only one?"

"I wasn't the only one. There were five men in there. We just sat in a circle on the floor, on a white sheet, and listened while one of the men talked."

"Did he tell you about the lists?"

"Yes, yes. He said a lot about lists. He talked all about them. He talked about the targeting, the paranoia that it's causing, and how unfair everything we must endure is. He was intense. Very intense. I don't know what happened to him before, but when he spoke, it was just hate."

"That doesn't sound like ACCL."

"I don't think it *was* ACCL, Stephen."

"Who do you think it was?"

"I don't know. But it didn't sound like a warning speech as much as anger . . . rage . . . pure rage."

"Maybe it was one of the volunteers who works with ACCL. Sebastin mentioned there are hundreds of volunteers working for them."

No response from Molly, so Stephen continued. "Did anyone else say anything?"

"No. Not at first. But the man who was speaking seemed to know the others, except for me and one other, Ali."

"Did anyone talk about what you should do now? Is there a way to get off these lists?"

"I, I don't know. They didn't talk about that. They just asked questions. They asked whether we've seen any signs of being watched, or anything out of the ordinary. They asked us about how we got on the lists, what we were doing, our backgrounds, all the standard questions, was I married, how long have I been in the U.S., where I last traveled . . . the usual."

"What did you tell them?"

"I answered the questions. What else could I do? I told them several times that I really didn't think that anyone was watching me. They repeatedly cautioned me to be vigilant in my lookout. Then they asked us how I thought the people who made the lists should be dealt with."

"What does that even mean? What did you say?"

There was an extra second of silence before Molly answered, "What was I supposed to say? What kind of question is that? I made up something. I basically said what Sahim Galab would say." She didn't want to elaborate, but there was no escaping it. "He would say that he detested the fact anyone who was studying, even peacefully, anything to do with Islam was automatically an enemy."

"That's all? Was that enough?"

"No. I guess I went on a bit. I don't remember it exactly. I just remember that I talked for a long time, longer than I wanted to. I probably said something about this being typical American aggression and that it should be dealt with severely. I couldn't tell if everyone bought it, especially coming from me."

"Why would you say that?" Stephen pleaded.

"I didn't know what else to do. They wanted an answer. What else was I going to say? I think Sahim would have said that." The adrenaline was dissipating now. She was thinking more clearly. "It's just like what I do on my web site—I just had to do it in person this time. How else was I going to find out what they were thinking if they didn't trust me?"

"I don't know, Molly. This really doesn't sound like the ACCL at all. We have to tell Sebastin about these volunteers."

"I don't think they were ACCL, Stephen, and I don't think they were volunteers, and I don't think they were warning me about being on a list."

The words hung in the air, waiting to be acknowledged. Molly quietly continued, "I think they were just trying to feel me out."

"For what? To join ACCL?" Stephen asked, hoping this was what Molly was referring to, but knowing full well it wasn't.

"No. I mean, I don't know. But I think it was to join something, just not ACCL," Molly replied, not wanting to mention anything more specific, lest it be true.

Stephen felt sick. What had he gotten her into? She had her suspicions. Stephen had his. And they were the same.

"What about the other person, Ali?"

"I don't know. He said he wasn't married and he talked about jobs and money a lot. That's all I know. What he wanted to do to the people who made the lists was a lot more disturbing and explicit than I was expecting. He's been thinking, fantasizing, about that a lot. He did refer to some of the posts he's made on EasternDiscussions. I tried, but I couldn't recognize him from what he said. I'm sure he used an alias. I don't know if I've ever noticed him before."

"Did anyone there know that EasternDiscussions is your site?"

"No, though it was brought up a couple of times. I bet that most of them have been on it. I doubt anyone had any idea I run it."

"Did you tell them you were there because of your research, because of EasternDiscussions?"

"Oh, God, no. Come on, Stephen. They take their posts and messages seriously. I can't tell them anything like that."

As the miles between the house and them grew, Stephen calmed down almost as much as Molly already had. "I wish we could find out more," Stephen heard himself say, though he would never have said it aloud if she were actually still in the house.

"I know. Me, too. But it was getting a little too intense. When they started in on Ali, I was done. I wasn't sure where it was headed at that point."

"And they just let you leave?"

"Of course they did. What else would they do? This was just our first meeting, Stephen. You know, maybe I'm reading the whole thing wrong. Maybe we're both jumping to the same, I'm going to guess, wrong conclusions about what was going on in there."

"Maybe. What's next?"

"We're supposed to meet again in a couple of weeks. I'll get an e-mail later to find out the specifics of when and where."

"You're not planning on going, are you?"

"Why don't you talk to Sebastin first, then we can figure it out from there?" Molly replied. She didn't cherish the thought of going back either, though these were exactly the research subjects she had been waiting for.

-FOUNDATIONS-

August 6, 2009.

Crashing from an adrenaline high, tired and ravenous, neither Molly nor Stephen was ready to go back to their apartment after the meeting in Milpitas. When the Ubatoo buildings appeared on the horizon, both agreed it was a good night to stop at one of Ubatoo's cafeterias. It was past 9 p.m., and thanks to their nerves, neither had eaten anything since that morning.

With food and loaner laptops in hand, they found an empty conference room and immediately hunkered down into their own private worlds in silence. It was almost 11:00 before Molly looked up at Stephen, only to find him staring back at her.

Molly spoke first. "Walk outside for a while? It's still early."

Molly held onto Stephen's hand as she led him out of the building into the cloudless quiet California night. It wasn't until they were well out of earshot of the buildings that Stephen spoke. "You know that just because you're on this list I made, doesn't mean you're on any official list—or that you ever will be. And even if you were, as soon as anyone checked, they'd see they made a mistake and your name would come right off. You know that, right?"

"I know. I also know you're really worried about it, probably more than I am. If I am on some list, though, it's not the end of the world. I've got nothing to hide. I haven't done anything wrong. Let them watch me," she said unconvincingly. "It's not your fault, Stephen. I wonder if you worked on your program some more, whether my name would fall off the list—maybe it's just a mistake? You did say it was a difficult project. Maybe we've worried about all this for nothing."

Maybe it really was nothing, maybe he was just wrong—a simple mistake. Molly's name was on the list, which was clear proof that he must be wrong, right? How many others like Molly were on the list? And how many were on the list for good reasons? Just how wrong was he? Then again, what about Molly and what she does, who wouldn't want to at least give her a second look? No, no, that's wrong. It was Molly—just Molly. His mind was reeling, stumbling through a chaotic maze of connections and conclusions being drawn, torn down, and re-created again.

Minutes passed before Molly spoke again. "What were you looking at while we were eating dinner back in the conference room?"

"Well, you mainly," Stephen replied, turning his head toward Molly.

Apparently that response warranted a hand squeeze, as Molly held on tighter. "I mean before that, when you were busily working away?"

"I was looking at Sebastin's e-mail account. I wanted to see if he had sent out any mails about tonight's meetings."

"Had he?"

"No. I didn't find anything. If he did send any, he didn't send them using his Ubatoo e-mail account. I also checked the accounts of the people he had been sending e-mail to in the last few weeks. There were only eighteen people he talked with regularly, and twelve of them used Ubatoo's e-mail. But, at least from those twelve, I couldn't find anything interesting."

"You can do that? You just read everyone's e-mails? Do you listen to their phone calls and watch what they do online, also?" Molly asked, surprised.

"We don't listen to phone calls."

"You do all the rest?"

"Sometimes. I had to do the same thing for ACCL, too, you know."

"I guess I do now. I just never figured that's what you did," Molly said. "I wish I had that kind of information for the people that I'm studying on EasternDiscussions. Why didn't you tell me about all of this?"

Stephen wound up apologizing, but not for anything he had antici-pated. He apologized for not sharing the resources he had. Before the walk ended, Stephen had promised to help Molly look up the e-mails and whatever other activities they could find on some of the posters on EasternDiscussions, despite Stephen's trepidation in doing so. First, this struck Stephen as crossing some fine, albeit arbitrary, line. Second, he didn't want to get Molly involved in this any more than she already was.

▼ ▼ ▼

In Building 11, the LCD screens were awash in pink, with Yuri and Kohan merrily talking and laughing away. When they saw Stephen and Molly walk through the doors, the laughing subsided, the LCDs were quickly turned off, and hastily Yuri stood up, as if he had been caught with his hand in the cookie jar.

"What were you two doing?" Molly asked suspiciously. She had met Kohan many times before and Yuri once or twice. Not hearing a response, Stephen volunteered one for them, "Watching people surf for porn."

"You two are a class act," Molly replied without a moment's hesitation. She walked over to Stephen's desk, opened her laptop, and started getting ready for her own investigations.

Yuri held out his hand for Stephen to shake. "I accepted the offer today. I thought about what you said, Stephen. I told Atiq I would accept."

"Hey, congratulations!" Stephen replied, shaking Yuri's hand. Today, with everything else on his mind, his congratulations were real.

"Kohan has told me about the project you are working on now, Stephen," Yuri continued. "I think it's wonderful you're even allowed to do this project here. I can't believe that too many companies, or even countries, would allow your project."

"Well, I haven't exactly told anyone about it yet, to tell you the truth. We'll see what happens when they find out what I'm doing."

"I'm still not even sure it'll work," Kohan piped in. Though he had been laughing with Yuri when Stephen walked in the building, he had steadily grown more morose since then—probably the spontaneous jealousy invoked by the mention of Yuri's job offer. Kohan was in no mood to be friendly, as he aggressively laid into Stephen's plan. But this wasn't the argument Stephen wanted to take on today. He left the two to discuss its possible merits or more likely, its many shortcomings.

Molly was ready. "Okay, there are six people I want to find out about. The first two are the angriest posters on my web site. I've been watching them for a while. The other four might have been the people from tonight's meeting—I want to see if I recognize them from their e-mails. Are six too many for you?" Molly asked.

Only six? He thought to himself how schizophrenic he was. Despite his apprehension in sharing Ubatoo's resources with Molly, it was hard to resist the urge to analyze everyone on her web site on the first go.

"Six is fine. What do you want to know about them? We could find out what they talk about in their e-mails, who they chat with, where they live, whatever you want," and then speaking louder than he needed to, to ensure that Kohan and Yuri heard, "even how much porn they look for."

Molly felt like a kid in a candy store. "Can I look at their e-mails first? Then maybe we can look at what they search for."

"No problem." Stephen opened Ubatoo's e-mail search and re-trieved the results for Molly, then let her take over.

While she was working, Stephen went to find an empty conference room. Despite the late hour, he wanted to call Sebastin. He wasn't sure what he was hoping to get from him. Just his reassurance that he'd look into today's meeting would be a good start. If Molly had a bad enough feeling about the meeting to actually leave early, the situation had to be much worse than she was letting on. But Sebastin didn't answer. Tomorrow afternoon he would go to the ACCL offices to see if Sebas-tin had returned or if they could at least reach him. Talking to anyone there would be comforting.

By the time he returned to Molly, she had closed her laptop and was arranging a large stack of papers. "What's all that?" Stephen asked.

"I printed out their e-mails."

Stephen was dumbfounded. "You *printed* them?" Looking at them was one thing, but printing them—so that physical evidence existed—that was another. Antiquated notion of evidence or not, some habits were hard to break.

"I'll shred them afterwards, I promise, but some of these are such good material for my thesis. Check out GR.Zadeh. I've been following his posts for days. He's been the most agitated, obnoxious poster on the site. And what he was posting was so tame compared to his e-mails.

Then, there's Tarik78, he's right up there with GR.Zadeh in how angry he is on the forums, but his e-mails don't even come close to his posts. Look how he writes in his e-mails when he's not posting—he's completely articulate and . . . normal. This is amazing—I've finally gotten into the heads of all the people in my study, and I did it without questioning them, without them knowing anything about it. Nobody ever has access to such untainted thoughts. This will absolutely make my thesis, Stephen."

This was too much to handle right now. "Did you at least find some information on the people you met tonight, the ones you thought might have been at the meeting? Maybe it'll shed some light on what the meeting was all about?"

"I don't know if they're the same people or not," she said, pointing to a second stack of papers. "They might be," Molly replied calmly.

"You haven't checked yet?"

"I'll do it in the car on the way home. Don't worry."

Stephen abruptly turned to leave without another word. She was taking this too lightly. The first thing she should have done was find out all she could about this night's meeting, not worry about what to write about.

Stephen's irritation was obvious. She assumed it was because she had printed the e-mails, so she tried explaining as she caught up with him. "I only printed their e-mails. I didn't need any of the other information you offered. I didn't even want to print them out and kill all those trees. I would have rather just forwarded copies of the e-mails to myself. But I figured that the way you track everyone's e-mail, it'd probably just be safer to print them and carry them home. Don't you think that makes sense?"

-ONE WAY-

July 29, 2009.

"Rajive here." The voice on the other end of the phone sounded tired.

"Rajive, it's Sebastin."

"Sebastin, where have you been? We were about to call out the troops to find you. Are you okay?"

"Listen, Rajive. I'm not sure."

"Did you get the list from Ubatoo?"

"That's what I wanted to talk to you about . . . What if I can't get it . . . I mean . . . for the price you're paying?"

Rajive's breath was barely audible in the moments he spent deciding what to say. "We're paying as much as we can, Sebastin. You knew the deal when we offered it to you."

"I'm going to need more. A lot more."

"I don't know what more I can do. Nobody is going to approve any more. Frankly, the list isn't worth that much."

"But what if it was? What if the names on the list were dead-on accurate? What if I was sure?"

"How could *you* possibly be sure?" Rajive replied impatiently.

Sebastin wanted to tell him he was sure because he knew the game that Rajive was playing, that he had figured out his little tricks with the two sets of books. He wanted to tell him that he already had the list, that he had already verified how good it was by checking it himself and that this was why he would set the terms from now on. What he really wanted to say was "Help me. I think that I really, really screwed up."

Instead, all he said was, "I have a lot of faith in the intern."

"Sebastin, even if the intern were God, he's not going to make a perfect list out of the books I gave you. They're books, Sebastin, that's all. It's impossible." Rajive's voice didn't reveal any of the uncertainty he had in his own words. "The contract stands, Sebastin. We're expecting the names from you. This isn't a game. If you have the list, tell me and let's finish this."

His last chance. "I . . . I have . . ." he could have finished that sentence in a lot of ways:

". . . the list"

". . . a buyer"

". . . proof of how good it is"

". . . a bad feeling"

Any of these would have saved him. But, instead, he said,

". . . I have to go. I'll call you when I have it."

The phone call ended.

▼ ▼ ▼

Twenty minutes later, there was a knock on the door of the *Hotel Georgian-de-Carmel*, room 151, in Santa Monica. Sebastin's room. Six hours and twenty minutes away from his home in Los Altos Hills.

M. Mohammad and the same two gentlemen from the last time they met walked in and overwhelmed the little room.

"Everything set?" M. Mohammad asked. No setup this time. No unnecessary questions.

Sebastin handed him a disk he had been clutching tightly in his hands.

Allahu Akbar, Allahu Akbar, Allahu Akbar.

In return, a package was placed in his shaking outstretched arms. He opened it, checked the contents because he knew it was expected of him to do so, and did all he could to stop from vomiting. Hopefully, it was all there, he was too nervous to count. "This isn't a game," he could hear Rajive saying again and again.

He looked M. Mohammad straight in the eyes, though all he wanted to do with every screaming atom in his body was run. Looking at M. Mohammad took all the resolve he had. When he spoke, his voice failed him. "When will you be contacting them?" Sebastin asked miserably.

There was no response.

Sebastin spoke again, looking away from M. Mohammad. "The information on all of their finances . . ." he said motioning to the disk in M. Mohammad's hand. ". . . is on schedule. I'll call you as soon as I have it."

His body was tensed, ready for the violence that might be. But the two men didn't move.

"I'll be back then, my friend, *insha'Allah.*"

-SEBASTIN'S FRIENDS-

August 10, 2009.

"What the hell is Sebastin doing? He was supposed to have checked in with us how long ago? And I'm just finding this out now?" Despite his anger, Alan Mayer's voice was barely audible over the drone of the two airplane engines swiftly pulling them closer to California.

"He's done this before. It's never been a problem. He's always come back to update us, every time," answered Rajive.

"So, if there aren't any problems, why am I on this plane headed to California?"

"He missed the final delivery. We suspect he's already obtained the list of names. He has not made contact with us to arrange his payment, and we haven't been able to reach him."

"We haven't paid him at all yet?"

"No, sir, not a dime. His full payment is contingent on completion—a list of at least 1,000 people who read, talked about, e-mailed about at least a few of the books in our list, CL-72B."

"Maybe he just doesn't have the list yet. What aren't you telling me, Rajive?"

"Our own intelligence, based on phone conversations, confirmed both by the National Security Administration as well as our own team at the National Counterterrorism Center, is that meetings across the country have been held in the past several days with a number of high-priority people that we have under active surveillance. That's what leads us to believe Sebastin already has the list," Rajive answered.

"Sebastin organized these meetings?" Alan asked, surprised.

"At least four calls were made by Sebastin. On these calls, he went as far as identifying himself as ACCL. As for all the rest, several of the other initial contacts came from his phone, and others were made from numbers that we were not, at the time, monitoring. The timing of the meetings corresponds too well with the phone calls. It's obviously too much of a coincidence for us to not connect all the dots to Sebastin."

"Meetings across the country? So, is ACCL now calling people on the list?" Alan asked, still not sure what Rajive was hinting at.

"No. That's what I thought at first. But that doesn't make sense—a bunch of rich dot-commers calling people on this list—for what? First, they're not even supposed to have the list. Sebastin was supposed to give it straight back to us, not get ACCL involved. Second, if ACCL actually did have the list, they'd be more organized, more professional— and much more public with it. We'd have heard about it on the nightly news by now. They'd be making some stink about watch lists, privacy, and civil rights. If there's one thing they do well, it's garner publicity. No, my guess is this isn't them."

"Do we have a transcript of any of the meetings?"

"No. We have transcripts of some of the phone calls—all of those were to initiate contact and arrange meetings. But no transcripts of the actual meetings."

Alan let the file he was holding fall to the table between him and Rajive. He rubbed his forehead slowly until his sallow skin glowed pink. He sometimes liked to declare that he was getting too old for this kind of stuff, but truth be told, this was exciting. He was out of the office after weeks behind a desk. Rajive could see the wheels spinning—in a few more seconds, Alan would doubtless arrive at the same conclusion Rajive had. It wasn't solely that Rajive enjoyed making Alan work a little, but when Alan reached the same conclusions on his own, things always went a bit more smoothly.

"So what do you think happened, Rajive? Are we paying a terror-ist to do our work—has he sold our list to someone else?" Alan asked. There it was.

"He's an opportunist, but I don't think he's a terrorist. I think he's found another buyer. I'm not sure there are too many other credible explanations."

"Let's be clear, Rajive. If our list has been sold, this 'opportunist,' as you put it, is a terrorist. Period. I presume he's already tried to renegotiate his contract?"

"He asked once, and only once. He never seriously thought we would. He gave up too quickly," Rajive stated decisively. "I don't think anything we could propose would do it for him. If the list is good enough, he'll get at least twenty times what we offered."

"Is the list good enough?"

"I think it is." Rajive paused a moment to let the words sink in. "What worries me is that he's already made contact with numerous individuals we've marked as high priority. Not just one or two. If his list wasn't good, maybe, just maybe, he would have found a few of these people from his list after making dozens of calls. But he didn't make dozens of calls—he called them one after the other. As it stands now, too many have been contacted in too short a time period. His list is good enough."

"Who has he contacted?"

"So far, the people we know about are either those who we were actively monitoring or those who were contacted via his phone—which we've been monitoring since the moment he made contact with Muratt Merdin. How many more people he's found, who may have been contacted via alternate means, we're looking into."

Alan exhaled loudly. This was going to get complicated fast. "So, who's buying the list?"

"Who wouldn't want it? I could name a dozen terrorist groups that would want it off the top of my head. Hamas, Al Qaeda, the PIJ, Hezbollah, you name it. This is a list of people who are ripe for the picking, if they haven't already been. For that matter, they might even make a great list of targets if you were from the other side of the desert," Rajive replied matter-of-factly.

First, before going further, Alan needed to distance himself from this project. "Look, I'm not the tech guy, Rajive. You are. I was under the impression this list was just to help us verify the intelligence we already had. Wasn't it supposed to be used to cross-reference our own list? I don't understand what a list of book readers would do by itself. I was told he wouldn't be able to do anything with the people he found."

Second, Alan needed someone to blame. "I thought you were careful? Didn't you, personally, put quite a few random books on that list, too? Just red herrings for Sebastin to try and track down—to make sure nobody could possibly figure out what was really going on? And don't tell me someone in our organization or the NSA was somehow incompetent enough to hand out our list to Sebastin. That, I just don't want to hear."

Alan's tactics to cover his own ass were nothing new. Rajive had seen this play out before. "No information was given out. And, of course, we do the cross-referencing back at our labs at NCTC. There's no reason for us to release our own list. And yes, we put in a large number of red herrings in the lists we gave Sebastin. I did it myself, just like the committee requested."

"Then tell me, Rajive, what use is Sebastin's list without our list?" Alan asked, eyes wide, relentlessly focused on Rajive.

"I suspect that he didn't *need* our list," Rajive finally replied. "There are two possibilities under active consideration. The first is that he already had access to NCTC's, our, list. If he did, yes, that would imply a major breach of security on our end. Not impossible, just the less likely of the two scenarios. The second option is that his list of names contains a number of viable recruits in itself, and he didn't need our list to cross-reference them."

"What the hell, Rajive? How could he possibly have our list? I thought we had enough random crap on that book list to make sure that any list he came up with would contain so many innocents it would be impossible for any of our targets to stand out— unless he actually had our list to see which of the names were on both lists, right?" Alan was seething now.

"There are plenty of places for leaks, Alan, as I'm sure you recall," Rajive replied, referring back to the summit held in Tysons Corner. "But, for what it's worth, I view that as the lower-probability scenario. More likely, someone did a lot more analysis than just finding the people interested in the books."

Alan, trying to calm himself, was in no hurry to continue. He had the entire plane ride to figure this out. He shook some ice out of his empty glass and chewed on it slowly as he looked out the window. The flickering light of the sun behind the clouds would have been worth noticing, on any other day. Today, though, they both had to deal with Sebastin and each other.

"Rajive, let me make sure I completely understand your plan. CL-72B contains *just* names of books, right, nothing more? You didn't give Sebastin any other info, did you?"

"Just books. But, as I tried to tell everybody before at the summit, people who bought these books are good to know, but if you look at the connections they have to other people, organizations, other web sites, you can start to re-create the intel that we have. It just takes a sufficiently motivated individual and an ungodly amount of perseverance, but it's possible. That's why we added all the red herrings. And as for them, I'm not sure how anyone would have solved that. Even if it's possible, I don't know who would, or even could, devote so much time and so many resources to that."

"The whole point of this exercise was to prioritize the people already on our list, wasn't it? Now, I'm hearing that you already know how to do all of this. Why was Sebastin involved? Why didn't your team do this work?"

Of course. Why hadn't they done it themselves? Rajive looked back incredulously. How many times had he asked for the resources, how many times had Alan said he would look into presenting it upward, to the decision-makers, when the time was right, when the economy was right? Of course, it had never happened.

Rajive replied, as coolly as he could, "Too little time. Too few resources. The usual."

Alan continued, undeterred by Rajive's inane response, "Damn it, Rajive. Sebastin is out there contacting the bastards we're actively watching, not just those who made it onto our list . . . that we're actually *actively* watching? How is that possible? If he can find a dozen people to contact in a couple days, people who we've struggled to put on the top of our lists for who knows how long . . . tell me again how he has a better list than we do?"

What was Rajive supposed to say? He could say I told you so, I told you this would eventually happen. He could try to explain it again to Alan, but he wouldn't pay enough attention to understand. Instead, he gave Alan a way out, something that wouldn't look bad when this mess made its way back to DC—and what he would say was true, too—just not the whole truth. "We don't have all the data we need. The data is much harder to come by when people aren't just handing it to you." No amount of resources, politicking, summits, or anything else was going to give them all the data Sebastin had access to.

"And people are willing to give all this data to Sebastin, and not to us?" Alan shook his head in disgust as he turned from Rajive.

"Alan, people didn't give the information to Sebastin. They gave it to Ubatoo. Sebastin just had to find someone at Ubatoo to hand it to him."

"So how did he convince Ubatoo to give him all this information and we can't convince them to give us the time of day?"

"ACCL is the darling of Silicon Valley right now. There's no deep secret to it—people just *want* to help them."

"Idiots. All of them, idiots," Alan said dismissively. "Which idiot in Ubatoo has been helping your friend, Sebastin?"

Rajive flipped through his files before responding about "his friend." "He has two contacts inside Ubatoo. The head of their data-mining division, a Dr. Atiq Asad—Asad was a former Berkeley professor, now a vice president at Ubatoo. Sebastin also worked with Stephen Thorpe, an intern—but the extent of his involvement is still not known. I'll read his file to figure out his role before we touch down."

"What do you think, Rajive? What happened to Sebastin? Have a change of heart? I guess a few million dollars just aren't enough for some people?"

"He already has a small fortune, so I suspect that the original reason he worked with us was a sense of patriotic duty. Maybe he decided a vacation home was more important. I don't know."

"Patriotic duty? Sebastin? You're giving him too much credit, Rajive. I bet he's like the rest—just a greedy S.O.B. from the start who would do anything for a quick buck, no matter how small the amount or how stupid the act," Alan countered. With that off his chest, he visibly relaxed, sat back and chewed on some more ice.

"About tomorrow—what do we do if Sebastin and ACCL are dead ends?" Alan asked.

"If I'm right, nobody else at ACCL will have any clue as to what's going on. Then it's time to talk with Dr. Asad and the intern. We need to start assessing what the full extent of the damage is."

"I can't wait to see Asad's face when they realize they've refused to give us access to their data, but they've been handing it over to some terrorist who's selling it to the highest bidder. This is going to be one hell of a train wreck." And this was the reason that Alan had to come on this trip. There was a chance, though it was Alan and Rajive's job to avoid it from happening, that this was about to become a very high-profile media frenzy. "Ubatoo hands data over to Unknown Terrorists," "Ubatoo spurns U.S.—Helps Terrorists Instead." There were a lot of bad, very public, endings to this story if not dealt with appropriately. Personally, Alan would have been fine with some press; the more the merrier. If handled with a little finesse and creativity, he was confident he could spin this story into a huge public-relations win for himself and even NCTC, but in today's world with president-mandated inter-agency cooperation and the explicit order to project a single unified focus— nothing doing. Everything had to be kept quiet. Rajive was a good man, but he wasn't ready for this.

"For their sakes, I hope Sebastin hasn't sold his list to anyone yet— it'll be ugly for Dr. Asad if he did," Rajive said, following up on Alan's thought.

"I presume that the team will be adequately briefed before we get there?"

Rajive didn't reply. It was more of a command than a question. With that, they leaned back in their chairs, loosened their ties and settled in for the few hours left on their journey. Within a few minutes, Alan was asleep. Rajive, though, still had to prepare for tomorrow.

-A TINKER BY ANY OTHER NAME-

August, 2008.

An enormous number of people had found their way onto "The List." When people talked about being on a watch list, what they usually meant, though they likely didn't know it, was either *TIDE*, the Terrorist Identities Datamart Environment, or the FBI's domestic terrorist watch list. Although TIDE, maintained by the NCTC, had been repeatedly subject to newer cleverer acronyms, the main characteristics stayed constant:

1. You don't want to be on it.
2. If you're on it, you probably don't know it.
3. There were many reasons you could be put on it and only a tiny number of reasons for you to ever be removed from it.
4. If you're on it, you probably know others who are on it.
5. If you're not on it, you probably know others who are on it.
6. There are a lot of people on it, and it will double in size before it gets a new acronym.

It was #6 that troubled those who worked with this list, not the fact that its name would change. The list grew too quickly. The problem was not in finding people to add to the list, it was in finding reasons to keep people off the list.

Within three years of the 9/11 atrocities, in not-so-fringe segments of society, on college campuses in parts of the U.S., and in much of

Europe, it was, sad to say, entirely fashionable to empathize with the terrorists, even while fastidiously denouncing their tactics. Youths, Muslim or not, were finding that the "angry teenager rebelling against the establishment" phase of life that had only twenty years ago meant a spiked haircut and too much colored hair gel, had come to mean "rebelling against American values." For too many, it meant at least empathizing with the world's frustrations toward America.

Fortunately, these frustrations typically amounted to bouts of angst and even self-discovery, but rarely to any action. Unfortunately for anyone in the business of eavesdropping, it was typically all talk. This meant the triggers for the first level of alarms that were in place to mark a person as "interesting" were perpetually being tripped. Further, with the easy availability of all types of information on the Internet, too many details and trigger words were readily available for the fastidious rebel to stumble upon. These words, when said by a person who had just activated a level-one alarm, would set off the second level of alarms. The more well-versed and intelligently you spoke of your dissatisfaction and frustrations with America, the more alarms you triggered.

The result was that the watch lists were enormous and expanding rapidly. The gargantuan amounts of data on "these people" far exceeded the capacity to analyze it. Data collection inside the NSA, FBI, CIA, NCTC, and everywhere else, was not the problem. The problem was knowing what to do with it. Until that was addressed, the mounds of evidence that may or may not be contained in the data collected were left untapped.

Insights on how to tackle this problem came from, curiously, one of the academic-outreach programs that the NSA had sponsored. In exchange for funding to support a graduate student, professors would reconfigure their work, or at least their student's work, to match the goals of the funding agency. In fact, such had been the case for Molly; her advisor's funding had come directly from the Department of Defense, one of the largest funders of anthropological research.

▼ ▼ ▼

At the same time that Harry Chaff walked into Professor Aore's lab at Georgia Tech, the blue skies of the last few precious days between summer's end and the start of classes swiftly turned to a dismal grey. Harry Chaff was the newly appointed Dean of the College of Computing and had been making his rounds of the faculty members' labs, getting to know his department. Dean Chaff loudly and awkwardly introduced himself from the doorway and added, "I'd like to hear about the work you're doing, is right now a good time?"

Had it been a few days later, when classes were in full swing, Professor Aore would have had the ready excuse of preparing for classes to avoid being disturbed. Instead, Professor Aore had no choice but to drop everything to accommodate Dean Chaff. Within ten minutes, he found himself demoing his latest research, trying to impress. Professor Aore, his students, and Professor Mikens from the linguistics department had been working on a new approach to online video recommendations. Based on a user's personal video viewing history (for example, DVDs rented or online videos watched), their newly created system would recommend other videos that the user would enjoy. The system, though steeped in the well-studied graph-theoretic mathematical techniques of finding stationary points in large graphs, was constructed with a far more accessible goal: to sell their invention to a dot-com and reap a portion of the lucrative rewards that were so easily handed out in Silicon Valley.

Professor Aore started his demo to Dean Chaff with a few compelling examples. "Imagine you've just seen a few movies and want to find another one to watch." He clicked on a few videos, *The Break-Up*, *The Holiday*, and *Monster-in-Law*." Then he sat back and let his system take over.

The screen sputtered out a few cryptic lines of gibberish, at the bottom of which appeared the automatically recommended movie titles. Professor Aore happily explained, "We've figured out what your tastes are and we've recommended that you watch *Bridget Jones's Diary*." Professor Aore watched as Dean Chaff sat rocking slowly back and forth in his chair, expressionless.

There really wasn't more to show at this point. Professor Aore tried to spell out the accomplishments for Dean Chaff, "To make this simple recommendation, we figured out that you're most like a twenty-five to thirty-five-year-old female," he said, pointing to some words in the lines of gibberish that had just scrolled by. "Then, we looked at the actors in these movies and matched them to similar actors." He pointed to another line, "We looked at the movies' genres, directors, viewers' reviews, professional reviews, and then we synthesized all of this information to give you movies you would most like," he concluded. Still nothing from Dean Chaff, just a slow back and forth in his squeaky chair.

Professor Aore waited expectantly before continuing. "Why don't you tell me some movies you like, and we'll see what it comes up with?"

To this, Dean Chaff responded quickly, with no hesitation, "In alphabetical order, my top three favorite movies are *Apollo 13*, *Close Encounters of the Third Kind*, and *Contact*." Professor Aore hurriedly found the movies and entered them into his system.

A moment later, Professor Aore was reading the results aloud. "It decided that you are likely a male—88 percent probability, and that you are over forty-five years old—64 percent probability. It recommended *2001: A Space Odyssey* for you."

Dean Chaff nodded his head approvingly in time with his rocking. "I've already seen that one, though," he replied. "What else?"

Professor Aore scanned further down the page, "*Battlestar Galactica?*"

The rocking and nodding was discernibly faster. "Really? The original or the remake?"

Professor Aore returned to his screen, trying to contain his quickly growing annoyance. The anger soon turned to alarm when he realized that nothing on his screen indicated which version of the movie was recommended. "Remake," Professor Aore guessed, voice cracking as he failed to suppress his anxiety.

"Well done!" Dean Chaff replied enthusiastically. He was impressed enough to give it further thought—but not by the underlying mathematics or even the potential for a sale to a dot-com. Instead, he imagined an untapped pipeline carrying copious amounts of funding straight from the NSA to Georgia Tech's College of Computing. "Does this thing work for anything other than movies?"

"Of course it does." Professor Aore stated defensively, as if merely questioning the system's broad usefulness was a direct insult cast upon the intellect of generations of his family. "The mathematics behind it are solid. Naturally, it'll work on any type of data."

"Perfect, I'd like you and Dr. Mikens to apply for a grant with the NSA—to help them catch terrorists. I think that this is just what they need . . ."

Though Dean Chaff never had it in him to find the right words to explain his notions enough to enthrall Professor Aore the way he would have liked, it was his job to find the connections between people and projects that others would normally miss. What the NSA needed, simply put, was to figure out the problem of *ranking*. Given that a million people were in the TIDE list, they needed to figure out which ones should be prioritized higher than others—which ones should make it to the top? Which ones were more likely to act rather than to just complain? What the NCTC needed was their own version of *tinkers* to help rank potential terrorists. And this, like ranking movies that were similar to each other, is exactly what Dean Chaff hoped Professor Aore's system could do. Though all of this should have been done from the start within the NSA or the NCTC, to do so demanded in-house experts with access to enormous amounts of data, years of hands-on experience and innovation, and most of all unwavering dedicated focus and support. And as Rajive had described in his presentation, these were not always cultivated in-house as they should have been.

Within a few months, Professor Aore and Professor Mikens had adapted their algorithm and submitted a grant that had been funded directly by the NSA. They had proposed completing a tightly directed morphological analysis of well-publicized web sites of known terrorism organizations and of terrorist supporters. They had matched the words, phrases, and idioms found on those web sites to pamphlets, newspapers, and other web sites from around the world. Based on the ones that matched closely, they derived a list of books, authors, pamphlets, and web sites that should be actively monitored. It was no different than finding and recommending similar movies. With this information, the NSA only had to find the people who read those pamphlets, had those books, or visited those web sites, and use this information to help prioritize the one million and growing names in the TIDE list.

Dean Harry Chaff may have been awkward, too abrupt, and unable to stay still, but his vague notion proved right. At the completion of their grant, the NSA offered Professors Aore and Mikens follow-up funding. This time, they were asked to create a tool that could be deployed autonomously behind the secure walls of the NSA, with no access given to the professors. The NSA wanted to repeat the same process on a confidential list of currently monitored, but far less publicized, web sites. These were the web sites on which the activities (postings, conversations, e-mails of the participants) were of interest to both the NSA and NCTC.

Enter Rajive.

Rajive took charge of the project. In a joint collaboration between the NSA and NCTC, their system was created and deployed behind secure walls.

The content of the web sites was analyzed, and, using the good professor's program, it was automatically matched to a list of books. From this, CL-72 was born, a list of books that were the closest matches to the documents that their program was asked to analyze. This was just one of the many CLs to emerge from the program. Each CL detailed some of the attributes and activities to look out for, besides just books and reading patterns, when hunting down would-be terrorists.

Perhaps most interesting was the fact that nobody could accurately articulate why any of the books or other attributes were actually on the list. The two professors who created the program didn't know anything about the conversations, e-mails, and web sites upon which the program was run (they had just handed over the program; nobody inside the NSA or NCTC told them the actual data that was going to be used) and therefore had no idea of what lists were created, nor the content of the lists (nor did they even know the existence of such lists). The government scientists, who actually ran the computer program, hadn't taken the time yet to fully understand the specifics of the algorithms. Needless to say, the expectations weren't high for the project.

▼ ▼ ▼

"I have a meeting in an hour, so just give me the highlights. Tell me what I should tell everyone about your project. I'll have about ten minutes," Alan said impatiently.

Sure. I'll spoon feed you months of work so you can gloss over it at your meeting. No problem, Rajive thought. "The most important thing you can tell them is that Professor Aore's and Mikens's work is completed, and it's deployed. We have 119 candidate lists, CLs, that we expect to get out of this. Once we have the people who match the lists, we can re-rank all the people in TIDE and any other terrorist lists we may have floating around—according to their importance to us."

"Sound like a good start. What do you call this program?"

"We don't have a name for it," Rajive replied.

"I can't present it without a name. Just make one up."

"How about Tide-Sorter?"

Alan contorted his face. "Tide-Sorter? Tide-Sorter? Come on Rajive, sounds like a laundry detergent. You're the whiz-kid. Think of a decent name. Give me an acronym. We need an acronym."

"I'll think about it."

"Fine. You were saying something about 119? 119 what?"

"We have 119 attributes of potential terrorists that we examine. The more attributes the would-be terrorists match, the more likely they are to be of high interest to us. Like CL-45, for example; it's a list of talks, lectures, and concerts. If the suspect went to those talks, his importance gets notched higher. CL-72 is a list of sixty books—read the books on the list, and that will up your importance to us, too. Some other examples—CL-11, that's a list of travel destinations. That's a particularly good one. Go to places on that list—like Iraq, Afghanistan, that will add a few more points to your name. We have 119 of these lists."

"That's what you've been working on? I can't present that. I'm going to walk into the meeting and tell them that we're finding terrorists by looking at what books they read? If they read one of your sixty books then they're a terrorist? You really want me to tell them that?"

"That's not all that there is to—"

Alan interrupted, "Or, better yet, if someone went to some concert or talk that you listed on CL-45, then we should be watching them? Rajive, what are you talking about? This is what you've been working on?"

Disgust, amusement, whatever the emotion on Alan's face, it wasn't appreciation. Unfortunately, Alan wasn't alone in this reaction. Rajive had been fighting resistance continuously throughout the development of the CLs. CL-1 through CL-119 were lists of TV shows, DVDs, symposiums, textbooks, universities, travel destinations, birthplaces, web sites and search queries, religious orientations, music, and so on that had also been matched with the good professors' program. When seen individually, the reaction to any of these lists ranged from skepticism to pure disbelief, even among the staff who ran the programs to create the lists.

"I know it sounds crazy. But think about all of these together, Alan. Individually, each one of these lists isn't important, but together, they're phenomenal. Together, these lists provide a comprehensive profile of known terrorists and terrorist supporters. When we aggregate the results, the decision of how to prioritize a person is simple: If the same person matches too many lists, for example by traveling to some place on CL-11, *and* using the phrases on CL-13, *and* searching for web sites on CL-91, logically they should be prioritized higher in the TIDE list. The more a person matches, the higher their priority is raised. It's about looking at the complete profile of the person. Not just one or two characteristics by themselves."

At least the disgust from Alan's face was dissipating. Alan asked, "And, where do you plan on getting all this information about these people? We don't have anything close to complete profiles on the million people on our lists."

"We've already started gathering the information. We're handing out individual CLs to a number of our partners. We're just asking them to return the names of anybody who matches them. For the airlines, who are always happy to work with us, we've given them the list of places on CL-11; they're returning a list of people who fly to any of those places. A list of stores, CL-61, and a list of products, CL-62, were handed over to credit card companies; the name of anyone who shops at any of the stores in CL-61 or buys an item from CL-62 will be given to us. CL-89 was given to phone companies; they're always more than happy to hand us phone records. TV shows on CL-19 were handed to cable and satellite providers. CL-83 was handed out to—"

"You have partners for all 119 CLs?"

"*TIPS!*" Rajive exclaimed proudly. "Let's call the system *TIPS*—Terrorist *I*dentity *P*rofiling and *S*orting."

"Sure. Whatever," Alan replied, irked to have his train of thought interrupted—even if it was to answer one of his own questions—though he did take a moment to write down the name. "So," he asked again, "do you have contacts for all the CLs?"

"No, not all of them. Anything related to the Internet is tough. If we can't gather it ourselves by our own online traffic surveillance, it's been difficult to find partners to help. No Internet company, except for a handful of minor players hoping to gain some small favor from us, is willing to hand out any information."

"So, what are you going to do?"

"We've got a number of middle men working with us to make contact into the companies where we don't have access. We've hired the usual contractors for the task.

"They're already in play?"

"Of course."

"Fine. Make sure you check them out carefully."

"Such sage wisdom and insight… That's why you're the boss," Rajive wanted to say. Instead, he replied, "Good idea. Thanks."

▼ ▼ ▼

Enter Sebastin.

When the National Counterterrorism Center, NCTC, came looking for discreet, patriotic contacts in Silicon Valley for a potentially lucrative payout—at least in terms of Washington, DC dollars—in exchange for some lightweight data, Sebastin's name popped up. Cory Waxman, a mutual acquaintance who worked in a venture capital fund that incubated companies primarily created to be acquired and integrated into DC's numerous intelligence agencies, had helped broker a small acquisition deal for iJenix to the Mahabishi Keiretsu. It was a deal of last resort. Nobody else, especially in DC, had wanted to acquire the company. Though the reasons weren't clear to Cory, what was obvious enough was that Sebastin had fared far less well than the other founders. To throw a few dollars his way, Cory gave Sebastin's name to Rajive. For Rajive, the fact that Sebastin was now associated with ACCL was workable. The non-profit's reputation as the poster child for vocal, trendy, white-hot, liberal charities might even be an asset to acquire the data from Silicon Valley techies.

Originally, Sebastin had been slated for handling a different CL, CL-91, one that listed web sites and search terms to look for in people's activities. However, someone more appropriate was found for that CL. Instead, Sebastin was eventually given the book list, CL-72. His goal was simple: Find all the people who purchased, looked for, read either online or in print, or ever were in any way interested in reading, the books on CL-72B.

The B designation was an indication that the list had been intentionally obfuscated. If anyone looked at CL-72, they would have seen a list that contained numerous book titles with very easily recognizable and unmistakable themes: terrorism, Middle East and Islamic studies, security, and extremist politics. To supplement the original books that were on CL-72, CL-72B was created. In CL-72B, numerous random books were mixed into the list to provide the viewer no immediately observable pattern of topics. It was Rajive who was tasked to select the books since he was in the room at the time it was decided that CL-72 needed to be augmented and since he, as he readily admitted, was no longer technical enough to help in the actual hard work being done.

To augment CL-72, Rajive simply scanned Amazon.com to find books with interesting covers that also matched the criteria given to him—not too popular, a wide variety of topics, and none related to the subject at hand. He added 900 books to the 60 originally on the list, just as requested. The obfuscation had worked well on Sebastin, too. Until Stephen had told Sebastin that there seemed to be two groups of books, Sebastin never noticed or thought to look that deeply. For Sebastin, the plan would have worked exactly as anticipated.

Enter Stephen.

Sebastin would have continued to be an ideal candidate for the task laid out had it not been for Stephen's desire to impress him. In the planning stages at NCTC, when it was decided to use outside sources to determine the people who matched the CLs, the possibility of the lists being intercepted was, of course, considered. The hypothetical adversaries may have been just as self-servingly motivated as Sebastin, but certainly did not have the resources and support that Stephen had to uncover the full potential of the lists. The combination of motivation and resources led to unanticipated outcomes. The results that Stephen came up with far surpassed finding the buyers of books that CL-72B had been intended to discover. He found the people who not only bought the books, but visited the same web sites, talked about the same subjects, and had similar profiles in many more ways than simply their choice of reading material. In short, he managed to re-create numerous other CLs, and in doing so, figured out how to take into account the evidence locked within them.

All of the data was put into Stephen's graph, and the connections between people, books, web sites, chats, and phone calls were naturally represented. Each connection revealed vital, if individually minute, pieces of evidence. The amount of data was massive and the computational requirements to do something meaningful with it even more gargantuan. But it was all completed in only one of Ubatoo's datacenters in India, while the local audience there slept and left the machines sitting idly waiting for someone to put them to good use. In these datacenters in India, resided the names of the people that NCTC would, beyond a doubt, find "interesting." At the moment of discovery, all these people were happily living their lives in the middle of the day, oblivious to their habits, personalities, and desires being systematically scrutinized and seconds later being marked for further examination by a program an intern had deployed on a farm of computers an ocean away.

Enter Molly.

These "interesting" people, like Molly, were flagged for review by Stephen, who was connected to Atiq, who was connected to Sebastin, who had found a connection into Rajive's plan.

And now, back to Rajive and Alan.

-WHEN IT RAINS-

August 11, 2009.

"I hate California," Alan would mutter to himself four times today.

Today was not going to be a good day. It wasn't often that Rajive and Alan made it to California, and when they did, the least they hoped for was good weather. That was not to be; a storm advisory was in effect. For Californians, it meant there was an unanticipated severe thunderstorm and that they should probably not venture outside. For those from any other part of the country who may be visiting California at the time, it meant there was an ever-present, and occasionally annoying, drizzle on a dreary day.

It was not just the weather that put Rajive and Alan in foul moods. It was two women who looked similar enough to be twins, with short muddy blond hair hanging limply to their chins, pasty white skin, the personalities of sloths overdosed on downers, and the imaginations of empty cardboard boxes. When Rajive and Alan had arrived at the local FBI office in the morning, the local team, led by these two women, were either not familiar with the concept of being prepared or were, more likely, being intentionally obtuse. The FBI perpetually put up obstacles; their modus operandi was to move slowly—always needing to build a case and work their way up the food chain. Neither Alan nor Rajive had the patience. Not only was this their project, but it was a matter of too much information being leaked to potentially too many unknown groups. Nobody even knew the extent of the information that Sebastin had, only that contact had already been made with people on his list, people who were already considered of high interest.

The leak had already begun. Action was needed now, not after weeks of mindless observation.

To make the morning worse, their first visit of the day, to the ACCL office, proved utterly useless. Not only was Sebastin nowhere to be found, but none of the others knew his whereabouts or when he might return. The office secretary showed them, without hesitation, all the meetings and appointments he had scheduled for the past several months. There was absolutely nothing to indicate any activity related to Ubatoo. At least upon first blush, it verified what Rajive suspected—Sebastin had not brought anyone from ACCL into the mix.

There was no point in wasting any more time at ACCL. They issued stern, albeit cryptic, warnings to the confused employees and volunteers who had stopped whatever they were doing for the little under two hours that Rajive and Alan had spent there. "All of ACCL is under investigation right now. For your own safety, please do not try to leave the premises without answering a few questions. Hopefully, the matter will be resolved shortly. Until then, be patient. That's all we can say at this point." All the bewildered onlookers could ascertain was that there was something important happening—something involving Sebastin given that his office contained the most agents. Beyond that, nobody was sure what was transpiring. This was what Alan had wanted. The two women from the local office would take up the work at ACCL. Rajive and Alan had other work to attend to at Ubatoo. Alan hoped, for Rajive's sake, that it wouldn't be another dead end. So far, he had seen nothing to indicate any level of confidence in Rajive on this project. It had been a poorly run operation from the start; he would have to make note of this immediately when he returned to DC.

▼ ▼ ▼

At Ubatoo, Rajive and Alan were escorted past the touristy displays, through the manicured lawns, and across grounds to Building 11. As they had requested, three agents were waiting for them at the entrance when they walked in. The receptionist escorted the party of five to Atiq's executive administrative assistant, Becky. From there, Becky took over. She led Rajive and Alan directly into Atiq's office. The other three agents stayed outside the door, and did their best, however unsuccessfully, to blend inconspicuously into the background. Now was not the time for them to call attention to themselves, despite the three agents' official uniform rain jackets with large FBI letters emblazoned on the back.

Rajive and Alan found Atiq seated at his desk, typing hurriedly away on his computer. It irked Alan a great deal that Atiq didn't instantaneously stop whatever it was he was doing to rise and greet them. Common courtesy dictated at least that much. Alan had, out of respect, taken a great deal of care not to cause a commotion and followed the usual visitor protocol in coming into Ubatoo and finding Atiq. Clearly this had not worked to his advantage, and he needed to reassert control.

As Becky was leaving the office, she offered to get coffee, tea, or something to drink. Atiq finally looked up and started to politely decline, but Alan spoke first. "Coffee now. In an hour, a little lunch. Cancel Dr. Asad's appointments for the rest of the day. He's not going anywhere."

Becky worriedly glanced over at Atiq. Atiq hadn't yet said a word.

"I'd like my coffee hot, no cream, lots of sugar," Alan said, noticing that Becky had not yet moved. Becky was staring straight at him now. He motioned to the door with a movement of his eyes.

Becky started to leave the office. Then, Alan spoke to Rajive, "Rajive, would you like anything?"

"I'm okay," Rajive replied somewhat too timidly for Alan's taste. Rajive wasn't inclined to take part in the showmanship—not yet. The name Atiq Asad was not a common one, and though for days he had thought he had seen the name before, until now he couldn't remember where. Seeing the books on Atiq's shelves helped put the pieces together. Course CSCI:457 at the University of North Dakota, Introduction to Large-Scale Commercial Data Gathering, a seminar class in which they reviewed academic papers about analyzing data from all forms of commerce—everything from shopping site design, to online and offline advertising, to data analysis and organization. They had spent two days reviewing one of Dr. Asad's papers. These two worlds should not have collided.

Of course, Atiq could see none of this in Rajive. Atiq's anger was visibly rising. He worked hard to calm himself. He would have to apologize a great deal to Becky later when these people left.

"Great. Thanks, Becky," Alan said, turning his back to Becky. And with that, Becky left the room and started to close the door behind her.

"Becky, one more thing," Alan yelled. He had waited until the door was almost fully closed to ensure he would have to yell loudly. "Make sure you get Stephen Thorpe ready to talk to me. I want him waiting outside this office the minute I'm ready for him."

"Now wait a second—" started Atiq.

"Dr. Asad," Rajive cut him off quickly but quietly. "It would be wise of you to let this go. This is not the battle to fight."

Atiq stared back at Rajive without saying anything further. Alan, who was still waiting for Becky to fully close the door, hadn't shifted his gaze to Atiq yet. He had heard everything Atiq and Rajive had said. That's better.

"Do you have any idea why we're here, Dr. Asad?" Alan asked.

"No. I certainly do not," Atiq snapped.

"We suspect you've been supplying information—information about potential people of interest to us—to terrorist groups."

Atiq stood motionless, unable to speak.

"It would be best for you, your family, and Ubatoo, if you cooperated with us so we can get to the bottom of this now."

Atiq's mind was reeling. His world shifted to slow motion. He saw Alan in front of him, watching him—then noticed the man's gun, His anger disintegrated into fear. He looked at Rajive, who rested his hands on his hips, pushing back his coat to also reveal a gun. Was this planned? Why were there guns in his office? What was happening?

An involuntary tremble surged through his body. He wondered if they had noticed. His palms were soaked and his legs would soon be unable to hold his weight. He wondered how much time had passed since someone had spoken.

He wanted to tell them so many things at once, but he wasn't sure where to start. What were they talking about? Obviously they had

mistaken him for someone else. Who would give them such information? But when he spoke, all he could stammer was "Who are you?" It
was not spoken aggressively, but in a meek voice that Atiq himself did
not recognize.

They each slid their hands across their chests, past their guns, and
pulled out their badges. He slowly rose to examine them, but his trem-
bles prevented him from focusing. Both Alan and Rajive had noticed
the violent shakes, the sweat on his palms and the gasps for air as he
had tried to speak. They noticed all of this, and more.

"Why don't you sit down, Dr. Asad?" Rajive suggested firmly.
"We're going to be here for a while."

Alan could barely suppress his smile.

-I AM A HEARTBEAT-

August 11, 2009.

Alan had plananed his shouts better than he had known. As he had yelled to Becky to find Stephen, he had no idea that Stephen was sitting in his cubicle, only twenty feet away from Atiq's office. Stephen had overheard the yelling and the commotion. So had the rest of the interns, as well as about a dozen of the other full-time employees, including William and Aarti, who had stepped out of their offices to investigate.

Andrew was the first to speak to Stephen, "What's going on? Is that really the FBI?"

"I have no idea why they're here." Stephen replied quietly. "I have no idea what's going on." He hadn't seen who was yelling for him. He had been staring at his monitor with his back to Atiq's office when the shouting began.

"The three outside there are from the FBI. I'm not sure about the one who was yelling, though. He may or may not be," Kohan replied. He had been paying attention to them since they walked in.

Stephen didn't turn to acknowledge Kohan. He walked straight to Becky. Becky thankfully recognized him, despite having had only a few occasions to talk to her. She took him aside before he reached her desk.

"What's going on in there, Becky?"

"Walk with me," Becky replied. She started walking to the cafeteria to get the coffee Alan had demanded.

"I think those two are from Homeland Security or something like that. I have no idea what they're doing here. That's all the front desk said before they were escorted to me. I first thought they were here on one of the usual information gathering sessions, or maybe a proposal for a collaboration. It sounds much more serious though."

"Is this a routine visit?" Stephen asked hopefully.

"No. We have tons of government organizations stopping by here all the time. Atiq usually winds up having to talk to them because of all the data mining. But these two are definitely not here on a general fact-finding trip. It sounds like Atiq is in some kind of trouble."

"Do you know what kind of trouble?"

"No. I was actually going to ask you if you knew what was going on," Becky replied. "They asked to see you, too, you know."

"I heard."

"Do you have any idea what this could be about?" she asked again.

He had quite a few ideas what this could be about. "No, I don't know," was all he said.

"Hmm. I better call Xiao's admin to see if she knows what's happening. Xiao will want to hear about this, if he hasn't already." Becky flipped open her cell phone, pressed a speed-dial button and was talking a moment later.

Stephen silently trailed behind her as she picked up the coffee.

"Xiao's coming down, too," she said finally, talking to Stephen.

"What do you think I should do?" Stephen asked.

"What do you mean? I think you should wait outside Atiq's office until they're ready for you. Do you want to grab some coffee too while we're here?"

"No."

When they returned to Atiq's office, Becky disappeared inside with Alan's coffee. Through the cracked doorway, Stephen caught Alan's eye. In those few instants, Stephen felt and heard only the pulsing of his own heartbeat. For a moment, a deluge of panic convulsed through him. Then the door closed, and he was staring at Becky's worried face.

He picked up his cell phone and sent a text message to Sebastin, but there was no reply. He called him. Still, no reply.

The panic was returning. He sent a text message to Molly. "Urgent. Go to the ACCL offices and find Sebastin. Tell him to come to the Ubatoo offices. Urgent."

A moment later, his phone chirped with a phone call. Everyone turned to watch him. He could see by the number displayed that it was Molly, but he didn't pick up. He composed a message back instead. "Can't talk. Trouble. Homeland Security and FBI are here. Not sure why. Get Sebastin."

A text reply came back: "On my way." He hoped she meant that she was going to find Sebastin and that she wasn't on her way to Ubatoo to see if he was okay.

Along with three men in FBI jackets, he sat outside Atiq's office, motionless except for his knee bouncing up and down frantically. He didn't notice the rest of the interns fixedly watching him instead of their computer screens.

▼ ▼ ▼

Within thirty minutes, Molly had left her post at GreeneSmart, had found the directions to the ACCL offices, and was walking into their front doors. She texted a message back to Stephen: "At ACCL now."

The office wasn't what she expected; there was silence instead of the buzz of activity she had been anticipating. As soon as she walked in, she was ushered to a table by a man with a FBI coat on. She signed in, and was told to wait with the others for questioning.

"I don't work here. I'm just here to see someone," she explained to the person behind the makeshift desk.

"Okay, Miss. We'll just be a few minutes. We just need to ask you a few questions and then you can get on out of here."

Four minutes passed. "Look, I just need to give a message to Sebastin from my boyfriend. I really don't know what's going on here." Everyone's eyes were on her. She wondered how long they had been there. The man behind the desk looked at her, her drenched GreeneSmart uniform, and her clashing orange backpack slung over one shoulder and said, "Sebastin's office is down the hall on the left. I think his assistant's in his office. Go ahead on down."

She left behind a hushed murmur of protest from the others waiting in the foyer, hurrying into the hallway before the guard could change his mind. She hastily walked the small corridor scanning the names on the plastic plaques until she found Sebastin's office. A woman was standing helplessly as two men rummaged through the contents of the desk and shelves that had been haphazardly dumped on the floor.

"You're looking for Sebastin?" the woman asked her, thankful for someone else to witness the disaster the two men were making. Both men in the room stopped their activity.

"Yes."

"He's not here. What can I help you with?" the woman said, moving toward her quickly and defiantly, happy for a moment's reprieve from watching the other two men in the room.

"I need to get him a message. Do you know when he'll be back?"

The two men kept staring.

"No. Sorry, I don't. But you can leave your message with me."

Molly surmised that there was no chance at this point it wouldn't be read by the other two. She replied, in as even a tone as she could muster, "Please tell him to call Stephen the moment he gets back in. He's waiting for his call."

"Stephen who?" asked the lady. Molly wrote his name down. The lady showed no reaction.

"Does he have Stephen's number?" the lady asked.

"Yes, he does. Do you know Stephen, by the way? Have you ever arranged any meetings between Sebastin and Stephen?"

"No. Sorry, the name and number don't ring any bells."

"You are Sebastin's assistant, right?"

"Yes. I'm the assistant for the whole office. But I don't know Stephen. Sorry."

Though she knew she shouldn't have, she lowered her voice and continued. Concerns about her own meeting last night were rising. "My name is Molly Byrne. I was invited to one of your meetings last night. It was in a house on Parkstone Way. Were you the one who arranged that meeting or was it someone else at ACCL?" The moment she said the words, her mouth went dry, and the turbulence of the blood pumping through her heart became deafening.

The lady's voice thrust her back to reality. "No. It wasn't me, and I don't think anyone here arranged any meetings this week. I would definitely know about that. I don't know of any facilities on Parkstone Way either. But you said it was in someone's house?"

"Yes. A few men were there. I think some were from here. The e-mail I received inviting me to the meeting looked like it came from ACCL."

"Sorry. I don't know anything about it. But it does sound a bit odd. We've never held meetings in people's houses. We have our own facilities or they're held here. But, if you want, I can check if someone else here knows anything about it."

Molly eyed the two men who had now gone back to looking at the few remaining files that weren't on the floor. "Don't bother right now. Looks like you have your hands full. I'll come back later, another day."

"That'd be best. Where did you say that you and Stephen were from again?"

She needed to think clearly. *Just make something up, anything.* "We just met Sebastin at a lecture he gave about ACCL. I work at GreeneSmart," she said, clutching her nametag. She was hoping it was true that he gave talks, and that the uniform was enough to dispel any doubts of her story.

"Okay. I'll make sure he gets this, that is if there's anything left of his office once these two are done with it," she said loudly, directing her comments to the two men behind her.

Molly walked back down the hall to find the same faces waiting in the same chairs. She walked past the desk where she had signed in earlier.

"Why don't you stick around a few minutes, Miss? We still have a few questions to ask you," a voice called out loudly.

She stopped in her tracks and turned around. She was about to say something about missing her shift at GreeneSmart or making up a lie about needing to pick up her kid from daycare, but said nothing instead. She sat down in the same chair she had risen from a few minutes earlier.

When she was certain nobody was taking note of her anymore, she opened her backpack and started typing on her phone to get a message to Stephen. "FBI here. Sebastin is not. Am stuck here for questioning. Are you ok?"

Before a message could come back, she found the man behind the makeshift desk staring directly at her. She put away her phone and her backpack and sat without moving. She listened for the phone to ring or for the beep of an incoming message, but neither came.

The man lied—it was not a few minutes. It was several hours before she was called back to Sebastin's office for questioning. Those hours gave her ample opportunity to let her mind wander. How many people on EasternDiscussions had had similar encounters? The more she thought about where she was and the stories that were posted on her web site, the more agitated she rightly became. This was not a good place to have walked into. Sahim would certainly have a lot to post about tonight.

Back in Sebastin's office, the two men who had been there during her last visit were gone. This time, only two women who looked like they may be twins were waiting in the room for her. No pleasantries, straight to business. One of them held the note on which she had scribbled Stephen's name and number. But it was the one without the note who started the questioning. "Stephen Thorpe is your boyfriend? Let's start there."

For the second time that day, she was overwhelmed by the sound of her heartbeat as the blood was swiftly pulled down, leaving her face ashen white.

on any other day. Again, he succinctly replied, "No, sir." Even as he said it, he knew that someday this would be remembered by Xiao as the lie that it was.

Xiao continued to look at Stephen for a second longer, as if trying to divine whether he was telling the truth or not. The attempted divination was interrupted with Atiq's office door opening. Xiao rushed in before anyone could step out and slammed the door behind him.

Within a minute, Rajive escorted Xiao out of the office and irritably called out Stephen's name. Stephen stumbled up from his chair, foot and leg asleep from the hours he had been sitting motionless. He gave Becky a final look of desperation, and limped into the office. Becky shut the door ever so quietly behind him.

▼ ▼ ▼

Stephen sat in the first available chair at a small conference table that Atiq had squeezed in his office. Neither Atiq, nor the other two, acknowledged his presence until Alan started talking.

"Do you know why you're here?" Alan asked.

"I think so," Stephen replied.

"Why don't you give us an update on what you've been doing? I think we'd all like to hear it."

"How much trouble am I in?"

"That's what we're trying to find out."

Stephen wasn't sure where to start. He figured that if Alan and Rajive were here, chances were they probably already knew more about what he had been doing than Atiq did. He hadn't told Atiq or Jaan anything about his latest project.

"I've been creating a tool that allows our users to see how likely they are to wind up on government watch lists."

Once again, the room was shrouded in silence. The three others, who had been absently looking in three different directions, were now intently watching him. None revealed whether this was the information they were looking for.

Stephen waited for someone, anyone, to say something. Nobody did, so he continued, unsure of what else to do. "I'm not sure how many details you want. It's basically a project for mining our users' behaviors,

-WHAT I DID THIS SUMMER-

August 11, 2009.

Waiting outside Atiq's office with three stoic guards arranged around the door and Xiao pacing back and forth was a nerve-racking experience. Stephen couldn't imagine how it could possibly get any worse inside the room. Xiao was an accumulation of nerves and energy waiting for the moment to explode. Between taking calls on his cell phone and having his assistants sprint from their offices every few minutes to ask him questions or remind him of missed meetings, Xiao would glance expectantly at Atiq's closed door. Other than Becky delivering lunch as she had been ordered, Atiq's door hadn't opened since he had arrived. For three hours, Stephen had done nothing but wait silently.

"You're Stephen, correct?" Xiao asked, finally noticing him.

"Yes, sir."

"They wanted to see you as well? Have you spoken to them yet?"

"No. I'm still waiting for them to call me in."

"Do you have any idea what this is about?"

Stephen wanted to tell him about all the work he had been doing with ACCL and *Watchlist*. He was certain that, under absolutely any other circumstances, it would be incredibly well received. But this was not one of those circumstances. He simply replied, "No, sir."

"You have no idea at all?" Xiao asked crossly.

Stephen had never spoken to Xiao before; most people at Ubatoo hadn't. He couldn't believe this was the first opportunity he was being given. What he would have done for even a few minutes of Xiao's time with their permission of course, to determine how likely it is that they will be suspects that are monitored on some government list."

"How far are you with this, Stephen?" Atiq asked. His lips were visibly quivering.

"I've generated the underlying association graph. The signals to propagate around it are sparse, but my hope is to bootstrap it with more basic mining and with more user-contributed information. The graph is pretty big. It's going to take roughly 800–1,000 machines to process the billions of connections in it. I haven't run it yet, though. There were a few bugs that slowed me . . ."

Alan was irritated with this blather. He interrupted loudly with a question, "Who else is working on this project with you?"

"Nobody yet. I've been trying to get interest, but so far no takers."

"Who else knows about this project?" Atiq asked.

"I've only told Yuri and Kohan the details. I think I told Aarti a little bit, too—but not much. I don't know who they've told."

"How does Sebastin Munthe fit into all of this?" Rajive asked.

Stephen was a bit puzzled. "He's the one who gave me the data to start with."

"CL-72B, you mean?" Rajive said.

"CL-72B? I don't know. It was a list of books from which I generated 5,000 names, that's all I know. I don't know if that's CL-72B."

"This work you are doing, this new project, it's for Sebastin? It's basically finding all the people who read those books?"

"No. No. This is my own project. I just did the little bit of work that Sebastin had for me for ACCL a while ago. I was just doing this as a research project, so I had something to show for the summer here."

"What work did you do—" Rajive started.

He was cut off by Stephen. "Oh. Sorry. Sorry to interrupt. But I just wanted to let you know that it's not about the people who read the books, by the way—that was just the seed set. From there I looked at their common online behavior—searches, web site visits, and so on. I found the people who had shared interests from the initial set of people who read some of the books on the book list that Sebastin gave me and expanded it greatly—"

"You did *all of this* yourself?" Alan interrupted.

"Yes. Why?"

Rajive sat quietly, taking it all in. *This is all it takes, one person.*

Alan continued. "Let's get back to the work you did for Sebastin."

Stephen gave the details of his analyses and the results he had found. About how the first list that Sebastin had given him was likely comprised of two interspersed parts, the first a set of random books, and the second the set of books that were probably of actual interest. Rajive shook his head side to side in disbelief, as he sunk back in his chair. All the hard work and planning was torn to bits because some kid thought a list of books "just felt stupid." Stephen justified all the extra work he had done for Sebastin because he couldn't convince himself of the importance of books by themselves. His audience listened without a word.

Stephen was feeling a bit more confident now. He was discussing material that he knew inside out. Surely, they could see he did his job well, that whenever he was asked to help someone, he did it whole-heartedly, and gave his best. Finally, he told them about the extensions to the projects that Sebastin had asked for in the restaurant. Along with this, though, he had to admit that he had not yet had time to complete that request. Stephen closed his review by asking if they would like to see all the lists he had generated for Sebastin—as long as it was okay with Atiq to show them. Atiq consented in utter resignation.

Stephen walked to Atiq's computer, as Atiq instinctively recoiled away. Stephen opened the e-mails he had sent to Sebastin. Together, all four scrolled through the lists quickly, with Rajive taking ample notes.

"Did you do any other work with Sebastin? Do you know what he was going to do with these lists?" asked Rajive.

"No, that's all the work I did. I was going to do more, but I ran out of time. As for Sebastin, I think he was going to contact the people on the list and arrange meetings to ensure they were aware their actions were getting them in trouble," Stephen replied. He hoped that was a satisfactory answer. He didn't want to tell them about the meeting Molly had attended unless he had to.

"Why the hell did you give him all this information?" Atiq roared suddenly. "Why?"

Stephen was taken aback at Atiq's anger. "It's all for ACCL. They are doing incredible work to ensure that our liberties are not taken away." He felt absolutely ludicrous touting the party line to Atiq, especially when he realized that he wasn't even sure that's what the party line was. He could have said a lot more, about how he fully supported their work, but this probably wasn't the audience for it.

"And secondly," Stephen continued, "you told me to."

Once again, all other motion and noise in the room halted.

"What are you talking about?" Atiq yelled.

"At the party, on the night after we won our internships for the summer, you said to give him all the data he wanted."

The two other men simply listened. This was exactly the type of thing they had hoped to hear.

"Why would I say that? I would never say anything like that!" he exclaimed. "Despite anything you may have thought I said, you should have known better. You're supposed to be smarter than that. You can't just give out this information to anyone who asks. That's, that's, that's just simply stupid. What were you thinking?"

Stephen sat upright in his chair like a chastised child. "I didn't give any information to anyone else. All the advertisers I worked with weren't given anything like this. But, Atiq, at the party, you even called Sebastin the 'moral conscience of Silicon Valley.' What else was I supposed to do?"

"Forget the party, Stephen. You should have known better. That party was probably only the second time I had ever met Sebastin. I barely remember him. His company was one of the hundreds of advertisers we invited to the party. For God's sake, Stephen."

"I thought it would be okay. You spoke so glowingly about him, and asked *me* in particular to help him. You've got to remember that, right? Then, when I saw what type of work ACCL did, it made sense."

"It was a party, Stephen. I spoke glowingly about everyone and with everyone. That's my job, to make sure all the people at that party like me, like Ubatoo, and want to keep spending their money here. That's what we do, Stephen. What else was I supposed to say there?"

The earth was slipping from underneath him. "Do you even know Sebastin at all? Hasn't he been talking to you on the phone about this project?" Stephen asked desperately.

"No. I haven't spoken with him since the party. It sounds like you're the only one who's been talking with him. Even if I did know him, though, Stephen, I would never have given him any of the information you did, even if he were my own flesh and blood."

"What else did you give him?" Rajive asked.

"I only gave him the lists that I just showed you. I didn't give him any code or anything. He can't replicate these results; he can't run the analyses again. He only has the lists." Stephen wasn't sure if this was any consolation to anyone but himself.

Rajive walked behind the desk to where Stephen was sitting and started clicking the mouse. "I need you to look at this," he called back to him. "This is the set of queries you made on Ubatoo's databases in the last three months; Atiq retrieved them for me. For the last thirty minutes before you came in here, Atiq and I were sitting here, trying to make sure we understood the magnitude and breadth of what you've done. I need you to look very carefully at this list. This is all your work, right? Are we missing anything?"

Every request for information for the advertisers, ACCL, or even to satisfy personal curiosity that Stephen had made from any of Ubatoo's data repositories was stored here. He didn't know that they were all logged and kept for posterity, though in retrospect, that should have been obvious. Almost every minute of his life at Ubatoo for the last few months was displayed on that screen, from his first day of selling diet pills, to his work on JENNY, his work for Sebastin, and even his own project. Every request for information he had ever made from Ubatoo's cloud—it was all there, shining brightly for anyone to see on Atiq's computer screen.

"It's mine. Yes, it's mine." He scrolled the page down. "Mine." Scrolled some more, "Mine. Mine. There's some other stuff in there too that I don't remember, but yes, almost all of it is mine."

Atiq started to ask a question about the material he didn't remember, but was interrupted by Alan. "You said something about meetings with the people on the list that you gave to Sebastin. What do you know about that?" Alan asked.

Stephen at first didn't hear Alan. Too much noise in his head was competing for attention. From the mass of scenarios he imagined, he couldn't find the one that made sense. "Where's Sebastin?" Stephen finally asked in a mumble.

But nobody answered. Alan just repeated his question.

Stephen exhaled deeply. He didn't know how to navigate this anymore. And now he had to tell them about Molly and the meeting. This wasn't going to go well. He knew, now, how it seemed. Too much was too suspicious. Statistically speaking, he knew nobody would believe that everything he had said and all he was about to say, was just coincidence. This was not going to go well.

-A PERMANENT POSITION-

August 11, 2009.

Stephen had been separated from Atiq when they were escorted from the Ubatoo grounds. At approximately 8:50 p.m., Atiq and Stephen found themselves in the parking lot of a nondescript office building forty minutes by car from Palo Alto. Stephen thought he saw signs indicating it was an FBI building, but wasn't sure, and wasn't going to ask. Before Stephen was allowed to exit the car, he glimpsed Atiq being escorted inside. He hadn't been able to look Atiq in the eye when they spoke at Ubatoo; it was good they weren't together now.

Unlike the movies, there was no storming of the Ubatoo offices with tear gas, and villains being thrown to the ground amidst urgent yells; there wasn't even any coercion or hardball tactics. Instead, there was a very irate Alan, and a slightly more understanding Rajive, who had taken them back to their own offices when they realized it was late and a lot more needed to be done. Sure, there were other officious looking guards who came with them, but the drama wasn't in the flashing lights or the blaring sirens. Rather, it was in having no idea what was coming next, and the knowledge that the more truths he told, the worse things were going to become.

Just like in the movies, the room he was in now was all too familiar. Fluorescent lights radiated a sickly blue-green blanket over everything and emitted a faint electrical buzz—dull enough to pass unnoticed had there been anything to distract him, but tortuously unceasing in the enveloping silence. A clean but old table stood nearby with nothing on it, and of course one-way glass adorned the wall. He had no idea if anyone was watching him or whether this was just the first empty room they could find.

Over what seemed like hours, he repeatedly believed he caught glimpses of silhouettes behind the glass, but each second glance revealed nothing. If he was being watched, he knew he wouldn't come across as the typical criminal. Nothing in his actions could be construed as being the slightest bit defiant. Whatever they wanted to know, he would tell them. The only fact that had not yet come out, though he assumed it would before the night was through, was how thoroughly Molly had created EasternDiscussions. So far, he had only mentioned that she had been invited to the suspicious meetings because of her research, not that she was running a web site that surely some division of Alan's organization was already monitoring.

When the door to the room finally opened, he had no concept of how long he had been sitting there. Had it been an hour? Had it been four? He was just relieved to have someone finally come in. He still clutched the vague hope that someone would understand his side of the story. It was Rajive who walked in—alone. If there was anyone who would at least listen to him, it would be Rajive.

"So," Rajive began. "We've looked up your girlfriend, Molly. She has quite the background, too, doesn't she?" Rajive unfolded a piece of paper he had in his hand and glanced at it before speaking again. "Her site, EasternDiscussions.com, is doing remarkably well. Some interesting messages on it, too. What's your involvement?"

Stephen stared back in dismay. There was nothing left to tell. "Rajive," Stephen called out his name in desperation. "Listen to me. I swear, I've never even read her site. She doesn't get involved in my work, and I don't get involved in hers. She's just doing it for her thesis. That's all there is to it. You can call her to verify, call her advisor, call anybody. That site has nothing to do with me."

"But you must have helped her get it started and running, right? I mean it's not completely her doing is it? Anthropology and Political Science? From what I remember, they're not usually the ones who are quite computer savvy enough to figure out how to get such a successful site up and running in just a month, or has Brown changed their curriculum that much?"

"Rajive, you know how this is. I know you do. I helped her get it set up, then she ran with it. The visitors come to the site and they post what they post. She studies it, that's all. I had nothing more to do with it."

"Then how did it get so popular so quickly Stephen? Are you sure it didn't have anything to do with Ubatoo? It's not common for sites to be *that* lucky, is it? That's just another coincidence, I guess?"

What did Rajive want to hear? He had helped her. But he had helped because it was Molly, not because of what she was doing.

"Stephen, help me out here. I used to be a bit of a computer guy, too. I'm impressed you even made it into Ubatoo, really, I am. I know that says a lot about how smart you are. I need to ask you, what happened? So far, looking over my notes, we have you giving private information about your users to someone who is likely selling it to one or more terrorist organizations. Then, we have you trying to launch a service that tells all people, including terrorists who are actively being watched, mind you, how likely it is that we are monitoring them. And, by the way, that's all based on information sources we still don't fully understand. As if that wasn't enough, now, within the last few hours, we learn that your girlfriend is the creator of what can only be described as a successful political, usually extremist, playground. Oh, and did I forget to mention that you attended, or well, according to you, drove your girlfriend to, a meeting that you yourself admit was likely some form of terrorist recruitment? Am I missing something, or is that enough?"

Stephen was not prone to crying. But he was on the verge of tears out of sheer frustration. "Rajive, you've got to believe me. I did all of this to impress Atiq and help Molly. You've got to ask Atiq, ask Molly. Just ask them. I didn't even want this internship. Molly will tell you. She's the one who encouraged me to try for this internship at Ubatoo. I was happy where I was before, at GreeneSmart."

"You know, we did ask Atiq. He denies knowing that you were working on any of this. He says he had absolutely no idea."

"He didn't, he didn't. He's not lying. He didn't ask me to do any of this. I keep telling you, I did it to impress him, to get a full-time offer, that's all. I don't know what else I can tell you. I was just trying to do something worthwhile. I thought Sebastin was, too. You should have heard Atiq at the party; he said so many good things about him. I just wanted—"

"Stephen, all I can tell you is that you should probably make other plans for your next career move. I don't think that full-time offer from Ubatoo is coming anytime soon." Rajive started toward the door. "Here's the thing, Stephen: We really need to find Sebastin. Do you pray, Stephen? If you don't, now's a good time to start. You should pray that Sebastin's not selling your list to anyone. It wouldn't be good for you if he was."

"I told you, I really don't know where he is. I have no idea. What about all of the rest of ACCL? They must know something."

"I hope you can think of something else to tell us. Stephen, for your sake, think. I mean really, really think hard." With that, Rajive left the room, and Stephen was again left looking at his broken-down reflection in the one-way mirror.

Stephen cradled his head in his hands and closed his eyes. The panic was setting in again and it took all his conviction to stop from utterly crumbling into himself. What else could he say? Where was Molly? What happened to Sebastin? *What now?*

-FOR ADAM-

August 11, 2009.

No more putrid stench of those who had been there before him. No more vision of bodies in rooms. It wasn't the Bellagio, but it was good enough. Ninety miles outside of Las Vegas in a dump of a casino near the Valley of Fire Park—home for the next several days.

Sebastin sat in the lounge with the waitresses in their skimpy slutty uniforms. They watched him as closely as he watched them, they made sure he was taken care of—all the drinks he wanted and all the attention he desired. He had been generous with his tips. This type of attention he liked. The offer of drinks he couldn't resist, but the offers for more would have to wait until later. First, he had to attend to business; M. Mohammad would be here soon. When M. Mohammad requested a meeting, to check up in person on Sebastin's progress, Sebastin couldn't decline. There was too much at stake—safety and money, for example.

Mohammad wasn't pleased to be traveling this far into the middle of nowhere, to the desert, to the Valley of Fire, in the heat of the summer. But this was the only condition for meeting that Sebastin was able to insist upon. He knew better than to be anyplace he could be found; if Rajive wasn't looking for him yet, he soon would be. Better to be somewhere else, anywhere else. He had already handed over the list of 5,000 to Mohammad, and had been paid in full. It wasn't much, but it was more than Rajive was going to pay. The bridge to Rajive had been burned—no, scorched—to ashes. He wouldn't be going back to Rajive now.

He was on his own. If this was his life now, dealing with M. Mohammad, then fine, this was his life. No more California, no more parties at *Il Fornaio*, no more interviews proudly presenting ACCL to the world. No more. Eventually, he was certain, he would make his escape, maybe after this delivery that Mohammad was coming to check on. If not this one, then maybe after the next. But it wouldn't be much more than that. A little bit more money, a little bit more spending cash to ease his way—and he would be done. Still nowhere as rich as Mark, or even Elizabeth or Nate. No, if he were in their shoes, he wouldn't be doing this. But he wasn't in their shoes, and that was reality. He might as well face it. Just a little bit more, and he would have enough, and he would call it quits.

When M. Mohammad came in, dressed as he always was, in a suit with no tie, the shameless stares of the locals and tourists alike brought a joy to Sebastin's heart. *Guess you're not quite American, enough, huh, Mohammad?* Motionless, Mohammad waited for his eyes to adjust to the dim light and the tacky swirling neon displays on the ceiling before finding his way to Sebastin.

Sebastin stood up to greet him, his hand outstretched.

Mohammad sat down at the table instead.

Sebastin sat down, too, smiling. Of course, Mohammad wouldn't shake his hand. He should have expected as much. Mohammad looked back at him with resentment in his eyes.

"What is this place, Sebastin? Why did you bring me here?"

"You were the one who wanted to meet," Sebastin replied, with the courage of knowing that these people all around him were his people—even if he didn't know them. They were his people, not Mohammad's.

"I have no list from you, Sebastin. Why?"

Sebastin took his time in answering. He wanted to play with Mohammad the same way he had played with him when they first met. "You already have the list. I gave it to you weeks ago."

"This is not a game, Sebastin. Where is the second list?"

"The one with everyone's financial information? That list?" Sebastin asked innocently.

Mohammad didn't answer for a long time. Sebastin suspected he was imagining what he would have done to him had they been alone.

But they weren't. This wasn't exactly Times Square, but there were enough people around that doing anything more than silently fuming wouldn't be possible.

"Yes, Sebastin. That list," Mohammad responded sternly.

Sebastin looked around the room and motioned for a waitress to come over—the oldest, most shriveled, most smoke-battered one he could find. He waited until she reached them before speaking. "I'd like another drink."

The waitress looked at Mohammad and then back to Sebastin. "How about your friend, there? What'll he have?"

Sebastin tore his gaze from the waitress to look at Mohammad. "I don't know. Why don't you ask him?" She looked back at him over her shoulder, and walked away instead. Sebastin might have felt bad for him, were he not enjoying this so much.

"You'll have your list, Mohammad, as soon as I have it."

"When?" he whispered, barely audible over the talking and laughing, the slot machines rattling their coins, and the video-poker machines announcing their presence to anyone nearby.

"As soon as I do."

He considered killing Sebastin right here. It would be worth it. It had been a mistake to meet here. It had been a mistake to work with Sebastin. Yet, he had given him a list of 5,000 brothers—5,000. It would take months to contact them all, but it would happen; it had already started. He must continue working with this *kafir*, must continue putting up with him and his kind. He must do it for Adam. For Adam. So his boy could grow up in a world without places like this. Where people, people like these, knew what it was to show respect and have dignity. Knew what it was to be . . . *better*. For Adam, he did this.

"I hope it is soon, Sebastin."

"I want to be done with this even more than you, Mohammad." It was the first real thing Sebastin had said to him. "I want to be done with this, with you, with everything."

His lips were dry and dusty and it hurt Mohammad to smile. "Me as well, my friend," Mohammad said. "Pray, Sebastin. Pray that we don't find out who your anonymous sources are before you do. Once we do, Sebastin, you'll be done with us, and us with you, once and for all.

Then there'll be no more need for you—," he scanned the room, taking in all its dirty filthy occupants, "—or your friends, anymore."

The haggard waitress returned with Sebastin's drink to find the two men staring at each other, saying nothing—Sebastin feeling dizzy as the minute tremors of the inevitable swelled ever larger to engulf him, and Mohammad feeling the peace of being able to speak the truth.

-FAITH-

The moment Atiq was allowed to leave, he rushed back to Ubatoo. He arrived there at approximately 10:30 a.m., bleary eyed with no sleep, frazzled from his night of questioning, and more terrified than he wanted to let on. The first stop was Jaan's office.

When Jaan saw Atiq, he jumped up to offer him a chair and something to drink. Atiq looked ready to collapse with every shallow breath. But he did his best to remain standing, determined to attend to all the emergencies that were surely going to need his attention today.

"Not now, Jaan. Listen to me. Do you know what's going on?"

Jaan had a slew of questions to ask Atiq, but he refrained. Jaan responded succinctly, "Yes. I heard about you and Stephen."

"Good. I need you to dig a little deeper. Something Stephen said when he was questioned bothered me. I gathered up all the commands and queries that I thought he ran on our databases. The problem is that he said that *most* of them looked familiar. He didn't recognize all of them."

Atiq paused for a moment. He was out of breath. "I need you to double-check me. What else did he look at? I tried to find all the potentially sensitive queries that any interns may have entered, not just Stephen. But with the NCTC guys watching me, it's possible I missed something. I want you to do that, too—look for anything in our records from the summer that I should know about. You know what to look for. I'll convey anything we find to Alan and Rajive. I know we have to cooperate with them, but come to me first. I want to make sure we contain the damage."

"I'll do it right now."

"Thanks, Jaan. I need to see Xiao. Come by my office when you have something."

As Atiq was turning to leave, Jaan called out "Atiq, are you okay?"

"I'll tell you about it later, Jaan. I'll be fine. Stephen, though, I don't know about him. We've got to figure out how this happened." Hesitatingly, he asked, "Jaan, I don't suppose you knew anything about this? I mean they didn't tell you, did they?"

"No, Atiq. Of course not!" Jaan answered, taken aback.

"You never checked up on them, did you? I mean just to find out what they were working on or if they needed any guidance?"

"I, I, I was going to . . ."

Atiq didn't need more of an answer. The next stop was Xiao's office. He was there, waiting. "Xiao. I'm back," Atiq called as he stepped through the door.

The worry etched on Xiao's face vanished when he saw Atiq. Xiao had been waiting in his office all night. Xiao walked straight over to him with outstretched arms to give him a long hug. Atiq hadn't expected that from him. "I wasn't sure when I was going to see you again, Atiq. Are you okay?"

"Yes. I'm trying to get to the bottom of everything. I have Jaan working on it now."

"They let you and Stephen out?"

"No. Stephen is still there. I don't know what will happen to him. Things were not looking good."

"But you're okay? How did you get out of this mess?"

"One of the men there, Rajive, must have convinced Alan to let me go. I don't really know. It must have been apparent that I had no idea what Stephen was doing. It's not over, though. There'll be plenty more for us to deal with, Xiao."

"I am happy to see you here, now," Xiao said, pausing as if deciding whether to say aloud what was on his mind. "I was really worried about you. These accusations are not to be taken lightly, Atiq. The world is not always kind in this day. And you, well, you are a Muslim, my friend. A few years ago, it might not have been the case that I would see you so soon. Things might have turned out differently then. Though you are innocent, of course, Atiq, you are also very lucky, I think. At least we can be thankful for that."

Atiq stopped pacing, stopped fidgeting, and stopped thinking. He let himself collapse into a chair. Nothing he had endured that night pained him as much as Xiao's last words. He wanted desperately to fall to his knees and prostrate himself in prayer. He had not once considered his religion through the entire night, not even once. Not once did he think about who he was. It had never crossed his mind to ask for strength, to accept his fate, to turn to his faith. He knew now, though, that his faith surely must have crossed everyone else's minds.

He felt ashamed—ashamed he had not prayed for months, nor even once during his ordeal today. He was distraught that he could have gotten so far away from his faith that even an event like this had not called him back. There would be many such moments of discovery through the months of introspection to come.

"How much of our information was leaked, Atiq?" Xiao asked for the third time.

Atiq snapped out of his thoughts. "I don't know yet. We're trying to figure it out now. I hope that Jaan will be able to tell us soon. I should go." And without waiting for a response, he headed out the door, and rushed back toward his office. He needed to call his family and tell them where he'd been all night.

Though he had left Jaan less than fifteen minutes ago, Jaan was waiting, laptop in hand, in his office. Atiq was about to ask Jaan to give him a second while he called his family, but Jaan started talking before Atiq had the chance. "I've found some disturbing news, Atiq."

-COUNTING BY TWO-

August 12, 2009.

At 1:30 p.m., Rajive received a call from Atiq urgently asking him and Alan to come back to Ubatoo. Atiq had more information to share—important information. It had been a long night for every-one—Stephen, Atiq, and Molly, as well as Rajive and Alan. Since the time Atiq had left, Rajive and Alan had spent hours reviewing notes, debriefing the agents who had scoured ACCL and interviewed its per-sonnel, and fending off reporters that had already whiffed the scent of a blood orgy in the making.

Earlier this morning, after learning about Molly's encounters from the agents at ACCL, Rajive had gone through the expected panic-stricken moments in front of Alan—blaming himself merci-lessly for not understanding what could be done with a list of books. Alan had waited patiently through the hysterics, and then succinctly informed him that, as of now, Rajive's management of the CL lists was to continue, unstopped. The CLs kept coming in, fleshing out the profiles of the men and women "of interest." Until they heard differ-ently, and Alan would try to ensure that they never did, no aspect of Rajive's program was to be changed. That was all that was said on the matter. Then they returned to the task of conveying all their information to those back at NCTC—to set much bigger wheels in motion.

Their calls to their home office had done the necessary job; an un-seen tempest was arising around them. While they made their way back to Ubatoo to find out what new surprise Atiq had in store for them, in the mayhem of their home offices in DC, hurried phone calls, frantic e-mails, and urgent meetings were taking place. In less than an hour, a full-scale search for Sebastin would be initiated, 5,000 people from Stephen's lists would have every aspect of their life scrutinized and recorded, this time by the NCTC, NSA, and FBI, and if all went well, the buyers of the list might be found, too.

"The way I see it, Rajive, whoever has that list is either going to try to sell it or is going to reach out to every single person on it. Once they start reaching out, it'll be too tempting not to call everyone, and we'll find them when they do."

"That's not what will happen. They'll do it over weeks, months, Alan. Maybe over years. They'll contact them through e-mails, phones, in letters, in person; we're not going to find them. You tell me how we're going to watch 5,000 people day and night for so long."

"Rajive, stop worrying. It's not doing us any good."

Rajive appreciated the attempt at consolatory words, if that's what they were, but they weren't working. "We just did their job for them. Before I came along, who knows how many people they had to contact just to get a single recruit? How many contacts they had to cull through, how many people they found who just weren't the right fit? How much time did they have to waste trying to find just a single one? That's what we had going for us. We had time. We had time to find out who they were recruiting and watch the handful of people they were about to convert. They made so many mistakes finding even one, we had a chance. Now, we gave them a list, Alan. We gave them 5,000 people in a single shot. They just have to pick up a phone, and there's an army waiting for them. We gave them a list on a silver platter. You tell me how we're going to catch them, Alan. You think we can watch *all* of them until they're contacted, until someone actually does something wrong? We just can't do it. We'll never be able to do it. Unless I built the damn bomb myself and strapped it to my chest, you tell me what else I could have done for them."

"Rajive," Alan snapped. "No more. I'm only going to say this once, and I promise you I will never say this again. It's not your fault. Nobody, and I mean nobody, could have seen this coming. Now calm down, we still have more work to do."

▼ ▼ ▼

What Atiq had asked Jaan to do was find other suspicious uses of the Touchpoints data-mining system over the past few months. Atiq wanted to know the extent of Stephen's violations and why it was that Stephen didn't acknowledge everything when they questioned him in Atiq's office. There was some material that he claimed not to recognize. What more was he hiding? Jaan was waiting with Atiq in his office when, at 2:41, Alan and Rajive walked in.

Becky was already on her way to get coffee for everyone. Atiq immediately rose to greet them, and introduced Jaan Ramamurthi, the architect and mastermind behind the data-mining system that allowed these analyses to be done so effectively.

Atiq started simply, "Jaan, this is your finding. Please tell them what you discovered this morning, and don't hold anything back."

Jaan stood up, turned his laptop around so everyone could see the screen, and presented his findings without emotion, just the facts. The laptop displayed lines of computer code that nobody there was paying attention to, but that held quite a bit of significance to Jaan.

"Atiq asked me to look into Stephen's work and database accesses over the past several months. I looked at the type of data he asked for, matched it with the projects he had been officially assigned, and verified the existence of the disparities you already know about."

Jaan clicked his mouse and the laptop went to the next screen. Judging from the line endings and whitespace, they were pretty certain it was a different page of computer code, but again, no one was paying attention to it. He continued, "I went ahead and expanded Atiq's request to see if we were missing anything in our review. I looked at all of the interns and newer full-time employee requests for information as well. What we found was that someone else also had requests for personal information not associated with any project she was tasked to do or was officially working on, and also seemed to be narrowly focused on many of the same people that Stephen found."

Rajive was fidgeting in his chair anxiously. *Not another one. This can't be.* Rajive interrupted, and blurted out his question, "This other person started with the list of books, too?"

"No. Aarti wasn't looking for books, but she was performing a very similar analysis for web site visits and searches that people had conducted, which led her to finding an extensive network of similarly profiled people. She pruned this down a bit by looking for similarities in their e-mails and friends. Though her list wasn't exactly the same as Stephen's—it was actually quite a bit longer than his. We noticed that Stephen used many of the same people's profiles and e-mails for his data analysis that Aarti used in hers. That's how we connected the two."

Alan spoke for the first time in the meeting—his words calm, even. "Was her information leaked out as well?"

"Yes. We're looking into that now."

"Jaan, was there anyone else who used your system to find information like this?" Alan asked, seemingly unperturbed.

"This is all we've found so far," Jaan answered, relieved.

Alan had his chin resting in his hand. He looked resigned. "Tell me, you two, how is it that everyone here has access to all of this information? Aren't there any rules here? Do any of you know what your employees are doing?"

Jaan started to answer, but Atiq raised his voice louder and immediately took charge, "There are very few people who have access to all this information. Many have access to small bits of it, but only a few have complete access. The two, Aarti and Stephen, are members of my group. We work to integrate the data, so yes, they had access to all of it."

"Hmmmm," Alan murmured. No words were necessary, his expression and tone conveyed everything there was to say.

"Clearly, our procedures need to be refined," Atiq conceded.

"Clearly," Alan mimicked. "Another *clear* fact that I don't understand, Dr. Asad, is how you, or one of your managers, or stars, or architects, or whatever you call yourselves, don't know what your subordinates are doing? Do you have any idea how much trouble they might be getting into right now? Who knows what someone in your group will do next?"

"I know. I know it must seem strange. My group's success is based on the fact that we hire only the best. If we had to dictate everything they did, they wouldn't be the best. Our breakthroughs come from what they invent when they're not doing what has been assigned to them."

"I think we can see where that leads, can't we?" His calm voice became a growl. "You two have no idea what you've done. Your whole company is broken, and you, you two . . ." He pointed at both Atiq and Jaan, who were looking back at him speechless. ". . . just sit here in your office and watch it happen. This is your fault. Nobody else's. Yours."

Next, Alan spoke directly to Rajive. "Take Jaan and find out all you can about Aarti. Find out where her information went and exactly what information she managed to hand out, and what this brilliant team has done this time." He turned to Atiq. "As for you, you need to immediately start checking everyone who has access to this data. We're going to get some of our guys in here. We're going to look at this data, too, and your records and anything else you might have. And we're going to find out just how much you screwed all of us over."

Atiq knew better than to fight this battle now. There would be time later for the drawn-out acrimonious conflict that would inevitably ensue if Alan moved forward with his notion of seeing Ubatoo's data and records. Nobody was going to see that data. But that confrontation was for another day.

▼ ▼ ▼

A little over two hours later, Alan and Rajive met in Ubatoo's parking lot.

The question of who Aarti was working for was already resolved. Earlier, Jaan had shown Rajive the data she had examined for her investigations. On a hunch, when he was alone, Rajive phoned his office, and gave them the list of web sites she had tracked and the list of individuals she had sent out in her final analysis. In fact, the exact same web site list comprised CL-91B. Further, the resulting people she had found corresponded exactly to the list that was returned from a contractor commissioned by NCTC. This was precisely how the plan was supposed to work. NCTC funds people who have connections inside massive data collection companies—they get the data, give it to NCTC, NCTC maintains deniability, and everyone is happy. The contractor, or middleman, isn't supposed to sell the information to another buyer, like Sebastin had. The list that Aarti had obtained was what was anticipated, just like all the other CLs they had successfully received—a large number of random people on the list, and a few people of interest. Only by looking at other CLs and finding the overlaps would the people of interest really be uncovered. Nobody, including any buyers who might intercept the list, would find much use in it—*almost* all of it was garbage; *almost* all of it was the names of innocent people.

Rajive was in a bind with Aarti. Obviously, he couldn't tell Jaan or Atiq that the information Aarti had gathered had already been funneled back to the NCTC, and that they would rather Ubatoo not press charges. If anyone at Ubatoo could show it was NCTC's money creating these leaks inside Ubatoo, any troubles encountered so far would pale in comparison to the problems they would face then. Instead, Rajive needed Jaan and Atiq to believe Aarti's information flow from Ubatoo was going into the terrorist world, like Stephen's had. Thanks to Stephen, there was no way to leave Aarti in place. She was, after all, as guilty as Stephen.

"What do you suggest we do with Stephen and Aarti?" Rajive asked Alan as they walked to the car.

"If Sebastin sold this data to the wrong people, it'll fall on Stephen. Ubatoo will hang him out to dry. I think it's already beyond our control. Rajive, forget about Stephen, your main concern should be that none of this gets connected to NCTC. I don't think that Sebastin will be talking much when we find him. He's the only one who can put this together, at least as far as CL-72B, right? Nobody else has any ties to the buyer, correct?"

"As far as I know."

"We have to keep NCTC out of this mess for as long as possible. You know that. Right, Rajive?"

"Yes. Yes, of course," Rajive replied irritably. "Sebastin got greedy. Let's give him what he deserves. But, about Stephen, he's not a terrorist, not even close. Did you hear him talking to us? He had no idea."

"At least we agree that we should go ahead and ruin Sebastin's life?" Alan said, the first smile on his face all day.

"What about Stephen? What about Aarti?"

"What do you want me to say? We should have done all this work in-house, Rajive. You know that." It was good that he wasn't facing Rajive to witness his resentment. "We ought to find someone like Atiq or Jaan—someone like those two to figure out how to make our people like Aarti and Stephen. No more mandated 'creativity time,' no more huge projects that are doomed to fail under their own weight. Next time, we can't afford to do this work outside our walls, Rajive. Look at Ubatoo, all that data, all that security and all the other crap they have in place, none of it matters. It just matters what one little intern decides to do. We can't take that risk again."

Rajive was furious. He stopped Alan before he walked any further. "I know all that. I'm the one who fed you these warnings for years. But now, Alan, what about Aarti and Stephen?"

"Stop the whining, Rajive. You've got more important things to worry about. What do you think? They did it to themselves, nobody forced them, and that's that."

"That's that," Rajive sniped back.

They didn't speak on the ride back to the local FBI office. It wasn't until they were pulling into the local FBI's parking lot that Alan threw Rajive a bone. "Look, you want to try to come up with something for Stephen and Aarti, be my guest. It's probably past the point that you or I could do anything for him, but maybe you can do something for Aarti. I'm not going to waste my time on this, but if you think you can save these kids, fine. Make sure NCTC comes out of this clean."

"Will do," Rajive replied quietly. Doors were opening—doors that had previously been locked. He was sure of it. But which ones? He needed to devote his full attention to swiftly reconfiguring his plans to find a place for Aarti and Stephen. But like Alan said, there were so many more important things to worry about.

-DISCONNECT-

It had now been more than twelve hours since Molly had last communicated with Stephen, and that was only via a short text message. The questioning she had endured, all told, had lasted more than seven hours. Her web site and its posts had been thoroughly scrutinized, with her dutifully sitting by and providing any insights when she could. Then, a new set of agents were brought in to uncover all she knew about the meeting she had attended, the one purportedly organized by ACCL. Nobody in the room believed that ACCL organized the meetings, but she had no more information to offer. She didn't know who the group really was and the agents didn't volunteer any information, if they had any.

Molly had endured the questioning voluntarily, and didn't think they had any right to make her stay, but never once thought of asking for a lawyer. She always believed, from the first fifteen minutes to the last, that she had done nothing wrong and that the questioning was on the verge of ending. She feared that if she had demanded a lawyer, if she was even allowed one, that it would make this nightmare all too real.

Eventually, the hours in a confined room, hashing and rehashing every detail she could remember, took their toll. She was physically sick, her head pounding, her hands trembling to the point where she had to press them tightly against her chest to stop the shaking. Had someone not called a taxi for her, she would have still been sitting in her car unable to move.

Molly returned to an empty apartment and sat in her usual place, in front of her computer, to rest for a minute before trying to muster enough energy to drink some water. Though she was convinced it would be physically impossible to sleep in her agitated state, when her body did shut down, she didn't have much say in the matter. She woke an hour later, still in front of her computer, still parched.

She tried to drink something. But as the glass fell from her hand and crashed onto the tile floor, Molly couldn't do anything but cry hysterically. She rested on the kitchen floor, trying to calm herself. Soon, her small shivers became violent shakes before she once again faded into sleep, broken glass surrounding her limp body.

▼ ▼ ▼

Fighting the heaviness of fading sleep and unrelenting exhaustion, Molly resumed her search for Stephen. He hadn't answered his cell phone or any of her text messages. She could only think of heading to Ubatoo to see if he might have gone there. When the receptionist was also unable to locate Stephen, Molly asked for Kohan and Yuri. Through the glass doors from the lobby, she soon saw them rushing toward her.

A loud and hurried exchange erupted between the three as they shared all they knew about Stephen and Atiq. But nobody had seen Stephen nor knew where he was. Kohan and Yuri both assumed that all of this turmoil was a direct result of the service that Stephen was trying to launch for his final intern project. Molly wasn't as certain, but she was too tired to convey all that had happened with ACCL. Someday she would tell them about her day, but not today. Today, she just listened, absorbing as much as she could.

"Can't you just track him on his phone?" Molly asked desperately.

Kohan reached in his pants pocket and handed her Stephen's phone. "Stephen left this in Atiq's office. Atiq gave it to me this morning to return to Stephen whenever I saw him. I think Atiq really wanted me to see if I could get any more information from it, but I'm not sure."

"Did you find anything on it?" Molly asked hopefully.

Kohan hesitated a moment before answering, but decided this was not the time to quibble over what was acceptable to look at in Stephen's life and what wasn't. "I checked everything I could. Everything that I found, you already know. He only tried to contact you and Sebastin."

"What do I do now?"

Yuri and Kohan looked away. The only thing she had learned from their exchange was that Atiq made it back. At least that was something—it left some hope for Stephen, too. She needed time to think.

▼ ▼ ▼

By the time she returned to her apartment, Ubatoo's news was already being aired on numerous TV stations. When a company that big makes a mistake, especially one involving privacy, terrorism, and a recognizable brand name like Ubatoo, the media coverage is immediate and immense.

The first image she saw on the screen was a still photo of Stephen's face. Atiq was talking in the background. "We're assessing the amount of private information that was leaked. We suspect it's limited to a few isolated individuals. We're contacting them now, and have already taken the necessary precautions to ensure this doesn't happen again."

"How long was Stephen Thorpe an employee at Ubatoo?" an attractive female reporter asked Atiq.

"He's been with us for almost three months, as an intern."

"An intern had access to all the information you collect on your users? Do you always allow that?"

"He had access to some of it, not all of it," Atiq replied. But Molly knew he was lying. "And we're reviewing the details of his access as well as what access will be given to our interns, as well as our employees, in the future."

"As I understand it, Thorpe supplied this data to ACCL, to a Sebastin Munthe. What terrorist organization was contacted? Was Thorpe in direct contact with them or was it Munthe? Is Ubatoo going to continue working with ACCL, given these developments?"

Atiq was taken aback that the reporter knew Sebastin's name. He wondered whether Alan and Rajive had something to do with this. He would have to think about that later. "I have to emphasize that we're just uncovering the details now. It's a very fluid situation. But I can assure you, that, as far as we know, Stephen had no contact with any terrorist organizations. Also, ACCL is a fine institution, and we respect the goals they are pursuing. It is specific individuals who are at fault, not ACCL and certainly not Ubatoo."

"It was Munthe who contacted them?"

"I don't know Munthe. All I can say is that I trust it was not Stephen."

"Do you know exactly what information was handed over to Al Qaeda, then?"

"Al-Qaeda? I don't know what you're talking about."

"Where are Stephen Thorpe and Sebastin Munthe now? And were there others involved? We're getting reports now that others from Ubatoo might be involved."

"I don't know. I presume that the FBI or CIA or whoever handles these matters has them. As for others being involved, as I said, it's a fluid situation. We're trying to figure this out, just like you are."

"So there are others?"

And so the questioning continued, filling a full seven minutes of the nightly thirty-minute news. This reporter had been lucky in finding Atiq as worn out as he was. What he might have revealed if the interview had gone on longer was anybody's guess. The seven minutes were sufficient, nonetheless, for all to hear Atiq's revelation of Stephen's role as the source of information. And so the inevitability of Mohammad's part in the remainder of Sebastin's life was cemented.

With no other options, Molly called Ubatoo and left a desperate message on Atiq's voicemail, pleading for any help in finding Stephen. Just telling her the right people to contact to make sure he was okay would be a start. She hoped Atiq would take pity on her and return her call, but it would be a week before she eventually heard from the man, and then only to apologize and inform her that he couldn't say anything, as much as he would like to.

That first night alone in her apartment, Molly did nothing more than lay curled on the couch, flipping channels from news story to news story, trying to find the latest details as they aired.

What would follow on TV in the coming week was a step-by-step unfolding of the events of the last few days as the trickle of information became a steady stream of a few facts, a lot of speculation, and even more opinion. Even Molly's name was mentioned, but thankfully that angle was not deeply pursued. Her phone, which rang constantly one day that week, was silent the next.

Seven days gone, and nothing had changed. She hadn't left the apartment or seen the sunlight behind the drawn curtains since the day she returned from Ubatoo. For a week, the news coverage had been relentless, and she never ventured more than a few feet from the TV. The news stories continued to escalate, the intensity of the words used elevating the severity of the alleged transgressions. Seven days was a long time to be alone. It was a long time to do nothing but be blanketed by distressed thoughts— a long time to dissect each possible "what if" and "maybe." All Stephen did was help Sebastin. What had Stephen done wrong? More was behind this than anyone was saying. The feeling made her long to be with people who still cared, people who wanted to know what was left unsaid.

The confusion and desperation of the seven days held few, if any, flashes of actual clarity, though at times she may have mistaken some moments as such. Her delusions and suspicions were numerous and intricate. Of all the theories and explanations she invented to understand all that had happened, each crumbled under the weight of a second glance, except for one.

She had been questioned. Stephen had been questioned. She was free, but Stephen wasn't. Who could take him and prevent him from contacting her? What had he done to warrant this? She was the one who created the web site and had attended the meeting. If anything, she should have been the one in custody, not Stephen. All he had done was tell her about the meeting. He had read her e-mail to find out about it. No, that wasn't the case; it was more than that. He knew she was on the list before she received her e-mail. He knew to look there. This insight, or more accurately, this recollection, put her on the first step to finding her own truth.

Stephen knew she would be on the list because he created the list. He knew everyone who was on the list, and had shared it with Sebastin. That Stephen wasn't with her today was an unmistakable sign that whatever he had found was credible. *If Stephen had done as much research on these people as he had offered to do for her that night at Ubatoo, Stephen probably knew everything about them—who they were, where they lived, their friends, their e-mails, and maybe much more. With all this in his head, how could he ever be set free?* She was here at home because all this wasn't about her or EasternDiscussions or the meetings she had attended. *This was about Stephen and what he knew. This was about Stephen and what he had uncovered in Ubatoo's data.*

She was close. Through a series of misconceptions, incomplete knowledge, and the steadfast belief that Stephen could not have done all he had been accused of, her final theory, the one she could not easily dispel, verged as close to the truth as any ever would. Perhaps it didn't matter that she didn't know and couldn't infer any more of the details of what had transpired. Even if she had, the anger and the consequences would have been the same.

She read again the private e-mails she had printed on that night at Ubatoo, from GR.Zadeh and Tarik78's accounts, the angriest and most vocal of the posters on her site. As Sahim, she initiated contact with both of them—the closest she had come to speaking to anyone in seven days. She wrote to them privately of her hypothesis, and asked only for their opinion, nothing more. Tarik78 was the first to reply. In his response, the reasoned writing and evenhanded consideration of her conjectures seemed well thought out. By the end of his e-mail, he affirmed the likely veracity of her theories. She believed Tarik78's response; he had understood all she was trying to convey.

The clarity that eluded her earlier had finally been found.

-SAHIM-

Seven days alone. Seven days and finally clarity had come. But who to tell? Who would believe her? Molly turned to the only place she could. She posted a message on her web site, EasternDiscussions.com. She needed everything these forums provided, support, a place to be among friends, and a place to be heard.

> Brothers,
>
> Have you all been watching the news? It seems that everyone is convinced more than ever that Ubatoo has been leaking their information to terrorist groups. Absurd. Do not believe it. I have many friends who know the accused person, Stephen, and they all proclaim that the charges and accusations are nothing but lies.
>
> Why, then, is all of this happening? The reasons are not always what they appear. But maybe this will help. Let me ask you, what government wouldn't want to know what Ubatoo knows? Wouldn't want to see the e-mails we've written and the friends that we have? How else could they credibly demand this information other than to create this sense of urgency and panic through the veil of terrorism? All of you who pray for peace must also pray that Ubatoo's information does not wind up in the wrong hands because of this. Think carefully of how all that Ubatoo knows about

us can be used by our enemies. No, it is better for all of our sakes that this box be left closed.

What will be next? Stephen is in custody now. What will become of him? I fear he will not be the last to suffer from this latest attempt by "our" government to crawl into every part of our lives — through any lies necessary. What lengths will they go to next, when such sickening witch hunts cannot mask their even worse true intentions?

Tell me, what should we do now?

—Sahim

Within five minutes she had a response. Within an hour, 20, and within three hours, well over 500. For EasternDiscussions.com, Ubatoo's indiscretions were exactly the event it needed to cement its long-term survival. Somehow, Sahim's posts always seemed to know more about Ubatoo than what was in the news. Users returned often to see what insights he might offer next. The large crowds on EasternDiscussions attracted even larger crowds, and the traffic to Molly's web site soared with new members needing a place to rant about the latest news and receive Sahim's wisdom. As Molly had documented already, controlling the opinion of a message board wouldn't be difficult. Her message boards became the playground of all things anti-U.S. Whether she just let it happen, or ensured that it did, is a matter of opinion.

Feeling empowered from her posting and the flood of responses it incited, she wanted to do more. But she didn't need to. She had already opened her readers' eyes to an alternate, deceitful, interpretation of the events taking place around them. Hundreds of posters on her site now passionately spoke of Ubatoo's data and how to most effectively harness it for their own use. For many, the Stephen on TV became a role model. Once the extent of the data collected by Ubatoo was made public, editorialized, and sensationalized, it was too much for anyone with a cause not to crave access. Next year, thousands of would-be Stephens would apply for internships. The intern candidate pool would swell to its largest ever.

▼ ▼ ▼

August 28, 2009.

After two weeks of nonstop coverage, Stephen Thorpe's moment was over. The next time Molly would see Stephen's face was when an old photo of him was shown on TV the day Sebastin's body was found in a hotel room ninety miles outside Las Vegas on August 28, 2009, apparently only hours after he was executed. The only new lead was a cocktail waitress who claimed to have last seen him with a "Suspicious, foreign-looking man." Sebastin's life and death became the talk of the media: Successful entrepreneur in Silicon Valley, working as the co-founder of a wildly successful activist group, who had sold his loyalties to the highest bidder, to a tragic end. The story was built for primetime news and glitzy breaking-news special reports. Neither Molly, Stephen, nor anyone else, would find out who the original buyer of the data was supposed to be or who the final buyer actually was. All of that information, if known, was diligently redacted for reasons of national security.

▼ ▼ ▼

It would be more than a month before she found a letter from Stephen waiting in her mailbox. She had never seen his handwriting before and it was left unsigned. He was okay, he missed her terribly, and he wasn't sure when, or even if, he'd ever be able to return. But if it were possible, he promised to contact her somehow whenever he could. He told her again how much he admired her for what she was doing, and wished her all the best in finishing her thesis, something he would have been much better off having done, if he had only remained on that path many years ago.

"Life and circumstances will be different if we can ever see each other again. As much as I want to, I can't change that," he wrote. The letter ended simply. There was so much more he would like to say, but for now, perhaps it was better left unsaid. No amount of her own brilliance, homework, or research could help her now. He was already resigned to something she was not prepared to endure.

She could not know it then, but with the appropriate amount of introspection she would eventually be able to pinpoint this moment as the one in which an important transition occurred. Life from then on would have little resemblance to her life just seconds before. She had started as an isolated researcher, studying the politics and science of message boards, and had become a devout participant in the lives she encountered there. She needed the support of people who still cared about the anger she was feeling and who shared in her venom—first toward the men who took Stephen, and then to all those unseen people who, through their silence, refused to do anything about it. She needed to be a part of the people who believed she should not sit idly by and wait for something to happen. She needed to act.

To her readers, she never revealed her real name or the extent of her rage, though the words she would go on to write were clear and unmistakable in their intent. Her endless flow of intensity needed a channel and her readers obliged by providing a clear one. The impassioned support, responses, and unwavering encouragement bestowed upon her from her ardent followers would give her the resolve needed to continue on her newfound path. In less time than she and Stephen had together, she would come to reinvent herself into someone primed to let her still fresh, still stinging, resentment overtake all else: Sahim.

-EPILOGUE: BEGINNINGS-

December 25, 2009.

"That's a pretty mean look you're giving the coffee machine," she said.

A small yelp escaped Stephen as he whirled around to find Aarti smiling at him. He figured the office was completely empty today. "What are you doing here?"

"Same as you, I imagine—might as well come into work. Not much else to do. My travel schedule seems to have been taken care of for me."

"Yeah, I know. Coffee's terrible here," Stephen replied, waiting for the antiquated vending machine to dispense its $0.75 of acrid sludge. He slammed the vending machine, hoping to convince it to at least hurry.

"Why don't you just write Molly again, Stephen? They didn't find out the last time. You haven't written her in months."

His gaze didn't waver from the vending machine, so she continued. "Stephen, you've been absolutely miserable. For her sake, and yours, write her again."

He looked up at her, as if to start the same conversation they'd had dozens of times before. But not again. Not today. He reached through the stream of coffee dispensing into his cup, and let the liquid scald his hand. With his cup half empty, he turned his back to her and started walking away.

"Hey. Wait. I have something for you," she opened her backpack and held out a small package neatly wrapped in red and green paper with a shiny gold ribbon. "Thought it might cheer you up."

He looked at her, then the package, then back at her. He took it from her hands slowly. "Thanks." He visibly relaxed his shoulders and stammered some apology for his behavior.

An awkward moment passed. Only when she looked like she might walk away did he speak again. "Do you have a second? I have something for you, too. It's in my office."

They turned to walk together through the empty building. "So why are you here today?" he asked again as they entered the musty concrete stairwell.

"What else was I supposed to do? No contact with family, no contact with friends, remember? Those are the terms for you and I," she smiled. Then, in her languid British accent, she added, "Screw Alan."

"Screw Alan, indeed," Stephen replied. "Prison would have been better for us. Cush life, white-collar criminal, playing golf all day, or whatever it is they do . . ."

"I'm not sure it would have been quite that good—not if Alan had his way. He'd have pushed the terrorist threat, made up some intent on our part, found the nearest firing squad, or just pulled the trigger himself if he had the chance. Not that Ubatoo would have minded. They would have had a field day with you and me. It would have been ugly. How Rajive managed this deal, I have no idea. Still, though, screw Rajive," she concluded.

"Yep, now we're just Rajive's play things. Screw Rajive," he agreed with a nod.

"By the way, I know it's Christmas, but since we're here, just curious. I don't suppose you've gotten anywhere tracking down the whereabouts of Rajive's newest top-priority urgent global menace have you?" The sarcasm in her voice was good to hear. She usually kept it in check during normal office hours.

"Dorothy, we're not in Ubatoo anymore. No, it's going to take some time. Hopefully, I'll be able to work my way through all the telephone transcripts by next week. Did you have any luck on your end?"

"Not yet. Still waiting to free up some computer resources so I can start analyzing their credit card transactions, too," she replied as she sat down in Stephen's windowless closet of an office.

"I don't think we'd be able to get the same resources even if we were still at Ubatoo. With all of the announced employee—especially intern—monitoring and the dozens of oversight committees they've promised to look into people's privacy, sounds like things are going to be a mess there, at least internally, for a long time."

"You think so? Even for Atiq's group? That would pretty much kill or cripple everything our . . . I mean his . . . group did."

Stephen tried to imagine life in Atiq's group with committees questioning all the experiments he ran that summer for the countless advertisers, for Jaan, for ACCL, for Sebastin. "I bet the rules apply to his group. After all, his group was the reason they were created. But I'd also be willing to bet you that Jaan either doesn't know about the rules and committees or, if he does, he never pays any attention to them. It's probably too mundane for him to think about, and—"

"—and Atiq will never even notice," she said, jumping to his conclusion for him.

"Until one of them winds up in here, with us," Stephen added with a smile.

He sat a moment sipping his coffee, letting the air of business adequately dissipate. It only took a few seconds, given neither wanted to be at work.

Stephen reached into his desk and pulled out her Christmas present carefully. "I don't know if you'll like it. It's an 1894 edition of *Pride and Prejudice*. It's not in the best condition, but I thought . . . anyway, I hope you like it. I know I should have wrapped—"

"I can't believe it! I've always wanted this—ever since I first read it. Thank you. Thank you so much," she leaned close and gave him a kiss on his cheek. "It's perfect. It really is."

Stephen reached across his desk and picked up his gift that he had set down when he walked in. He tore away the holiday wrapping paper—the complete *Freddie Krueger's Nightmare on Elm Street* series. "I love horror movies," he exclaimed. "How did you know I liked . . ."

The fluorescent lights did nothing to diminish the shimmer in her eyes and her happy joyful smile—a smile that had been missing for months. She held up her book and beamed. "The same way you knew *exactly* what I wanted, I suspect."

The End

Acknowledgments

Writing is often regarded as a lonely pursuit. True as that is, publishing one's writing requires interacting with many people. I am greatly indebted to the Princeton University Press, in particular to Vickie Kearn and her excellent team, for guiding me through this process. My appreciation for her constant encouragement and kind words cannot be overstated.

At Google, my managers and wonderful colleagues have all been supportive of my writing pursuits. Life would have been difficult, and certainly far less interesting, had it been any other way.

I have sought the critique and selfishly requested the time of many family members and friends throughout this process. For all those who read early drafts and provided such thoughtful feedback, I would like to express how indebted I am to you for your help. Let me assure you again that any mean glances, muttering, and rolling eyes that might have initially been construed as my being defensive, were just my own unique ways of saying thank you.

I would like to give special thanks to Todd Wiggins. He had the misfortune of being the first "outsider" to read my first (of many) "final versions." Todd, I officially apologize for putting you through that. Although, beware, if you let me, I would do it again—your insightful critique helped reshape the book from the first page to the last.

To the person to whom I should say the most, my wife, Kaari, I'm at the greatest loss for words. In a year in which our lives were turned upside down, she made the time to read countless drafts, provide unfathomable amounts of reassurance, and give endless encouragement at all hours of the day and especially the night. She did this all while having to endure the great variety of moods and insecurities inherent in an "aspiring writer." I don't know how she did it. I am, truly, in awe. Thank you.

Finally, a note to my two children, Ashwin and Emma. My daughter is at the age where books are more tasty than interesting. She seemed to enjoy the drafts. My son declared this to be the "best book ever," long before it was finished. Someday, when you're old enough to read it, I hope you still like it. This book is for you two.

— Shumeet Baluja

Know More

The Silicon Jungle is a work of fiction. The companies, people, numbers, and anything else that can be misconstrued as fact, are fictional. Really.

The research for this book was often exciting, sometimes scary, and always thought provoking. For those who want to read more, I've provided a few places to start your search. Note, all the links and references below are provided for information and sometimes amusement. The thoughts expressed on them are their own—not mine. Their perspectives are yours to consider or ignore. All of them provide ample fodder for the imagination—whether you're a mathematician, a conspiracy theorist, or both.

All the best in your pursuits.

First and foremost, documents addressing data mining and civil liberties:

Executive Committee on SIGINT—KDD (2003), "Data Mining" Is NOT Against Civil Liberties, by the Executive Committee on ACM Special Interest Group on Knowledge Discovery and Data Mining. See *SIGKDD.org*: http://www.sigkdd.org/civil-liberties.pdf.

Thuraisingham, B. (2002) "Data Mining, National Security, Privacy and Civil Liberties." *SIGKDD Explorations Newsletter* 4, 2 (Dec. 2002), 1–5.

Carafano, J. (2007) "Promoting Security and Civil Liberties: The Role of Data Mining in Combating Terrorism," The Heritage Foundation (Jan. 10, 2007). http://www.heritage.org/Research/Homeland Security/tst010907a.cfm

The Privacy Policy of a few organizations, in their own words (as found in April, 2009):

Microsoft:
http://privacy.microsoft.com/

Google:
http://www.google.com/privacy.html

Yahoo:
http://privacy.yahoo.com

Facebook:
http://www.facebook.com/policy.php

MySpace:
http://www.myspace.com/index.cfm?fuseaction=misc.privacy

YouTube:
http://www.youtube.com/t/privacy

Amazon:
http://www.amazon.com/gp/help/customer/display
.html?nodeId=468496

TRUSTe:
http://www.truste.org/

References

Chapter: Touchpoints
Chapter: An Understatement

Assael, H. (2005) "A Demographic and Psychographic Profile of Heavy Internet Users and Users by Type of Internet Usage," *Journal of Advertising Research*, 45:1: 93–123.

Ayers, I. (2007) *Super Crunchers: Why Thinking-by-Numbers Is the New Way to Be Smart*, Bantam.

Bilchev, G. and Marston, D. (2003) "Personalised Advertising—Exploiting the Distributed User Profile," *BT Technology Journal* 21, 1 (Jan. 2003), 84–90.

Claypool, M., Le, P., Wased, M., and Brown, D. (2001) "Implicit Interest Indicators." In *Proceedings of the 6th International Conference on Intelligent User Interfaces* (Santa Fe, New Mexico, United States, January 14–17, 2001). IUI '01. ACM, New York, NY, 33–40.

ClickZ (1999) "Engage Launches Profile Based Web-Wide Ad Network," *ClickZ* (Oct. 13, 1999), http://www.clickz.com/216871.

Fink, J. and Kobsa, A. (2000) "A Review and Analysis of Commercial User Modeling Servers for Personalization on the World Wide Web," *User Modeling and User-Adapted Interaction* 10, 2–3 (Feb. 2000), 209–49.

Fox, S., Karnawat, K., Mydland, M., Dumais, S., and White, T. (2005) "Evaluating Implicit Measures to Improve Web Search," *ACM Trans. Inf. Syst.* 23, 2 (Apr. 2005), 147–68.

Germanakos P., Tsianos N., Lekkas Z., Mourlas C., and Samaras G. (2008) "Realizing Comprehensive User Profile as the Core Element of Adaptive and Personalized Communication Environments and Systems," *The Computer Journal Advance Access* published online on April 4, 2008.

Guo, F., Liu, C., Kannan, A., Minka, T., Taylor, M., Wang, Y., and Faloutsos, C. (2009) "Click Chain Model in Web Search," *Proceedings of the 18th International Conference on World Wide Web, WWW-2009*, 11–20.

Hassan, A., Jones, R., and Klinkner, K. L. (2010) "Beyond DCG: User Behavior as a Predictor of a Successful Search," *Proceedings of the Third ACM International Conference on Web Search and Data Mining* (New York: February 4–6, 2010). WSDM '10. ACM, New York: 221–30.

Jansen, B. (2007) "Preserving the Collective Expressions of the Human Consciousness," *Query Log Analysis: Social and Technological Challenges: A Workshop at the 16th International World Wide Web Conference.*

Joachims, T. and Radlinski, F. (2007) "Search Engines that Learn from Implicit Feedback," *Computer* 40, 8 (Aug. 2007), 34–40.

Karagiannis, T. and Vojnovic, M. (2009) "Behavioral Profiles for Advanced Email Features," *Proceedings of the 18th International Conference on World Wide Web, WWW-2009*, 711–20.

Katz, R. (2009) "Tech Titans Building Boom," *IEEE-Spectrum Online*, http://www.spectrum.ieee.org/feb09/7327.

Kelly, D. and Teevan, J. (2003) Implicit Feedback for Inferring User Preference: A Bibliography. *SIGIR Forum* 37, 2 (Sep. 2003), 18–28.

Markoff, J. (2008) "You're Leaving a Digital Trail. What about Privacy?" *The New York Times* (Nov. 29, 2008), http://www.nytimes.com/2008/11/30/business/30privacy.html.

McDonald, J. (2008) "China Reports It's Tied U.S. for Most Internet Users," *USA Today.com*, 4/24/2008, http://www.usatoday.com/tech/products/2008-04-24-3250683510_x.htm.

Narayanan, A. and Shmatikov, V. (2009) "De-anonymizing Social Networks," *IEEE Symposium on Security and Privacy*, 2009.

Pasca, M., Lin, D., Bigham J., Lifchits, A., and Jain, A. (2006) "Names and Similarities on the Web: Fact Extraction in the Fast Lane," *Proceedings of the 21st International Conference on Computational Linguistics and 44th Annual Meeting of the Association for Computational Linguistics* (COLING-ACL-06), 809–16.

Shankland, S. (2009) "Google Uncloaks Once-Secret Server," *CNET News* (Apr. 1, 2009), http://news.cnet.com/8301-1001_3-10209580-92.html.

Smith, G., and Ashman, H. (2009) "Evaluating Implicit Judgments from Image Search Interactions," *Proceedings of the WebSci '09: Society On-Line*, 18–20.

Song, Y., and Leung, T. (2006) "Context-aided Human Recognition—Clustering," *Proceedings of the 9th European Conference on Computer Vision*, 382–95.

Stamou, S. and Efthimiadis, E. N. (2010) "Interpreting User Inactivity on Search Results," *Advances in Information Retrieval: Proceedings of the 32nd European Conference on IR Research* (ECIR).

Story, L. (2008) "To Aim Ads, Web Is Keeping Closer Eye on You," *The New York Times*, March 10, 2008, http://www.nytimes.com/2008/03/10/technology/10privacy.html.

Thomas G., *Method and Apparatus for Determining Behavioral Profile of a Computer User.* Patent #5848396.

Vishwanath, K., Greenberg, A., and Reed, D. (2009) "Modular Data Centers: How to Design Them?" *High-Performance Distributed Computing, Proceedings of the 1st ACM Workshop on Large-Scale System and Application Performance*, 3–10.

Yan J., Liu N., Wang G., Zhang W., Jiang Y., and Chen Z. (2009) "How Much Can

Behavioral Targeting Help Online Advertising?" *Proceedings of the 18th International Conference on World Wide Web, WWW-2009*, 261–70.

Youn, S., Lee, M., and Doyle, K. (2003) "Lifestyles of Online Gamers: A Psychographic Approach," *Journal of Interactive Advertising*, 3:2.

Zetter, K. (2009) "Yahoo, Verizon: Our Spy Capabilities Would 'Shock,' 'Confuse' Consumers," www.wired.com (Dec. 1, 2009), http://www.wired.com/threatlevel/2009/12/wiretap-prices

Zheng, Y. T., Zhao, M., Song, Y., Adam, H., Buddemeir, U., Bissaco, A., Brucher, F., Chua, T. S., and Neven, H. (2009) "Tour the World: Building a Web-Scale Landmark Recognition Engine," *Computer Vision and Pattern Recognition Conference*, 2009.

A recent job posting for Yahoo.com:
http://www.job.com/my.job/sup/appTo=32758541/p=1/jsOn=1.

Chapter: Mollycoddle

Eliot, T. S. (1917) "The Love Song of J. Alfred Prufrock," *Prufrock and Other Observations*.

Chapter: Anthropologists in the Midst
Chapter: Subjects
Chapter: Control

Abbasi, A. (2007), "Affect Intensity Analysis of Dark Web Forums," *Intelligence and Security Informatics, 2007 IEEE*, May 23–24, 2007, 282–88.

ANI. (2008) "Extremist Groups Using Facebook, MySpace, YouTube to Recruit Members," *ANI* November 20th, 2008, http://www.thaindian.com/newsportal/india-news/extremist-groups-using-facebook-myspace-youtube-to-recruit-members_100121244.html.

Bermingham, A., Conway, M., McInerney, L., O'Hare, N., and Smeaton, A. (2009) "Combining Social Network Analysis and Sentiment Analysis to Explore the Potential for Online Radicalisation," *2009 International Conference on Advances in Social Network Analysis and Mining*.

Bickart, B., and Schindler, R. M. (2001) "Internet Forums as Influential Sources of Consumer Information," *Journal of Interactive Marketing*, vol. 15, no. 3, 31–40.

Blakely, K. (2009) "Reaching the Masses on Their Own Time: The Parallel between Viral Marketing and Psychological Operations," *IOSphere: The Professional Journal of Joint Information Operations*, Spring 2009, http://www.au.af.mil/info-ops/iosphere.htm.

Chau, M. and Xu, J. (2006) "A Framework for Locating and Analyzing Hate Groups in Blogs," *PACIS 2006 Proceedings*, http://www.fbe.hku.hk/~mchau/papers/Blog_PACIS.pdf.

———. (2007) "Mining Communities and Their Relationships in Blogs: A Study of Online Hate Groups," *Int. J. Hum.-Comput. Stud.*, vol. 65, no. 1 (Jan. 2007), 57–70.

Choi, J. and Danowski, J. (2002) "Making a Global Community on the Net—Global Village or Global Metropolis?: A Network Analysis of Usenet Newsgroups," *Journal of Computer-Mediated Communication*, vol. 7, no. 3.

Conway, M. (2007) "Terrorism and the Making of the 'New Middle East': New Media Strategies of Hizbolla and al Qaeda," in Seib, Philip (ed.) *New Media and the New Middle East*, Palgrave Macmillan.

Crilley, K. (2001) "Information Warfare: New Battlefields Terrorists, Propaganda, and the Internet," *Aslib Proceedings* (Jul./Aug. 2001), 53, 7.

DiMaggio P., Hargittai E., Neuman, W., and Robinson J. (2001) "Social Implications of the Internet," *Annual Review of Sociology* (2001), 27.

Dringus, L. P. and Ellis, T. (2005) "Using Data Mining as a Strategy for Assessing Asynchronous Discussion Forums," *Comput. Educ.* 45, 1 (Aug. 2005), 141–60.

Efaw, J. M. (2009) "Social Networking Services: The New Influence Frontier," *IO-Sphere: The Professional Journal of Joint Information Operations.* Winter, 2009. http://www.au.af.mil/info-ops/iosphere.htm.

EFYtimes.com. (2007) "Wonders of Internet Now in Remote Villages," *EFYtimes.com*, http://www.efytimes.com/efytimes/fullnews.asp?edid=18592.

Gerstenfeld, P. B., Grant D. R., and Chiang, C. P. (2003) "Hate Online: A Content Analysis of Extremist Internet Sites," *Analyses of Social Issues and Public Policy*, vol. 3, no. 1, 29–44.

Hawkey, M. A. (2008) "Depression, the Internet, and Ethnography: A Study of Online Support Forums and the Methodology Used." A thesis presented in partial fulfillment of the requirements for a Master of Arts degree in Social Anthropology at Massey University, Albany Campus, http://muir.massey.ac.nz/handle/10179/618.

James, M. (2003) "Sustainable Internet Access for the Rural Poor? Elements of an Emerging Indian Model," *Futures*, 35, 461–72.

Johnson, T. and Kaye, B. (2004) "Wag the Blog: How Reliance on Traditional Media and the Internet Influence Credibility Perceptions of Weblogs among Blog Users," *Journalism & Mass Communication Quarterly*, vol. 81, no. 3 (Autumn 2004), 622–42.

Kravets, D. (2009) "Lawyer: FBI Paid Right-Wing Blogger Charged with Threats," www.wired.com, August 19, 2009, http://www.wired.com/threatlevel/2009/08/lawyer-fbi-paid-right-wing-blogger-charged-with-threats/.

Krishnamurthy, S. (2003) "Communication Across Borders: Experiences of Rural Indian Women in Using Cyber Cafes." Paper presented at the annual meeting of the International Communication Association.

Madon, S. (2000) "The Internet and Socioeconomic Development: Exploring the Interaction," *Information Technology and People*, vol. 13, no. 2, 85–101.

Nicholson, C. (2009) "Bringing the Internet to Remote African Villages," *The New York Times*, http://www.nytimes.com/2009/02/02/technology/internet/02kenya.html.

O'Hara, K. and Stevens, D. (2009) "The Devil's Long Tail: Religious Moderation and Extremism on the Web," *Proceedings of the WebSci '09: Society On-Line*.

Ray, B. and Marsh, G. E. (2001) "Recruitment by Extremist Groups on the Internet," *First Monday*, vol. 6, no. 2. http://firstmonday.org/htbin/cgiwrap/bin/ojs/index.php/fm/article/viewArticle/834.

Schafer, J. (2002) "Spinning the Web of Hate: Web-Based Hate Propagation by Extremist Organizations," *Journal of Criminal Justice and Popular Culture*, vol. 9, no. 2 (2002), 69–88, http://www.albany.edu/scj/jcjpc/vol9is2/schafer.html.

Sterns, K. (1999) "Hate and the Internet," *Policy Archive*, http://hdl.handle.net/10207/13673.

Thomas, T. (2007) "Hezballah, Israel, and Cyber PSYOP," IOSphere: *The Professional Journal of Joint Information Operations*, (Winter 2007), http://www.au.af.mil/info-ops/iosphere.htm.

———. (2003) "Al Qaeda and the Internet: The Danger of 'CyberPlanning,'" *Parameters*, vol. 33.

Veile, B. (2003) "Hate and the Internet Curriculum," *document created for Gonzaga University Institute for Action Against Hate*, http://guweb2.gonzaga.edu/againsthate/hateandInternet.pdf.

Waltman, M. (2003) "Stratagems and Heuristics in the Recruitment of Children into Communities of Hate: The Fabric of Our Future Nightmares," *Southern Communication Journal*, vol. 69, no. 1, 22–36.

Waltman, M. and Haas, J. (2007) "Advertising Hate on the Internet," in *Internet Advertising: Theory and Research*, D. Schumann, E. Thorson (eds), Lawrence Erlbaum & Associates Publishers.

Zhou, Y., Reid, E., Qin, J., Chen, H., Lai, G. (2005) "US Domestic Extremist Groups on the Web: Link and Content Analysis," *IEEE Intelligent Systems*, vol. 20, no. 5, 44–51.

Zhou, Y., Qin, J., Lai, G., Reid, E., and Chen, H. (2006) "Exploring the Dark Side of the Web: Collection and Analysis of U.S. Extremist Online Forums," *Proceedings of the IEEE International Conference on Intelligence and Security (ISI 2006)*, San Diego, CA, May 23–24, 2006.

Chapter: Patience

Rayner, G. (2008) "Groups Linked to September 11 Hijackers Spark Fury over Conference," *Telegraph.co.uk*, Dec. 28, 2008, http://www.telegraph.co.uk/news/uknews/

3966501/Muslim-groups-linked-to-September-11-hijackers-spark-fury-over-conference
.html.

Chapter: Working 9 to 4

TopCoder. (2006) "AOL, Bloomberg, UBS, and NSA Announced as Sponsors/Patrons
of 2006 TopCoder Collegiate Challenge: UBS and National Security Agency Continue Involvement with Leading Collegiate Computer Programming Contest," Press
Release June 6, 2006, TopCoder.com, http://www.topcoder.com/tc?module=Static&
d1=pressroom&d2=pr_060606.

———. (2007) "Students from Russian Federation, China, Indonesia, and United
States Win 2007 TopCoder Collegiate Challenge," Press Release November 5, 2007,
TopCoder.com, http://www.topcoder.com/tc?module=Static&d1=pressroom&d2=pr_
110507.

Chapter: Predicting the Future and 38 Needles

Ali, K. and van Stam, W. (2004) "TiVo: Making Show Recommendations Using a
Distributed Collaborative Filtering Architecture," *Proceedings of the Tenth ACM
SIGKDD International Conference on Knowledge Discovery and Data Mining* (Seattle,
WA, Aug. 22–25, 2004). KDD '04. ACM, New York, 394–401.

Cohen, W. (2005) "Enron Email Dataset," Carnegie Mellon University web site,
http://www.cs.cmu.edu/~enron/.

Kamvar, M. (2008) "Using Context to Improve Query Formulation and Entry from
Mobile Phones," thesis, Computer Science, Columbia University, http://www
.maryamkamvar.com/publications/Kamvar.pdf.

Kamvar, M. and Baluja, S. (2007) "The Role of Context in Query Input: Using Contex-
tual Signals to Complete Queries on Mobile Devices," *Proceedings of Mobile HCI.*

———. (2008) "Query Suggestions for Mobile Search: Understanding Usage Patterns,"
*CHI '08: Proceedings of the Twenty-Sixth Annual SIGCHI Conference on Human Fac-
tors in Computing Systems.* New York: ACM, 1013–16.

Li, W., Hershkop, S., and Stolfo, S. J. (2004) "Email Archive Analysis through Graphi-
cal Visualization," *Proceedings of the 2004 ACM Workshop on Visualization and Data
Mining for Computer Security* (Washington, DC, Oct. 29).

Martin, S., Sewani, A., Nelson, B., Chen, K., and Joseph, A. D. (2005) "Analyzing
Behavioral Features for Email Classification," *Second Conference on Email and Anti-
Spam* (CEAS 2005).

Stolfo, S. J., Hershkop, S., Hu, C., Li, W., Nimeskern, O., and Wang, K. (2006)
"Behavior-based Modeling and Its Application to Email Analysis," *ACM Trans. Internet Technol.*, 6, 2.

Tyler, J. R., Wilkinson, D. M., and Huberman, B. A. (2003) "Email as Spectroscopy: Automated Discovery of Community Structure within Organizations," *Communities and Technologies*, Huysman, M., Wenger, E., and Wulf, V. (eds.), Kluwer B., Deventer V., The Netherlands, 81–96.

Zaslow, J. (2002) "If TiVo Thinks You Are Gay, Here's How to Set It Straight," The *Wall Street Journal Digital Network*, Tuesday November 26, 2002, http://online.wsj.com/article_email/SB1038261936872356908.html.

Zeitchik, S. (2008) "Technology Gets Personal: Can Algorithms Predict Our Tastes in Movies and Books?" *The Wall Street Journal Digital Network*, July 18, 2008, http://online.wsj.com/article/SB121633741917263835.html.

Chapter: Euphoria and Diet Pills

Chavez, P. (2009) "Consumer Watchdog Wrong on Medical Records Claim," *Google Public Policy Blog*, http://googlepublicpolicy.blogspot.com/2009/01/consumer-watchdog-wrong-on-medical.html.

Crounse, B. (2006) "The Future with Electronic Medical Records: Effective, Flexible, Affordable: Hospitals, Physicians Need Systems that Share Information, Require Less Training, Reduce Log-in Headaches," http://www.microsoft.com/industry/healthcare/providers/businessvalue/housecalls/clinicalworkflow.mspx.

Fried, I. (2007) "Microsoft Plans Medical-Record Service," CNET News, Oct. 4, 2007, http://news.cnet.com/Microsoft-plans-medical-record-service/2100-1011_3-6211575.html.

Goldstein, A. (2008) "Microsoft, Google, Consumers Endorse Health Privacy Standards," Bloomberg (June 25, 2008), http://www.bloomberg.com/apps/news?pid=20601087&sid=a38Kg3O.d86k.

Google Health. (2009) http://www.google.com/health.

Healy, B. (2009) "Electronic Medical Records: Will Your Privacy Be Safe?" *U.S. News & World Report*, USNews.com (Feb. 17, 2009), http://www.usnews.com/health/blogs/heart-to-heart/2009/02/17/electronic-medical-records-will-your-privacy-be-safe.html.

Kluger, J. (2009) "Electronic Health Records: What's Taking So Long?" *Time, Health & Science* (Mar. 25, 2009), www.time.com, http://www.time.com/time/health/article/0,8599,1887658,00.html.

Kohavi, R., Mason, L., Parekh, R., and Zheng, Z. (2004) "Lessons and Challenges from Mining Retail E-Commerce Data," *Machine Learning* 57, 1–2, 83–113.

Newcomb, K. (2008) "Where's Search Heading? Ask Yahoo's Chief Scientist," *Search Engine Watch*, March 20, 2008, http://searchenginewatch.com/3628767.

Nielsen Wire. (2009) "Ad Buyers Bulk Up Spending as Consumers Diet," *Nielsen Wire* (Jan. 13, 2009), http://blog.nielsen.com/nielsenwire/consumer/ad-buyers-bulk-up-spending-as-consumers-diet/.

Rodgers, Z. (2008) "ISPs Collect User Data for Behavioral Ad Targeting," *ClickZ* (Jan. 3, 2008), http://www.clickz.com/3628004.

Song, Q. and Shepperd, M. (2006) "Mining Web Browsing Patterns for E-commerce," *Computers in Industry* 57, 7 (Sep. 2006), 622–30.

Chapter: The Life and Soul of an Intern

DiRomualdo, T. (2005) "Is Google's Cafeteria a Competitive Weapon?" *Wisconsin Technology Network, WTN News* (Aug. 30, 2005), http://wistechnology.com/articles/2190/.

Jung, C. (2009) "Inside the Café at Facebook Headquarters," *Food Gal: Musings on Food, Wine, Laughter and Life,* http://www.foodgal.com/2009/08/inside-the-cafe-at-facebook-headquarters/.

Knowledge@Wharton. (2008) "Don't Touch My Perks: Companies that Eliminate Them Risk Employee Backlash," *FTPress, Financial Times* (Sept. 25, 2008), http://www.ftpress.com/articles/article.aspx?p=1235052.

Microsoft. (2010) "Silicon Valley Lab Internship Program," http://research.microsoft.com/en-us/jobs/intern/about_ca.aspx.

Olsen, S. (2007) "Wooing Interns to Silicon Valley," *cNet.com* (July 3, 2007), http://news.cnet.com/Wooing-interns-to-Silicon-Valley/2100-1014_3-6194777.html.

Ramirez, M. (2005) "Tray Chic: At Work, Cool Cafeterias, Imaginative Menus," *The Seattle Times* (Nov. 21, 2005), http://seattletimes.nwsource.com/html/living/2002634266_cafes21.html.

Chapter: Hallucinations and Archetypes

Eirinaki, M. and Vazirgiannis, M. (2003) "Web Mining for Web Personalization," *ACM Trans. Internet Technol.,* 3, 1, 1–27.

Hu, J., Zeng, H., Li, H., Niu, C., and Chen, Z. (2007) "Demographic Prediction Based on User's Browsing Behavior," *Proceedings of the 16th International Conference on World Wide Web,* http://www2007.org/papers/paper686.pdf.

Jones, R., Kumar, R., Pang, B., and Tomkins, A. (2007) "I Know What You Did Last Summer: Query Logs and User Privacy," *Proceedings of the Sixteenth ACM Conference on Conference on information and Knowledge Management.*

Linden, G., Smith, B., and York, J. (2003) "Amazon.com Recommendations," *IEEE Internet Computing 7,* no. 1 (Jan.–Feb. 2003), 76–80.

Resnick, P. and Varian, H. R. (1997) "Recommender Systems," *Communications of the ACM 40,* 3 (Mar. 1997), 56–58.

Ruffo, G., and Schifanella, R. (2009) "A Peer-to-Peer Recommender System Based on Spontaneous Affinities," *ACM Trans. Internet Technol.,* 9, 1.

Spertus, E., Sahami, M., and Buyukkokten, O. (2005) "Evaluating Similarity Measures: A Large-Scale Study in the Orkut Social Network," *Proceedings of the Eleventh ACM SIGKDD International Conference on Knowledge Discovery in Data Mining.*

Vozalis, M. G. and Margaritis, K. G. (2004) "Collaborative Filtering Enhanced by Demographic Correlation," *presented at the AIAI Symposium on Professional Practice in AI, of the 18th World Computer Congress,* Toulouse, France, August 22–27, 2004, 393–402.

Chapter: Candid Cameras

Chan, S. P. (2009) "New Microsoft Bing Maps Show Streetside Views," *The Seattle Times,* December 2, 2009, http://seattletimes.nwsource.com/html/microsoftpri0/2010405191_somenewmapandsearchfeaturesformicrosoftbing.html.

CNN Staff. (2009) "Gang of Villagers Chase Away Google Car," http://www.cnn.com/2009/WORLD/europe/04/03/google.anger/index.html.

Corank.com. (2009) "Welcome to the Funny Side of Google Street View," http://streetviewgallery.corank.com/.

Culotta, A., Bekkerman, R., and McCallum A. (2004) "Extracting Social Networks and Contact Information from Email and the Web," *First Conference on Email and Anti-Spam* (2004), http://www.cs.umass.edu/~culotta/pubs/culotta04extracting.pdf.

Ghia, A. (2009) "Google to Fund 'Video Street View' for Central London," *The Register* (Apr. 1, 2009), http://www.theregister.co.uk/2009/04/01/watch_out_london/.

Kolakowski, N. (2009) "Microsoft Bing Now Features Updated Maps, Twitter Feed," eWeek.com (Dec. 2, 2009), http://www.eweek.com/c/a/Windows/Microsoft-Bing-Now-Features-Updated-Maps-Twitter-Feed-592395/.

Mills, E. (2005) "Amazon A9 Takes It to the Streets," *CNet News* (Aug. 15, 2005), http://news.cnet.com/2100-1032_3-5833916.html.

Skinner, F. (2009) "Even If God Isn't Watching You, Google Is," *TimesOnline,* March 27, 2009, http://www.timesonline.co.uk/tol/comment/columnists/frank_skinner/article5982700.ece.

Chapter: Negotiations and Herding Cats

Gallagher, A. and Chen, T. (2009) "Using Context to Recognize People in Consumer Images," *IPSJ Transactions on Computer Vision and Applications,* vol. 1, 115–26.

Rowley, H., Baluja, S., and Kanade, T. (1998) "Neural Network-based Face Detection" *IEEE-Transactions on Pattern Analysis and Machine Intelligence, IEEE-PAMI,* vol. 20, no. 1, 23–38.

Stone, Z., Zickler, T., and Darrell, T. (2008) "Autotagging Facebook: Social Network Context Improves Photo Annotation," *Proc. First IEEE Workshop on Internet Vision*, 2008.

Viola, P. and Jones, M. J. (2004) "Robust Real-Time Face Detection," *International Journal of Computer Vision*, vol. 57, no. 2, 137–54.

Zhao, W., Chellappa, R., Phillips, P., and Rosenfeld, A. (2003) "Face Recognition: A Literature Survey," *Computing Surveys*, vol. 35, no. 4, 399–459.

Chapter: Giving Thanks

Associated Press. (2007) "Surveillance Cameras Get Smarter: New Devices Can Watch, Interpret What They're Seeing," *MSNBC.com* (Feb. 25, 2007), http://www.msnbc.msn.com/id/17330942/.

Collins, R. T., Lipton, A. J., and Kanade, T. (2000) "Introduction to the Special Section on Video Surveillance," *IEEE Transactions on Pattern Analysis and Machine Intelligence*, vol. 22, no. 7 (July 2000), 745–46.

Dick, A. R. and Brooks, M. J. (2003) "Issues in Automated Visual Surveillance," *Proceedings of VIIth Digital Image Computing: Technique and Applications*, 195–204.

McCahill, M. and Norris, C. (2002) "CCTV in London," Working Paper No. 6, Center for Criminology and Criminal Justice, University of Hull, http://www.urbaneye.net/results/ue_wp6.pdf.

McCue, C. (2007) *Data Mining and Predictive Analysis: Intelligence Gathering and Crime Analysis*, Butterworth-Heinemann.

O'Toole, A. J., Harms, J., Snow, S. L., Hurst, D. R., Pappas, M. R., Ayyad, J. H., and Abdi, H. (2005) "A Video Database of Moving Faces and People," *IEEE Trans. Pattern Anal. Mach. Intell.*, vol. 27, no. 5 (May 2005), 812–16.

Chapter: Truth Lies and Algorithms

Anderson, C. (2004) "The Long Tail," *Wired* (Oct. 2004), http://www.wired.com/wired/archive/12.10/tail.html.

———. (2009) *The Long Tail: Chris Anderson's Blog*, http://longtail.typepad.com/the_long_tail/.

Bello, S. (2006) "The Long Tail of YouTube," *Change Is Good Blog* (July 2006), http://changesgood.wordpress.com/2006/07/04/the-long-tail-of-youtube/.

Brin, S. and Page, L. (1998) "The Anatomy of a Large-Scale Hypertextual Web Search Engine," *Comput. Netw.*, 107–17. http://infolab.stanford.edu/~backrub/google.html.

Croft, B., Metzler, D., and Strohman, T. (2009) *Search Engines: Information Retrieval in Practice*, Addison Wesley.

Grimes, C., Tang D., and Russell, D. M. (2007) "Query Logs Alone Are Not Enough," *Query Log Analysis: Social and Technological Challenges*, A Workshop at the 16th International World Wide Web Conference.

Hoffman, H. (2005) "On the Trail of the Long Tail," *Yahoo! Search Blog*, http://ysearchblog.com/2005/02/17/on-the-trail-of-the-long-tail/.

Huff, D. and Geis, I. (1993) *How to Lie with Statistics*, W.W. Norton & Co.

Huffman, S. (2008) "Search Evaluation at Google," *Google Blog* (Sept. 15, 2008), http://googleblog.blogspot.com/2008/09/search-evaluation-at-google.html.

Manber, U. (2008) "Introduction to Google Search Quality," *Google Blog* (May 20, 2008), http://googleblog.blogspot.com/2008/05/introduction-to-google-search-quality.html.

Norvig, P. (2007) "Warning Signs in Experimental Design and Interpretation," *Norvig.com*, http://norvig.com/experiment-design.html.

Search Engine Watch (2007) "How Search Engines Rank Web Pages," *Search Engine Watch* (Mar. 15, 2007), http://searchenginewatch.com/2167961.

Singhal, A. (2008) "Introduction to Google Ranking," *Google Blog* (July 9, 2008), http://googleblog.blogspot.com/2008/07/introduction-to-google-ranking.html.

———. (2008) "Technologies Behind Google Ranking," *Google Blog* (July. 16, 2008), http://googleblog.blogspot.com/2008/07/technologies-behind-google-ranking.html.

Yoshida, Y., Ueda, T., Tashiro, T., Hirate, Y., and Yamana, H. (2008) "What's Going on in Search Engine Rankings?" *Proceedings of the 22nd International Conference on Advanced Information Networking and Applications—Workshops* (Mar. 25–28, 2008).

Chapter: A Drive through the Country

All Points Blog. (2009) "Tracking LBS Apps on iPhone, Android." http://apb.directionsmag.com/archives/5457-Tracking-LBS-Apps-on-iPhone,-Android.html.

Gorlach, A., Heinemann, A., and Terpstra, W. (2004) "Survey on Location Privacy in Pervasive Computing," *Privacy, Security and Trust within the Context of Pervasive Computing*, The Kluwer International Series in Engineering and Computer Science.

Gundotra, V. (2009) "See Where Your Friends Are with Google Latitude," Google Blog, http://googleblog.blogspot.com/2009/02/see-where-your-friends-are-with-google.html.

Reardon, M. (2006) "Mobile Phones that Track Your Buddies," *cNet news* (Nov. 14, 2006), http://news.cnet.com/Mobile-phones-that-track-your-buddies/2100-1039_3-6135209.html.

———. (2007) "Sprint to Offer Loopt Friend-Tracking Service," *cNet news* (July 17, 2007), http://news.cnet.com/8301-10784_3-9745834-7.html.

———. (2008) "Verizon Wireless Adds Friend-Finding Service," *cNet news* (Mar. 28, 2008), http://news.cnet.com/8301-10784_3-9905438-7.html.

———. (2009) "AT&T Launches Family-Tracking Service," *cNet news* (Apr. 15, 2009), http://news.cnet.com/8301-1035_3-10219786-94.html.

Yahoo. (2009) "Yahoo Fire Eagle," http://fireeagle.yahoo.net/.

Zheng, Y., Xie, X., and Ma, W. (2009) "Mining Interesting Locations and Travel Sequences from GPS Trajectories," *Proceedings of the 18th International Conference on World Wide Web, WWW-2009*, 791–800, http://research.microsoft.com/apps/pubs/?id=79440.

Chapter: Control

Cui, H., Mittal, V., and Datar, M. (2006) "Comparative Experiments on Sentiment Classification for Online Product Reviews," *Proceedings of the Twenty-First National Conference on Artificial Intelligence (AAAI-06)*, July 16–20, 2006, Boston, Massachusetts.

Lerman, K., Blair-Goldensohn, S., and McDonald, R. (2009) "Sentiment Summarization: Evaluating and Learning User Preferences," *12th Conference of the European Chapter of the Association for Computational Linguistics (EACL-09)*.

Manufacturing & Logistics IT. (2007) "McAfee Inc. Exposes the Psychological Warfare Used by Cybercriminals," www.logisticsit.com, http://www.logisticsit.com/absolutenm/templates/article-news.aspx?articleid=3147&zoneid=26.

Pang, B. and Lee, L. (2008) "Opinion Mining and Sentiment Analysis," *Foundations and Trends in Information Retrieval*, vol. 2, 1–135.

Wikipedia. (2009) "Psychological Operations," *Wikipedia: The Free Encyclopedia*, http://en.wikipedia.org/wiki/Psychological_operations.

Chapter: A Tale of Two Tenures

Alexanian, J. (2006) "Publicly Intimate Online: Iranian Web Logs in Southern California," *Comparative Studies of South Asia, Africa, and the Middle East* vol. 26, no. 1 (2006),134–45.

Lutz, C. (2008) "Selling Our Independence? The Perils of Pentagon Funding for Anthropology," *Anthropology Today*, vol. 24, no. 5 (Oct. 2008), 1–3, http://www.brown.edu/Administration/International_Affairs/international/documents/LutzReadings4.pdf.

McPherson, M. and Schapiro, M. (1999) "Tenure Issues in Higher Education," The *Journal of Economic Perspectives*, vol. 13, no. 1 (Winter), 85–98.

Chapter: Thoughts Like Butterflies
Chapter: Core-Relations
Chapter: Collide

Abbasi, A. and Chen, H. (2005) "Applying Authorship Analysis to Extremist-Group Web Forum Messages," *IEEE Intelligent Systems*, vol. 20, no. 5 (Sep. 2005), 67–75.

Azran, A. (2007) "The Rendezvous Algorithm: Multiclass Semi-supervised Learning with Markov Random Walks," *Proceedings of the 24th International Conference on Machine Learning* (Corvalis, Oregon, June 20–24, 2007). Z. Ghahramani, Ed. ICML '07, vol. 227, ACM, New York, 49–56.

Baluja, S., Seth, R., Sivakumar, D., Jing, Y., Yagnik, J., Kumar, S., Ravichandran, D., and Aly, M. (2008) "Video Suggestion and Discovery for YouTube: Taking Random Walks through the View Graph," *Proceedings of the 17th International Conference on World Wide Web*, WWW '08. (Beijing, China, April 21–25, 2008).

Egghe, L. and Rousseau, R. (1990) *Introduction to Informetrics*, Elsevier.

Gerwehr, S. and Daly, S. (2005) "Al Qaida: Terrorist Selection and Recruitment," *RAND National Security Research Division and McGraw-Hill Homeland Security Handbook*, Kamien, D. (ed). McGraw-Hill, http://www.rand.org/pubs/reprints/2006/RAND_RP1214.pdf, http://www.rand.org/pubs/authors/g/gerwehr_scott.html.

Gibson, D., Kleinberg, J., and Raghavan, P. (1998) "Inferring Web Communities from Link Topology," *Proceedings of the 9th ACM Conference on Hypertext and Hypermedia*.

Gross, P. L. K. and Gross, E. M. (1927) "College Libraries and Chemical Education," *Science* 66, 385–89.

Jiang, L., Wang, J., An, N., Wang, S., Zhan, J., and Li, L. (2009) "Two Birds with One Stone: A Graph-based Framework for Disambiguating and Tagging People Names in Web Search," *Proceedings of the 18th International Conference on World Wide Web*, WWW-2009, 1201–2.

Kleinberg, J. (1998) "Authoritative Sources in a Hyperlinked Environment," *Proc. 9th ACM-SIAM Symposium on Discrete Algorithms*.

Lotka, A. J. (1926) "The Frequency Distribution of Scientific Productivity," *Journal of the Washington Academy of Sciences*, vol. 16, 317–23.

MEMRI. (2007) "The Enemy Within: Where Are the Islamist/Jihadist Web Sites Hosted, and What Can be Done About It?" *The Middle East Media Research Institute*, http://memri.org/bin/latestnews.cgi?ID=IA37407.

Nicolaisen, J. (2002) "The J-Shaped Distribution of Citedness," *Journal of Documentation*, vol. 58, no. 4, 383–95.

Reid, E. and Chen, H. (2007) "Internet-Savvy U.S. and Middle Eastern Extremist Groups." *Mobilization: An International Quarterly*, vol. 12, no. 2 (2007), 177–92.

Zhu, X. (2005) "Semi-Supervised Learning with Graphs," Ph.D. thesis, Carnegie Mellon University, CMU-LTI-05-192.

Chapter: Apple Pie

Binyon, M. (2007) "Why Medical Schools Provide Islamic Extremists with Fertile Recruiting Grounds," *The Times and TimesOnline* (July 4, 2007), http://www.timesonline.co.uk/tol/news/uk/crime/article2023018.ece.

Chapter: The Yuri Effect
Chapter: Sebastin's Friends
Chapter: Fables of the Deconstruction
Chapter: A *Tinker* by Any Other Name

America.gov. (2008) "The United States Identifies 42 Foreign Terrorist Organizations," *America.gov* (Apr. 30, 2008), http://www.america.gov/st/peacesec-english/2008/April/20080429115651dmslahrellek0.9584772.html

Auchard, E. (2006) "Google Rejects DOJ Bid for Search Info, Rivals Including Microsoft and Yahoo Have Already Complied with the Demand," *Computerworld.com* (Feb. 18, 2006), http://www.computerworld.com/printthis/2006/0,4814,108843,00.html.

Bamford, J. (2008) *The Shadow Factory: The Ultra-Secret NSA from 9/11 to the Eavesdropping on America*, New York: Doubleday.

Bell, R., Koren, Y., and Volinsky, C. (2007) "Chasing $1,000,000: How We Won the Netflix Progress Prize," *ASA Statistical and Computing Graphics Newsletter*, vol. 18, no. 2.

CorpWatch. (2009) *CorpWatch: Holding Corporations Accountable*, Web site, http://www.corpwatch.org/.

Cuomo, C., Shaylor, J., McGuirt, M., Francescani, C. (2009) "'GMA' Gets Answers: Some Credit Card Companies Financially Profiling Customers," *abcNews.com* (Jan. 28, 2008), http://abcnews.go.com/GMA/GetsAnswers/story?id=6747461&page=1.

DeYoung, K. (2007) "Terror Database Has Quadrupled in Four Years" *The Washington Post*, March 25, 2007, http://www.washingtonpost.com/wp-dyn/content/article/2007/03/24/AR2007032400944_pf.html.

Eisler, P. (2009) "Terrorist Watch List Hits 1 Million," *USA Today* (Mar. 10, 2009), http://www.usatoday.com/news/washington/2009-03-10-watchlist_N.htm.

Frommer, D. (2006) "Callers Can't Hide," *Forbes* (May 11, 2006), http://www.forbes .com/2006/05/11/wireless-nsa-voip_cx_df_0511security.html?boxes=custom.

———. (2006) "AT&T Slapped in NSA Suit," *Forbes* (May 17, 2006), http://www .forbes.com/2006/05/17/nsa-wiretap-att_cx_df_0517nsa.html.

———. (2006) "Paper Pulls Back on Spy Story," *Forbes* (June 30, 2006), http://www .forbes.com/2006/06/30/wiretap-nsa-phone_cx_df_0630nsa.html.

———. (2006) "Judge Hangs Up on NSA Spy Program," *Forbes* (Aug. 17, 2006), http://www.forbes.com/2006/08/17/NSA-wiretap-spying_cx_df_0817nsa .html?boxes=custom.

Hillhouse, R. J. (2007) "Exclusive: Intel Outsourcing at Heart of Gonzales Controversy," *The Spy Who Billed Me: Outsourcing the War on Terror* (July 30, 2007), http:// www.thespywhobilledme.com/the_spy_who_billed_me/2007/07/corporate-spyin .html.

Holzer, J. (2006) "Did the NSA Break the Law?" *Forbes* (May 11, 2006), http://www .forbes.com/2006/05/11/nsa-wiretap-bush_cx_jh_0511NSA.html?boxes=custom.

National Counterterrorism Center. (2009) "Terrorist Identities Datamart Environment," www.nctc.gov. http://www.nctc.gov/docs/Tide_Fact_Sheet.pdf.

Park, S. and Pennock, D. (2007) Applying Collaborative Filtering Techniques to Movie Search for Better Ranking and Browsing," *Proceedings of the 13th ACM SIGKDD International Conference on Knowledge Discovery and Data Mining*, http:// research.yahoo.com/node/261.

Roney, M. (2006) "Verizon NSA Suit Could Add Risk," *Forbes* (May 15, 2006), http:// www.forbes.com/2006/05/15/verizon-communications-0515markets07.html.

Singel, R. (2008) "Judge Orders YouTube to Give All User Histories to Viacom," *Wired-Blog*, http://blog.wired.com/27bstroke6/2008/07/judge-orders-yo.html.

———. (2009) "FBI Mishandles Terror Watch List," *Wired-Blog*, http://www.wired .com/threatlevel/2009/05/fbi-gets-f-in-handling-terror-watch-list-ig-finds/.

———. (2009) "Newly Declassified Files Detail Massive FBI Data-Mining Project," *Wired-Blog*, http://www.wired.com/threatlevel/2009/09/fbi-nsac/.

Stern, J. (2006) "Flights of Fancy; Many Muslim Youth Espouse Jihad as a Fad," *Globe and Mail*, June 12, 2006, http://belfercenter.ksg.harvard.edu/publication/1562/ flights_of_fancy_many_muslim_youth_espouse_jihad_as_a_fad.html.

Stuckey, M. (2008) "AmEx Rates Credit Risk by Where You Live, Shop," *MSNBC .com* (Oct. 7, 2008), http://www.msnbc.msn.com/id/27055285/.

Vilches, J. (2007) "Judge Orders TorrentSpy to Hand Over User Data," *Techspot* (June 11, 2007), http://www.techspot.com/news/25642-Judge-orders-TorrentSpy-to-hand-over-user-data.html.

Wakeman, N. (2000) "Contractors Spy Dollars in NSA Outsourcing," *Washington Technology* (June 16, 2000), http://washingtontechnology.com/articles/2000/06/16/ contractors-spy-dollars-in-nsa-outsourcing.aspx.

Zabarenko, D. (2010) "U.S. Counterterror Agency Lacks 'Google-like' Search," *Reuters* (Jan. 20, 2010), http://www.reuters.com/article/idUSTRE60J5FA20100120.

Chapter: What I Did This Summer

Adar, E. (2007) "User 4XXXXX9: Anonymizing Query Logs," *Query Log Analysis: Social and Technological Challenges: A Workshop at the 16th International World Wide Web Conference.*

Xiong, L. and Agichtein, E. (2007) "Towards Privacy Preserving Query Log Publishing," *Query Log Analysis: Social and Technological Challenges: A Workshop at the 16th International World Wide Web Conference.*